The best projects from a year of *Bead&Button* magazine

Creative Beading

Vol. 8

KALMBACH BOOKS

Kalmbach Books
21027 Crossroads Circle
Waukesha, Wisconsin 53186
www.Kalmbach.com/Books

Published in 2013
17 16 15 14 13   1 2 3 4 5

Manufactured in China

ISBN: 978-0-87116-768-2
EISBN: 978-0-87116-769-9

The material in this book has appeared previously in *Bead&Button* magazine. *Bead&Button* is registered as a
trademark.

Editor: Erica Swanson
Technical Editor: Julia Gerlach
Art Director: Lisa Bergman
Layout Designer: Carole Ross
Illustrator: Kellie Jaeger
Photographers: William Zuback and James Forbes

Publisher's Cataloging-in-Publication Data
Creative beading : the best projects from a year of Bead&Button magazine.

   v. : ill.

   Annual
   Vol. [1] (2006)-
   Description based on: vol. 7 (2012).
   Latest issue consulted: vol. 7 (2012).
   Material in each volume appeared in the previous year's issues of Bead&Button magazine.
   Includes index.

   1. Beadwork—Periodicals. 2. Beads—Periodicals. 3. Jewelry making—Periodicals. I. Kalmbach Publishing Company. II. Title:
Bead&Button magazine.

TT860 .C743
745.594/2

Contents

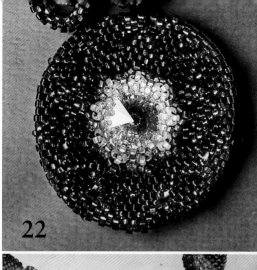

22

33

40

58

102

126

129

137

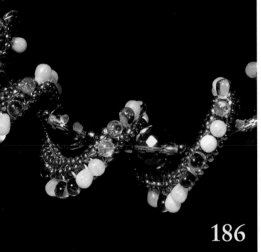

162

168

186

196

OTHER TECHNIQUES 234

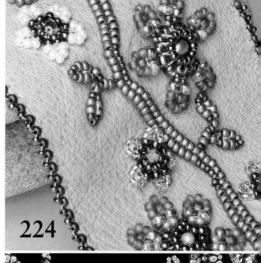

224

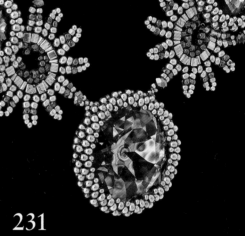

231

238

251

Introduction

Welcome to *Creative Beading, Volume 8*, our annual compendium of the best projects from a year of *Bead&Button* magazine. Beads continue to inspire creative people around the globe, as the beautiful pieces in this book attest. Designed by beaders from places far and wide, including the United States, Canada, Europe, Japan, South Africa, and Russia, the pieces in this volume represent a wide gamut of styles.

From gorgeous gallery-quality necklaces to timeless everyday bracelets and earrings, the jewelry you'll find in these pages features techniques beloved by today's beader, including the classics like peyote stitch and herringbone as well as new introductions, such as soutache bead embroidery. Old standbys or new favorites, all the projects and techniques are presented with the complete, easy-to-follow instructions that *Bead&Button* is known for.

The projects in the volume have been grouped into three categories—single stitch projects, multi-stitch projects, and other techniques. Each section contains projects representing a full range of difficulty levels, from easy to challenging, so regardless of your expertise, you'll be able to find projects that you can get done quickly as well as those that will keep your beading fingers busy. So dive in and feed your need to bead with *Creative Beading, Volume 8*.

Happy beading!

Julia Gerlach
Editor, *Bead&Button*

Tools & Materials

Excellent tools and materials for making jewelry are available in bead and craft stores, through catalogs, and on the Internet. Here are the essential supplies you'll need for the projects in this book.

TOOLS

Chainnose pliers have smooth, flat inner jaws, and the tips taper to a point. Use them for gripping, bending wire, and for opening and closing loops and jump rings.

Roundnose pliers have smooth, tapered, conical jaws used to make loops. The closer to the tip you work, the smaller the loop will be.

Use the front of a **wire cutters'** blades to make a pointed cut and the back of the blades to make a flat cut. Do not use your jewelry-grade wire cutters on memory wire, which is extremely hard; use heavy-duty wire cutters, or bend the memory wire back and forth until it breaks.

Crimping pliers have two grooves in their jaws that are used to fold and roll a crimp bead into a compact shape.

Make it easier to open split rings by inserting the curved jaw of **split-ring pliers** between the wires.

Beading needles are coded by size. The higher the number, the finer the beading needle. Unlike sewing needles, the eye of a beading needle is almost as narrow as its shaft. In addition to the size of the bead, the number of times you will pass through the bead also affects the needle size that you will use; if you will pass through a bead multiple times, you need to use a thinner needle.

A **hammer** is used to harden wire or texture metal. Any hammer with a flat head will work, as long as the head is free of nicks that could mar your metal. The light ball-peen hammer shown here is one of the most commonly used hammers for jewelry making.

A **bench block** provides a hard, smooth surface on which to hammer wire and metals pieces. An anvil is similarly hard but has different surfaces, such as a tapered horn, to help form wire into different shapes.

bench block

chainnose pliers

roundnose pliers

wire cutters

crimping pliers

hammer

split-ring pliers

beading needles

Tools & Materials

head pin

eye pin

jump rings

split ring

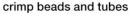

crimp beads and tubes

clasps

earring findings

FINDINGS

A **head pin** looks like a long, blunt, thick sewing pin. It has a flat or decorative head on one end to keep beads on. Head pins come in different diameters (gauges) and lengths.

Eye pins are just like head pins except they have a round loop on one end instead of a head. You can make your own eye pins from wire.

A **jump ring** is used to connect components. It is a small wire circle or oval that is either soldered closed or comes with a cut so it can be opened and closed.

Split rings are used like jump rings but are much more secure. They look like tiny key rings and are made of springy wire.

Crimp beads and tubes are small, large-holed, thin-walled metal beads designed to be flattened or crimped into a tight roll. Use them when stringing jewelry on flexible beading wire.

Clasps come in many sizes and shapes. Some of the most common (clockwise from the top left) are the toggle, consisting of a ring and a bar; slide, consisting of one tube that slides inside another; lobster claw, which opens when you pull on a tiny lever; S-hook, which links two soldered jump rings or split rings; and box, with a tab and a slot.

Earring findings come in a huge variety of metals and styles, including (from left to right) lever back, post, hoop, and French hook. You will almost always want a loop (or loops) on earring findings so you can attach beads.

WIRE

Wire is available in a number of materials and finishes, including brass, gold, gold-filled, gold-plated, fine silver, sterling silver, anodized niobium (chemically colored wire), and copper. Brass, copper, and craft wire are packaged in 10- to 40-yd. (9.1–37 m) spools, while gold, silver, and niobium are sold by the foot or ounce. Wire thickness is measured by gauge—the higher the gauge number, the thinner the wire. It is available in varying hardnesses (dead-soft, half-hard, and hard) and shapes (round, half-round, square, and others).

STITCHING & STRINGING MATERIALS

Selecting beading thread and cord is one of the most important decisions you'll make when planning a project. Review the descriptions below to evaluate which material is best for your design.

Threads come in many sizes and strengths. Size (diameter or thickness) is designated by a letter or number. OO and A/O are the thinnest; B, D, E, F, and FF are subsequently thicker. **Cord** is measured on a number scale; 0 corresponds in thickness to D-size thread, 1 equals E, 2 equals F, and 3 equals FF.

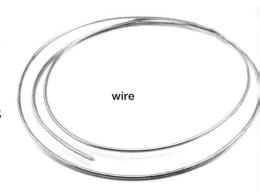

wire

Parallel filament nylon, such as Nymo or C-Lon, is made from many thin nylon fibers that are extruded and heat-set to form a single-ply thread. Parallel filament nylon is durable and easy to thread, but it can be prone to fraying and stretching. It is best used in beadweaving and bead embroidery.

Plied nylon thread, such as Silamide, is made from two or more nylon threads that are extruded, twisted together, and coated or bonded for further strength, making them strong and durable. It is more resistant to fraying than parallel filament nylon, and some brands do not stretch. It's a good material to use for twisted fringe, bead crochet, and beadwork that needs a lot of body.

Plied gel-spun polyethylene (GSP), such as Power Pro or DandyLine, is made from polyethylene fibers that have been spun into two or more threads that are braided together. It is almost unbreakable, it doesn't stretch, and it resists fraying. The thickness can make it difficult to make multiple passes through a bead. It is ideal for stitching with larger beads, such as pressed glass and crystals.

Parallel filament GSP, such as Fireline, is a single-ply thread made from spun and bonded polyethylene fibers. It's extremely strong, it doesn't stretch, and it resists fraying. However, crystals will cut through parallel filament GSP, and smoke-colored varieties can leave a black residue on hands and beads. It's most appropriate for bead stitching.

Polyester thread, such as Gutermann, is made from polyester fibers that are spun into single yarns and then twisted into plied thread. It doesn't stretch and comes in many colors, but it can become fuzzy with use. It is best for bead crochet or bead embroidery when the thread must match the fabric.

Flexible beading wire is composed of wires twisted together and covered with nylon. This wire is stronger than thread and does not stretch. The higher the number of inner strands (between 3 and 49), the more flexible and kink-resistant the wire. It is available in a variety of sizes. Use .014 and .015 for stringing most gemstones, crystals, and glass beads. Use thicker varieties, .018, .019, and .024, for heavy beads or nuggets. Use thinner wire, .010 and .012, for lightweight pieces and beads with very small holes, such as pearls. The thinnest wires can also be used for some bead-stitching projects.

flexible beading wire

nylon threads

parallel filament GSP

Tools & Materials

SEED BEADS

A huge variety of beads is available, but the beads most commonly used in the projects in this book are **seed beads**. Seed beads come in packages, tubes, and hanks. A standard hank (a looped bundle of beads strung on thread) contains 12 20-in. (51 cm) strands, but vintage hanks are often much smaller. Tubes and packages are usually measured in grams and vary in size.

Seed beads have been manufactured in many sizes ranging from the largest, 5º (also called "E beads"), which are about 5 mm wide, to tiny size 20º or 22º, which aren't much larger than grains of sand. (The symbol º stands for "aught" or "zero." The greater the number of aughts, e.g., 22º, the smaller the bead.) Beads smaller than Japanese 15ºs have not been produced for the past 100 years, but vintage beads can be found in limited sizes and colors. The most commonly available size in the widest range of colors is 11º.

Most round seed beads are made in Japan and the Czech Republic. **Czech seed beads** are slightly irregular and rounder than **Japanese seed beads**, which are uniform in size and a bit squared off. Czech beads give a bumpier surface when woven, but they reflect light at a wider range of angles. Japanese seed beads produce a uniform surface

and texture. Japanese and Czech seed beads can be used together, but a Japanese seed bead is slightly larger than the same size Czech seed bead.

Seed beads also come in sparkly cut versions. Japanese **hex-cut** or hex beads are formed with six sides. **2-** or **3-cut** Czech beads are less regular. **Charlottes** have an irregular facet cut on one side of the bead.

Japanese **cylinder beads**, otherwise known as Delicas (the Miyuki brand name), Toho Treasures (the brand name of Toho), and Toho Aikos are extremely popular for peyote stitch projects. These beads are very regular and have large holes, which are useful for stitches requiring multiple thread passes. The beads fit together almost seamlessly, producing a smooth, fabric-like surface.

Bugle beads are thin glass tubes. They can be sized by number or length, depending on where they are made. Japanese size 1 bugles are about 2 mm long, but bugles can be made even longer than 30 mm. They can be hex-cut, straight, or twisted, but the selection of colors, sizes, shapes, and finishes is limited. Seed beads also come in a variety of other shapes, including **triangles, cubes,** and **drops**.

In stitches where the beads meet each other end to end or side by side — peyote stitch, brick stitch, and square stitch — try using Japanese cylinder beads to achieve a smooth, flat surface. For a more textured surface, use Czech or round Japanese seed beads. For right-angle weave, in which groups of four or more beads form circular stitches, the rounder the seed bead, the better; otherwise you risk having gaps. Round seed beads also are better for netting and strung jewelry.

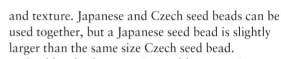

seed beads

cube beads

triangle beads

drop beads

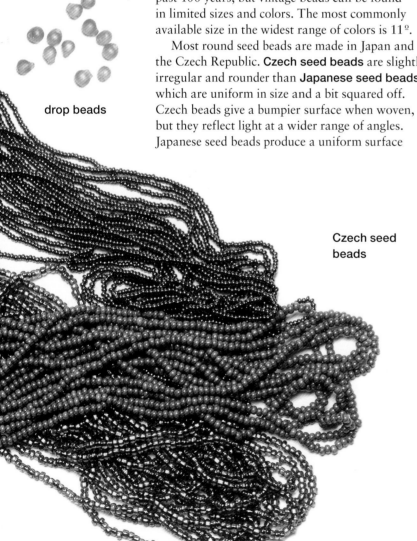

Czech seed beads

triangle twisted bugle beads

hex-cut beads

Basics

THREAD AND KNOTS

Adding thread

To add a thread, sew into the beadwork several rows or rounds prior to the point where the last bead was added, leaving a short tail. Follow the thread path of the stitch, tying a few half-hitch knots (see "Half-hitch knot") between beads as you go, and exit where the last stitch ended. Trim the short tail.

Conditioning thread

Use beeswax or microcrystalline wax (not candle wax or paraffin) or Thread Heaven to condition nylon beading thread and Fireline. Wax smooths nylon fibers and adds tackiness that will stiffen your beadwork slightly. Thread Heaven adds a static charge that causes the thread to repel itself, so don't use it with doubled thread. Both conditioners help thread resist wear. To condition, stretch nylon thread to remove the curl (Fireline doesn't stretch). Lay the thread or Fireline on top of the conditioner, hold it in place with your thumb or finger, and pull the thread through the conditioner.

Ending thread

To end a thread, sew back through the last few rows or rounds of beadwork, following the thread path of the stitch and tying two or three half-hitch knots (see "Half-hitch knot") between beads as you go. Sew through a few beads after the last knot, and trim the thread.

Half-hitch knot

Pass the needle under the thread bridge between two beads, and pull gently until a loop forms. Cross back over the thread between the beads, sew through the loop, and pull gently to draw the knot into the beadwork.

Overhand knot

Make a loop with the thread. Pull the tail through the loop, and tighten.

Square knot

[1] Cross one end of the thread over and under the other end. Pull both ends to tighten the first half of the knot.
[2] Cross the first end of the thread over and under the other end. Pull both ends to tighten the knot.

Stop bead

Use a stop bead to secure beads temporarily when you begin stitching. Choose a bead that is different from the beads in your project. Pick up the stop bead, leaving the desired length tail. Sew through the stop bead again in the same direction, making sure you don't split the thread. If desired, sew through it one more time for added security.

Surgeon's knot

[1] Cross one end of the thread over and under the other twice. Pull both ends to tighten the first half of the knot.
[2] Cross the first end of the thread over and under the other end. Pull both ends to tighten the knot.

Crochet
Slip knot and chain stitch

[1] Make a slip knot: Leaving the desired length tail, make a loop in the cord, crossing the spool end over the tail. Insert the hook in the loop, yarn over, and pull the cord through the loop.
[2] Yarn over the hook, and draw through the loop. Repeat this step for the desired number of chain stitches.

Beaded backstitch

To stitch a line of beads, come up through the fabric from the wrong side, and pick up three beads. Place the thread where the beads will go, and sew through the fabric right after the third bead. Come up between the second and third beads, and go through the third bead again. Pick up three more beads, and repeat. For a tighter stitch, pick up only one or two beads at a time.

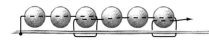

Basics

STITCHES

Brick stitch

[1] To work the typical method, which results in progressively decreasing rows, work the first row in ladder stitch (see "Ladder stitch") to the desired length, exiting the top of the last bead added.

[2] Pick up two beads, sew under the thread bridge between the second and third beads in the previous row, and sew back up through the second bead added. To secure this first stitch, sew down through the first bead and back up through the second bead.

[3] For the remaining stitches in the row, pick up one bead per stitch, sew under the thread bridge between the next two beads in the previous row, and sew back up through the new bead. The last stitch in the new row will be centered above the last two beads in the previous row, and the new row will be one bead shorter than the previous row.

Increasing

To increase at the start of the row, repeat step 1 above, then repeat step 2, but sew 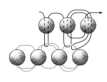 under the thread bridge between the first and second beads in the previous row. To increase at the end of the row, work two stitches off of the thread bridge between the last two beads in the previous row.

Herringbone stitch
Flat

[1] Work the first row in ladder stitch (see "Ladder stitch") to the desired length, exiting the top of an end bead in the ladder.

[2] Pick up two beads, and sew down through the next bead in the previous row (a–b). Sew up through the following bead in the previous row, pick up two beads, and sew down through the next bead (b–c). Repeat across the first row.

[3] To turn to start the next row, sew down through the end bead in the previous row and back through the last bead of the pair just added (a–b). Pick up two beads, sew down through the next bead in the previous row, and sew up through the following bead (b–c). Continue adding pairs of beads across the row.

Tubular

[1] Work a row of ladder stitch (see "Ladder stitch") to the desired length using an even number of beads. Form it into a ring to create the first round (see "Ladder stitch: Forming a ring"). Your thread should exit the top of a bead.

[2] Pick up two beads, sew down through the next bead in the previous round (a–b), and sew up through the following bead. Repeat to complete the round (b–c).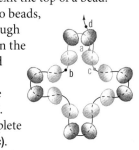

[3] You will need to step up to start the next round. Sew up through two beads — the next bead in the previous round and the first bead added in the new round (c–d).

[4] Continue adding two beads per stitch. As you work, snug up the beads to form a tube, and step up at the end of each round until your rope is the desired length.

Twisted tubular

[1] Work a ladder and two rounds of tubular herringbone as explained above.

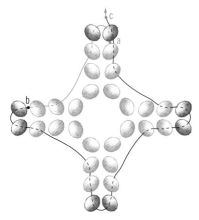

[2] To create a twist in the tube, pick up two beads, sew down through one bead in the next stack, then sew up through two beads in the following stack (a–b). Repeat around, adding two beads per stitch. Step up to the next round through three beads (b–c). Snug up the beads. The twist will begin to appear after the sixth round. Continue until your rope is the desired length.

Ladder stitch
Making a ladder

[1] Pick up two beads, and sew through them both again, positioning the beads side by side so that their holes are parallel (a–b).
[2] Add subsequent beads by picking up one bead, sewing through the previous bead, then sewing through the new bead (b–c). Continue for the desired length.

This technique produces uneven tension, which you can correct by zigzagging back through the beads in the opposite direction or by choosing the "Crossweave method" or "Alternative method."

Crossweave technique

[1] Thread a needle on each end of a length of thread, and center a bead.
[2] Working in crossweave technique, pick up a bead with one needle, and cross the other needle through it (a–b and c–d). Add all subsequent beads in the same manner.

Alternative method

[1] Pick up all the beads you need to reach the length your project requires. Fold the last two beads so they are parallel, and sew through the second-to-last bead again in the same direction (a–b).

[2] Fold the next loose bead so it sits parallel to the previous bead in the ladder, and sew through the loose bead in the same direction (a–b). Continue sewing back through each bead until you exit the last bead of the ladder.

Forming a ring

With your thread exiting the last bead in the ladder, sew through the first bead and then through the last bead again. If using the "Crossweave method" or "Alternative method" of ladder stitch, cross the threads from the last bead in the ladder through the first bead in the ladder.

Basics

Peyote stitch

Flat even-count

[1] Pick up an even number of beads, leaving the desired length tail **(a–b)**. These beads will shift to form the first two rows as the third row is added.

[2] To begin row 3, pick up a bead, skip the last bead added in the previous step, and sew back through the next bead, working toward the tail **(b–c)**. For each stitch, pick up a bead, skip a bead in the previous row, and sew through the next bead until you reach the first bead picked up in step 1 **(c–d)**. The beads added in this row are higher than the previous rows and are referred to as "up-beads."

[3] For each stitch in subsequent rows, pick up a bead, and sew through the next up-bead in the previous row **(d–e)**. To count peyote stitch rows, count the total number of beads along both straight edges.

Flat odd-count

Odd-count peyote is the same as even-count peyote, except for the turn on odd-numbered rows, where the last bead of the row can't be attached in the usual way because there is no up-bead to sew through.

Work the traditional odd-row turn as follows:

[1] Begin as for flat even-count peyote, but pick up an odd number of beads. Work row 3 as in even-count, stopping before adding the last bead.

[2] Work a figure-8 turn at the end of row 3: Pick up the next-to-last bead (#7), and sew through #2, then #1 **(a–b)**. Pick up the last bead of the row (#8), and sew through #2, #3, #7, #2, #1, and #8 **(b–c)**.

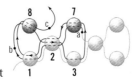

[3] In subsequent odd-numbered rows, pick up the last bead of the row, sew under the thread bridge between the last two edge beads, and sew back through the last bead added to begin the next row.

Tubular even-count

Tubular peyote stitch follows the same stitching pattern as flat peyote, but instead of sewing back and forth, you work in rounds.

[1] Start with an even number of beads tied into a ring (see "Square knot").

[2] Sew through the first bead in the ring. Pick up a bead, skip a bead in the ring, and sew through the next bead. Repeat to complete the round.

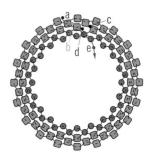

[3] To step up to start the next round, sew through the first bead added in round 3 **(a–b)**. Pick up a bead, and sew through the next bead in round 3 **(b–c)**. Repeat to complete the round.

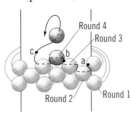

[4] Repeat step 3 to achieve the desired length, stepping up after each round.

Tubular odd-count

[1] Start with an odd number of bead tied into a ring (see "Square knot").

[2] Sew through the first bead into the ring. Pick up a bead, skip a bead in the ring, and sew though the next bead. Repeat to complete the round. At the end of the round, you will sew through the last bead in the original ring. Do not step up. Pick up a bead, and sew through the first bead in the previous round. You will be stitching in a continuous spiral.

Bezels

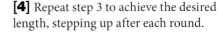

[1] Pick up enough seed beads to fit around the circumference of a rivoli or stone, and sew through the first bead again to form a ring **(a–b)**.

[2] Pick up a bead, skip the next bead in the ring, and sew through the following bead **(b–c)**. Continue working in tubular peyote stitch to complete the round, and step up through the first bead added **(c–d)**.

[3] Work the next two rounds in tubular peyote using beads one size smaller than those used in the previous rounds **(d–e)**. Keep the tension tight to decrease the size of the ring.

[4] Position the rivoli or stone in the bezel cup. Using the tail thread, repeat steps 2 and 3 to work three more rounds on the other side of the stone.

Increasing

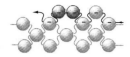

[1] At the point of increase, pick up two beads instead of one, and sew through the next bead.

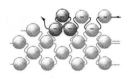

[2] When you reach the pair of beads in the next row, sew through the first bead, pick up a bead, and sew through the second bead.

Decreasing

[1] At the point of decrease, sew through two up-beads in the previous row.

[2] In the next row, when you reach the two-bead space, pick up one bead.

Zipping up or joining

To join two sections of a flat peyote piece invisibly, match up the two pieces so the end rows fit together. "Zip up" the pieces by zigzagging through the up-beads on both ends.

Right-angle weave
Flat strip

[1] To start the first row of right-angle weave, pick up four beads, and tie them into a ring (see "Square knot"). Sew through the first three beads again.

[2] Pick up three beads. Sew through the last bead in the previous stitch (a–b), and continue through the first two beads picked up in this stitch (b–c).

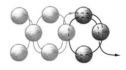

[3] Continue adding three beads per stitch until the first row is the desired length. You are stitching in a figure-8 pattern, alternating the direction of the thread path for each stitch.

Adding rows

[1] To add a row, sew through the last stitch of row 1, exiting an edge bead along one side.

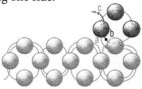

[2] Pick up three beads, and sew through the edge bead your thread exited in the previous step (a–b). Continue through the first new bead (b–c).

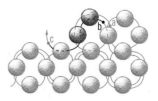

[3] Pick up two beads, and sew back through the next edge bead in the previous row and the bead your thread exited at the start of this step (a–b). Continue through the two new beads and the following edge bead in the previous row (b–c).

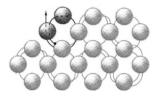

[4] Pick up two beads, and sew through the last two beads your thread exited in the previous stitch and the first new bead. Continue working a figure-8 thread path, picking up two beads per stitch for the rest of the row.

Square stitch

[1] String all the beads needed for the first row, then pick up the first bead of the second row. Sew through the last bead of the first row and the first bead of the second row again. Position the two beads side by side so that their holes are parallel.

[2] Pick up the next bead of row 2, and sew through the corresponding bead in row 1 and the new bead in row 2. Repeat across the row.

Basics

Crimping

Use crimp beads to secure flexible beading wire. Slide the crimp bead into place, and squeeze it firmly with chainnose pliers to flatten it. For a more finished look, use crimping pliers:

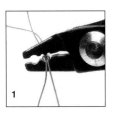

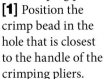

[1] Position the crimp bead in the hole that is closest to the handle of the crimping pliers.

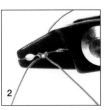

[2] Holding the wires apart, squeeze the pliers to compress the crimp bead, making sure one wire is on each side of the dent.

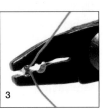

[3] Place the crimp bead in the front hole of the pliers, and position it so the dent is facing the tips of the pliers. Squeeze the pliers to fold the crimp in half.

Opening and closing loops and jump rings

[1] Hold a loop or a jump ring with two pairs of pliers, such as chainnose, flatnose, or bentnose pliers.

[2] To open the loop or jump ring, bring the tips of one pair of pliers toward you, and push the tips of the other pair away from you.

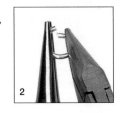

[3] The open jump ring. Reverse the steps to close.

Plain loop

[1] Using chainnose pliers, make a right-angle bend in the wire directly above a bead or other component or at least ¼ in. (6 mm) from the end of a naked piece of wire. For a larger loop, bend the wire further in.

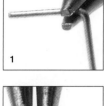

[2] Grip the end of the wire with roundnose pliers so that the wire is flush with the jaws of the pliers where they meet. The closer to the tip of the pliers that you work, the smaller the loop will be. Press downward slightly, and rotate the wire toward the bend made in step 1.

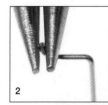

[3] Reposition the pliers in the loop to continue rotating the wire until the end of the wire touches the bend.

[4] The plain loop.

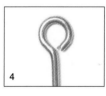

Wrapped loop

[1] Using chain-nose pliers, make a right-angle bend in the wire about 2 mm above a bead or other component or at least 1¼ in. (3.2 cm) from the end of a naked piece of wire.

[2] Position the jaws of the roundnose pliers in the bend. The closer to the tip of the pliers that you work, the smaller the loop will be.

[3] Curve the short end of the wire over the top jaw of the roundnose pliers.

[4] Reposition the pliers so the lower jaw fits snugly in the loop. Curve the wire downward around the bottom jaw of the pliers. This is the first half of a wrapped loop.

[5] To complete the wraps, grasp the top of the loop with one pair of pliers.

[6] With another pair of pliers, wrap the wire around the stem two or three times. Trim the excess wire, and gently press the cut end close to the wraps with chainnose pliers.

Loops, wrapped above a top-drilled bead

[1] Center a top-drilled bead on a 3-in. (7.6 cm) piece of wire. Bend each wire end upward, crossing them into an X above the bead.

[2] Using chain-nose pliers, make a small bend in each wire end so they form a right angle.

[3] Wrap the horizontal wire around the vertical wire as in a wrapped loop. Trim the excess wrapping wire.

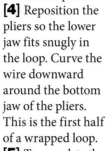
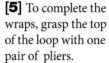
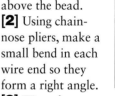

Single-Stitch Projects

PEYOTE STITCH

Fireflower

Create a sparkling centerpiece with lively layers of delicate peyote petals

designed by **Lauren M. Miller**

Attach the clever bail rings to opposite ends of the centerpiece to transform it into a bracelet focal.

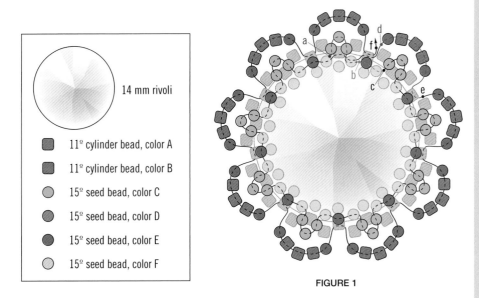

14 mm rivoli

▪ 11º cylinder bead, color A

▪ 11º cylinder bead, color B

● 15º seed bead, color C

● 15º seed bead, color D

● 15º seed bead, color E

○ 15º seed bead, color F

FIGURE 1

materials

purple/red necklace 16 in. (41 cm)
- 14 mm rivoli (Swarovski, golden shadow)
- **2** 6 mm round crystals (Swarovski, tanzanite)
- **2** 4 mm bicone crystals (Swarovski, tanzanite)
- 11º cylinder beads
  2 g color A (Miyuki 105, transparent garnet)
  4 g color B (Miyuki 135, rainbow moonlit purple)
- 15º seed beads
  1 g color C (Miyuki 578, gilt-lined pale gold opal)
  2 g color D (Toho 52113, silver-lined milky pomegranate)
  5 g color E (Toho 2124, silver-lined lilac opal)
  10 g color F (Toho 576, gilt-lined gray)
- Fireline 6 lb. test
- beading needles, #12

green/pink bracelet colors:
- 14 mm rivoli (Swarovski, celadon)
- 11º cylinder beads
  color A (Miyuki 0308, matte metallic rainbow rose/green)
  color B (Miyuki 0327, matte metallic rainbow dark green/teal)
- 15º seed beads
  color C (Toho 995, gold-lined rainbow aqua)
  color D (Toho 115, transparent amethyst luster)
  color E (Miyuki 453, metallic forest green iris)
  color F (Miyuki 551, gilt-lined white opal)

Use several peyote stitch techniques to make this colorful pendant, then suspend it from several strands of seed beads.

step by step

Rivoli bezel

[1] On 2 yd. (1.8 m) of Fireline, attach a stop bead (Basics), leaving a 10-in. (25 cm) tail. Pick up 36 color A 11º cylinder beads, and sew through the first A to form a ring.

[2] Work two rounds of tubular peyote stitch (Basics) using As.

[3] Continuing in tubular peyote, work two rounds using color C 15º seed beads. Retrace the thread path of the last round to secure the thread, exiting a C in the second-to-last round. Don't end the working thread.

[4] Place the 14 mm rivoli into the ring so the front of the rivoli lies against the rounds of Cs. Using the tail and tight tension, work two rounds with color D 15º seed beads. End the tail (Basics).

Bezel embellishments

Work the bezel embellishment rounds from the front of the rivoli to the back, stepping up through one round of the bezel for each embellishment round. For clarity, the embellishments shown in **figure 1** are omitted in **figures 2** and **3**.

Picots

[1] Using the working thread, pick up three Cs, and sew through the next C in the same round of the bezel (**figure 1, a–b**). Pick up a color E 15º seed bead, and sew through the next C in the same round of the bezel (**b–c**). Repeat these two stitches to complete the round. Sew through the next A, C, and A in the bezel (**c–d**). Your thread should be exiting an A in the bezel adjacent to a single E added in this step. This will position your thread so the next round of picots will sit behind the three-bead picots added in this step.

[2] Pick up an E, three color B 11º cylinder beads, and an E. Skip an A in the same round of the bezel, and sew through the next A (**d–e**). Repeat this stitch to complete the round (**e–f**). Step up through the adjacent A in the next round in the bezel and the A in the round after that, positioning your thread so the small petals added in the next round will sit between two five-bead picots added in this step, and the medium petals will sit directly behind them.

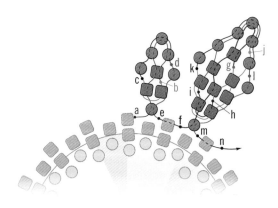

FIGURE 2

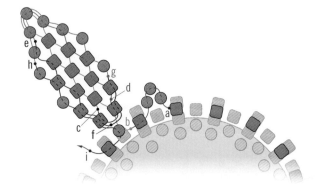

FIGURE 3

Petals

[1] Make a small petal: Working in flat peyote stitch (Basics), pick up a D, two As, and three Ds. Skip the last three Ds, and sew back through the last A picked up **(figure 2, a–b)**, creating a picot at the tip of the petal. Pick up an A, and sew through the first A picked up at the start of this step in the opposite direction **(b–c)**. Pick up a D, and sew through the next three Ds **(c–d)**. Pick up a D, and sew through the next A and the following D **(d–e)**. Sew through the next A in the same round of the bezel **(e–f)**.

[2] Make a medium petal: Working in flat peyote stitch, pick up a D, four As, and three Ds. Skip the last three Ds, and sew back through the last A picked up **(f–g)**. Work one stitch with an A **(g–h)**, then pick up an A, and sew through the first A picked up at the start of this step in the opposite direction **(h–i)**. Work one stitch with an A and one stitch with a D, sewing through the three Ds at the tip of the petal **(i–j)**. Work a stitch with a D and a stitch with an A, then sew through two As on the other edge of the petal **(j–k)**. Work a stitch with a D, sewing through the five Ds at the tip of the petal **(k–l)**. Work a stitch with a D, and sew through the next A and D **(l–m)**. Sew through the next A in the same round of the bezel **(m–n)**.

[3] Repeat steps 1 and 2 to complete the round, then step up through the next A in the following round of the bezel. Flip the bezel over to work the final round of petals and picots.

[4] Create a base round for the large petals: Pick up an A, and sew through the next A in the same round of the bezel. Repeat to complete the round, and end the working thread.

[5] Add 1 yd. (.9 m) of Fireline (Basics) to the bezel, exiting an A added in step 4, and positioning the thread to exit an A that sits between a small and medium petal. The small picots you'll make next should sit behind the medium petals, and the large petals should sit behind the small petals.

[6] Make a small picot: Pick up three Ds, and sew through the next A in the same round of the bezel **(figure 3, a–b)**.

[7] Make a large petal: Pick up a D, six As, and three Ds. Skip the last three Ds, and sew back through the last A. Work two stitches using As **(b–c)**. Pick up an A, and sew through the first A picked up at the start of this stitch in the opposite direction **(c–d)**. Work two stitches with As and one stitch with a D, sewing through the three Ds at the tip of the petal **(d–e)**. Work a stitch with a D and two stitches with As **(e–f)**. Sew through the next two As on the other edge of the petal **(f–g)**. Work two stitches with Ds, sewing through the five Ds at the tip of the petal **(g–h)**. Work two stitches with Ds, then sew through the next A and D, and continue through the next A in the same round of the bezel **(h–i)**.

[8] Repeat steps 6 and 7 to complete the round, and end the working thread.

Peyote rings

[1] Make a large ring: On 1 yd. (.9 m) of Fireline, attach a stop bead, leaving a 6-in. (15 cm) tail. Pick up 90 Bs, and sew through the first B picked up to form a ring. Work one round of tubular peyote using Bs, three rounds using Es, and four rounds using Bs. Zip up (Basics) the first and last rounds. Sew through the beadwork to exit a B in the third round from the last round of Es. End the tail but not the working thread.

[2] Make a medium ring: On 1 yd. (.9 m) of Fireline, attach a stop bead, leaving a 6-in. (15 cm) tail. Pick up 36 Bs, and sew through the first B picked up to form a ring. Work one round of tubular peyote using Bs, three rounds using Es, and two rounds using Bs. Zip up the first and last rounds, and sew through the beadwork to exit a B in the outer round of the ring. End the tail but not the working thread. Make a second medium ring.

[3] Make a small ring: On 18 in. (46 cm) of Fireline, attach a stop bead, leaving a 6-in. (15 cm) tail. Pick up 24 Bs, and sew through the first B picked up to form a ring. Work one round of tubular peyote using Bs, three rounds using Es, and two rounds using Bs. Zip up the first and last rounds, and sew through the beadwork to exit a B in the outer round of the ring. End the tail, but not the working thread. Make a second small ring.

a

b

c

d

e

DESIGN NOTE:
To create a bracelet, make one more medium peyote ring and two more small rings. Connect them opposite each other on the large ring of the centerpiece.

Toggle bar

[1] On 18 in. (46 cm) of Fireline, attach a stop bead, leaving a 6-in. (15 cm) tail. Pick up 13 Bs, and work 10 rows of flat odd-count peyote stitch (Basics). Zip up the end rows, and end the tail.

[2] Using the working thread, sew through the center of the tube, and pick up a D, a 4 mm bicone crystal, and a D. Skip the last D, and sew back through the 4 mm and D. Repeat to add a 4 mm embellishment on the other end of the tube, then end the working thread.

Assembly

[1] Using the thread from the large ring, sew through the D at the tip of one of the large petals. Sew through the next B in the same round of the large ring (photo a). Continue through the next eight Bs in the ring, exiting the fifth B in the same round from the previous petal tip. Repeat this step to complete the round, and end the thread.

[2] Arrange the two small rings next to each other. Using the thread from one of the small rings, sew through a B in the

outer round of the other small ring and back through the B on the first small ring. Retrace the thread path several times, then sew through two Bs on the outside of the first small ring (photo b). Make a second connection in the same manner, then sew through four Bs on the outside of the first small ring.

[3] Connect a B from the first small ring to a B in the outer round of the large ring as in step 2, but make only one connection instead of two (photo c). Retrace the thread path, and end the thread. Using the thread from the second small ring, connect it to a corresponding B in the outer round of the large ring, retrace the thread path, and end the thread.

[4] Center the medium ring above the two small rings. Use the thread from the medium ring to connect it to a B in the outer round of each of the small rings (photo d). Retrace the thread path of each connection, and end the thread.

[5] Add 3 yd. (2.7 m) of Fireline to the remaining medium ring, exiting a B in the outer round. Pick up a 6 mm round

crystal and 18–20 in. (46–51 cm) of color F 15º seed beads. Sew through the medium ring of the pendant from back to front, an adjacent small ring from front to back, the other small ring from back to front, and the medium ring from front to back (photo e). Pick up a 6 mm, and sew through a B in the middle of the toggle bar. Sew back through the 6 mm, and pick up the same number of Fs as you did at the start of this step. Retrace the thread path through the pendant rings, and sew through the 6 mm of the toggle ring and a B in the outer round of the ring. Complete two more strands of Fs in the same manner, and end the thread.

Bella's pearls

The Belle Époque of the late
19th century meets the 21st
century in this contemporary
take on a fashion standard

designed by **Cynthia Rutledge**

Wire-wrapped chain
adds a delicate and
romantic touch to
this lovely necklace.

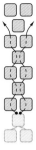

FIGURE 1

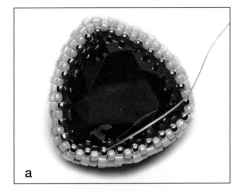

a

b

c

materials

lavender necklace 18 in. (46 cm)
- 20 x 20 mm trillion CZ (lavender)
- 8 mm pearl (Swarovski, white)
- 28 3 mm pearls (Swarovski, cream)
- 2 g 11º cylinder beads (Miyuki 0505, dark gold higher metallic)
- 6 11º seed beads (Miyuki 457L, bronze metallic)
- 15º seed beads
  2 g color A (Miyuki 457L, bronze metallic)
  1 g color B (Toho 460I, purple/bronze metallic AB)
- 8 mm cone (gold)
- S-hook clasp (gold)
- 24 in. (61 cm) wire-wrapped bead chain (gold vermeil with 3.5–4 mm white pearls)
- 6 4 mm 22-gauge jump rings (gold)
- nylon beading thread conditioned with microcrystalline wax or Thread Heaven
- beading needles, #12
- 2 pairs of pliers
- wire cutters

garnet/silver necklace colors:
- 20 x 20 mm trillion CZ (garnet)
- 8 mm pearl (Swarovski, white)
- 3 mm glass pearls (Czech, white)
- 11º cylinder beads (Miyuki DB0021, nickel plated)
- 11º seed beads (Toho 711, nickel-plated silver)
- 15º seed beads
  color A (Toho 0711, nickel-plated silver)
  color B (Miyuki 1428, dyed silver-lined wine)
- 8 mm cone (silver)
- wire-wrapped garnet bead chain (sterling silver)

The bezel around this trillion-cut CZ is pretty and also practical — a sculptural peyote "throne" on the back protects against the stone's pointed terminus. The bezel's pearl detailing then draws the eye upward to a scalloped necklace chain of wrapped loops and more pearls.

step by step

Trillion bezel

Rounds 1–3

[1] Thread a needle on each end of 2 yd. (1.8 m) of conditioned thread (Basics). Pick up 52 11º cylinder beads, leaving a 24-in. (61 cm) tail.

[2] With the working thread, stitch a row of flat even-count peyote stitch (Basics) using cylinders until you sew through the first cylinder from step 1.

[3] Join the ends to form a ring: Wrap the peyote strip around your finger, and with each needle, sew through the first several beads on the appropriate edge of the beadwork (figure 1). Snug up the beads.

Rounds 4 and 5

[1] Using the working thread, work two rounds of even-count tubular peyote (Basics) with 26 color A 15º seed beads in each round, stepping up after each round. This will form the back of the bezel, and the trillion will sit in the cradle created by these two rounds.

[2] Sew through the beadwork to exit an A in the first round of As just added. Do not end the working thread.

Rounds 6 and 7

[1] Place the trillion in the bezel with the back of the stone (the point) resting on rounds 4 and 5. Using the tail, work a round of peyote using As on the front of the trillion, and step up.

[2] Work a round of peyote using color B 15º seed beads (photo a), and end the tail (Basics).

Trillion throne

[1] With the working thread exiting an A in round 4 of "Trillion bezel," work a round of 26 peyote stitches off of the As in round 4 using cylinders (photo b), and step up.

[2] Work five more rounds of peyote using cylinders (photo c), stepping up after completing each round. Sew

DESIGN NOTE:

You can adapt this project to fit a 23 mm Swarovski crystal triangle with a few changes: Pick up 60 11º cylinder beads in step 1 of "Trillion bezel," and then work one more round of peyote in step 3 before adding the 15ºs in step 4. Pick up 33 3 mm pearls in step 2 of "Ring of pearls" instead of 27.

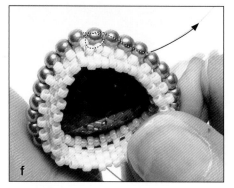

through the beadwork to exit a cylinder in the third round of the throne.

Ring of pearls

[1] Work a round of peyote using cylinders, creating a ledge **(photo d)** on which to anchor the pearls. Step up. Leave this thread for step 5 of "Beaded chain."

[2] On 1 yd. (.9 m) of conditioned thread, pick up 27 3 mm pearls, leaving a 9-in. (23 cm) tail, and wrap the pearls around the throne so they rest on top of the ledge created in the previous step **(photo e)**. Tie the pearls into a ring with a square knot (Basics).

[3] Rotate the ring of pearls on the ledge to align the working thread with a corner cylinder in the ledge. Pick up an A, and sew through the corner cylinder. Pick up an A, sew through the pearl your thread exited at the start of this step, and continue through the next three pearls **(photo f)**.

[4] Pick up an A, and sew through an adjacent cylinder in the ledge. Pick up an A, sew through the pearl your thread exited at the start of this step, and continue through the next three pearls. Repeat to the next corner.

[5] Repeat steps 3 and 4 to complete the round, but note that the cylinder

at one corner will not be positioned directly at the corner. To anchor the pearl at this corner, exit the corner pearl, pick up an A, sew through the adjacent cylinder in the ledge, pick up an A, and sew through the next cylinder in the ledge. Pick up an A, sew through the corner pearl, and continue through the next three pearls in the ring **(photo g)**. The two pearls you anchor after this corner will need to be attached to the ledge in the same manner.

[6] Once you've anchored the ring of pearls to the ledge, retrace the thread path, and end the working thread and tail.

Beaded chain

[1] Cut two 2¾-in. (7 cm) lengths of chain, two 3½-in. (8.9 cm) lengths of chain, and two 4½-in. (11.4 cm) lengths of chain. Trim each end of the chain as necessary to make sure the loops on each end are uncut.

[2] Open a 4 mm jump ring (Basics), and attach one end of a 2¾-in. (7 cm) chain and one end of a 3½-in. (8.9 cm) chain.

[3] Open a jump ring, and attach the other available ends of the two chains and one end of a 4½-in. (11.4 cm)

h

i

j

chain, making sure the longest chain is not between the two shorter chains.

[4] Open a jump ring, and attach the available end of the 4½-in. (11.4 cm) chain and half of the clasp.

[5] Using the thread from step 1 of "Ring of pearls," sew through the beadwork to exit a corner cylinder added in step 1 of "Ring of pearls." Make sure this is a corner with just one corner cylinder; the corner with two cylinders will be used to attach the "Pearl dangle."

[6] Pick up five As, sew through the first jump ring you used to attach the two shorter chains, and sew through a corresponding cylinder in the last round of cylinders added in the throne. Check to make sure the shorter of the two chains will fall to the inside of the necklace.

[7] Pick up an A, and sew through the middle three of the five As picked up in step 6. Pick up an A, and sew through the cylinder your thread exited at the start of step 6 as shown in **photo h** (for clarity, the jump ring and chain are not shown). Retrace the thread path, and do not end the thread.

[8] Repeat steps 2–7 for the other side of the necklace.

[9] Sew through the beadwork to exit the cylinder in the ledge preceding the remaining corner. Leave this thread for step 3 of "Pearl dangle."

Pearl dangle

[1] On 24 in. (61 cm) of conditioned thread, center nine As, an 11º seed bead, a 3 mm pearl, an 8 mm cone from top to bottom, an 11º, an 8 mm pearl, and three 11ºs. Skip the last three 11ºs, and sew back through the 8 mm pearl, the 11º, the cone, and the 3 mm pearl. Pick up an 11º and nine As **(photo i)**.

[2] With one thread, sew back through the 11º above the 3 mm pearl to form a loop. Retrace the thread path through the dangle, and end the thread. Repeat this step with the other thread.

[3] Using the remaining thread from step 9 of "Beaded chain," pick up 15 As and the two loops of the dangle. Skip the two corner cylinders, and sew through the following cylinder **(photo j)**. Sew through the beadwork to retrace the thread path, and end the thread.

Fashion
at your
fingertips

Create a chic ring
with pearl and
crystal accents

designed by **Aasia Hamid**

This design makes a great
statement or cocktail ring.

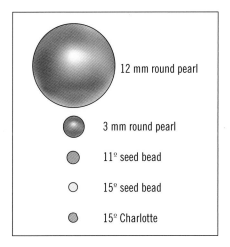

- 12 mm round pearl
- 3 mm round pearl
- 11º seed bead
- 15º seed bead
- 15º Charlotte

materials

bronze ring 1 in. (2.5 cm) diameter

- 12 mm round pearl (Swarovski, antique brass)
- 3 mm round pearls
  14 color A (Swarovski, antique brass)
  14 color B (Swarovski, copper)
- 14 2 mm round crystals (Swarovski, crystal copper)
- 3–5 g 11º seed beads (Miyuki 311, topaz gold luster)
- 3–5 g 15º seed beads (dark brown)
- 1–3 g 15º Charlottes (gold)
- Fireline 6 lb. test
- beading needles, #12
- bobbin (optional)

red ring colors:

- 12 mm round pearl (Swarovski, Bordeaux)
- 3 mm round pearls
  color A (Swarovski, Bordeaux)
  color B (Swarovski, coral)
- 2 mm round crystals (Swarovski, crystal copper)
- 11º seed beads (opaque red)
- 15º seed beads (Miyuki 309, dark red gold luster)
- 15º Charlottes (gold)

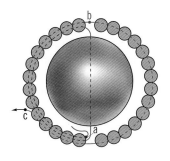

FIGURE 1

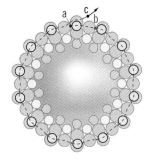

FIGURE 2

Make finery for your finger in coordinating or contrasting colors.

stepbystep

Bezel

[1] On 1½ yd. (1.4 m) of Fireline, pick up 14 11º seed beads and a 12 mm pearl, leaving a 12-in. (30 cm) tail. Sew through all the 11ºs again **(figure 1, a–b)**. Pick up 14 11ºs, and sew through the first few 11ºs picked up at the start of this step **(b–c)**.

[2] Work a round of tubular peyote stitch (Basics) using 11ºs, and step up through the first 11º picked up in this round.

[3] Repeat step 2 twice so you have a total of five peyote rounds with 11ºs.

[4] Work a round of tubular peyote stitch with 15º seed beads, and step up through the first 15º seed bead picked up in this round.

[5] Work a round of tubular peyote stitch with 15º Charlottes, then wind the working thread around a bobbin.

[6] Using the tail, work three rounds of tubular peyote stitch as follows: one round with 11ºs, one round with 15º seed beads, and one round with 15º Charlottes. End the tail (Basics).

Embellishment

[1] With the working thread, sew through the beadwork to exit an 11º in the second round of 11ºs from the inner edge of the bezel.

[2] Working in circular peyote stitch, pick up a 15º seed bead, and sew through the next 11º **(figure 2, a–b)**. Repeat to complete the round, and step up through an 11º in the next round of the bezel, working away from the inner edge **(b–c)**.

[3] Repeat step 2 twice, but on the second repeat, step up through the first 15º seed bead added in that embellishment round.

[4] Pick up a 15º seed bead, an 11º, and a 15º seed bead, and sew through the

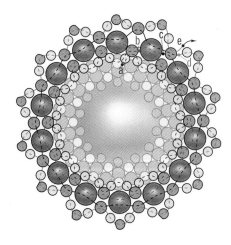

FIGURE 3

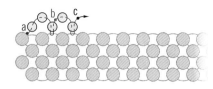

FIGURE 4

next 15º seed bead in the round. Repeat to complete the round, and step up through the first 15º seed bead and 11º added in this round **(figure 3, a–b)**.

[5] Pick up a color A 3 mm pearl, and sew through the center 11º in the next stitch of the previous round. Repeat to complete the round, and step up through the first A added in this round **(b–c)**.

[6] Pick up an 11º, and sew through the next A in the previous round. Repeat to complete the round, and step up through the first 11º added in this round **(c–d)**.

[7] Pick up a 15º seed bead, a 15º Charlotte, and a 15º seed bead, and sew through the next 11º in the previous round. Repeat to complete the round **(d–e)**, and sew through the beadwork to exit a 15º seed bead in the center round of 15º seed beads added in step 3.

[8] Pick up a color B 3 mm pearl, and sew through the next 15º seed bead in the round. Repeat to complete the round, and step up through the first B added.

[9] Pick up an 11º, and sew through the next B in the previous round. Repeat to complete the round, and sew through the beadwork to exit a 15º seed bead in the first round of 15º seed beads added in step 2.

[10] Pick up a 15º Charlotte, a 2 mm round crystal, and a 15º Charlotte, and sew through the next 15º seed bead in the round. Repeat to complete the round, and end the thread. The round with 2 mm crystals is the top of the bezel.

Band

[1] Add 18 in. (46 cm) of Fireline (Basics) to the bezel, and sew through the beadwork to exit a 15º seed bead

in the second round from the bottom. Working in flat even-count peyote stitch (Basics), pick up an 11º, and sew through the next 15º seed bead. Repeat to work a second stitch.

[2] Using the 11ºs added in step 1 as a base, work a band of peyote stitch four beads wide and long enough to fit around your finger when connected to the other side of the bezel.

[3] Zip up (Basics) the last row of 11ºs to the 15º seed beads opposite the 15ºs your thread exited in step 1.

[4] Retrace the thread path to reinforce the join, and sew through the beadwork to exit an edge 11º of the peyote band.

[5] Pick up three 15º seed beads, and sew under the thread bridge between the next pair of 11ºs on the edge and back through the last 15º seed bead added **(figure 4, a–b)**.

[6] Pick up two 15º seed beads, and sew under the next thread bridge and back through the last 15º seed bead added **(b–c)**.

[7] Repeat step 6 for the length of the band.

[8] Sew through the beadwork to exit the other edge of the band, and repeat steps 5–7. End the thread.

DESIGN NOTES:
Play with materials:
• **Use any type of 12 mm round bead for the center.**
• **Try fringe drops or fire-polished beads for one or both rounds of 3 mms.**
• **Use color B 11º seed beads instead of 2 mm round crystals.**

FLAT AND TUBULAR PEYOTE STITCH

Ride the
wave

Undulating waves
of peyote stitch
tumble 'round
a sturdy core

designed by
Kris Empting-Obenland

materials

necklace 34 in. (86 cm)

- 9º seed beads
  70 g color A (matte gray)
  30 g color B (matte purple)
  30 g color C (matte dark red)
  10 g color D (red AB)
  10 g color E (matte light red)
  40 g color F (matte red-orange)
  30 g color G (matte yellow-orange)
  10 g color H (silver-lined yellow-orange)
- 10 g 6º seed beads, color H (silver-lined yellow-orange)
- yarn, color A (for necklace core and marking the position of the wave)
- nylon beading thread, size D
- beading needles, #10
- 5.5–6.5 mm crochet hook
- **5** safety pins
- necklace form (optional)

DESIGN NOTE:

This necklace won the November 2011 Etsy Beadweavers "Totally twisted" challenge. I used purple thread throughout my piece, which pulls together the warm and cool colors in the necklace. Since the beads are matte transparent, the thread plays an active role in the overall design.

a

b

Get caught up in the rhythm of increasing peyote stitch and color gradations to create this stunning neck piece. The spiraling, overlapping waves create a dynamic necklace that is full of life.

The necklace pictured on p. 33 is made with 9ºseed beads. If 9ºs prove too difficult to locate, use 8º, 10º, or 11º seed beads instead, adjusting the number of beads in the initial ring of the rope as needed. In the step-by-step photos, we used 8º seed beads, beginning with a ring of 13 beads.

stepbystep

Crochet/peyote rope

[1] Make a slip knot in the center of a 14–15-ft. (4.2–4.6 m) length of yarn.

Working with both ends together, work in chain stitch (Basics) until the cord is about 1 yd. (.9 m) long.
[2] On a comfortable length of thread, pick up 17 color A 9º seed beads, and tie them into a ring with a square knot (Basics), leaving a 6-in. (15 cm) tail. Using As, work in odd-count tubular peyote stitch (Basics) around the crocheted core until the rope is about 34 in. (86 cm) or the desired length. End and add thread (Basics) as needed.
[3] Add or remove stitches in the crocheted core until the core is the same

c

length as the beadwork. Join the ends of the core: Replace the hook in the last loop. Slide the hook into the first stitch, yarn over with the tail **(photo a)**, and pull the tail all the way through the stitch. Trim the tail to about 1–2 in. (2.5–5 cm), and push it into the peyote tube.

[4] Rotate one end of the peyote rope to add some twist, align the ends, and zip them up (Basics and **photo b**).

[5] Arrange the rope on a necklace form or put it on yourself. Determine where you want the wave to begin and end. Cut a 1½-yd. (1.4 m) length of yarn, and wrap it 12 times around the rope between the beginning and ending points, spacing the wraps farther apart near the central portion and closer together at the ends **(photo c)**. Tie the ends of the yarn around the rope.

[6] Attach a safety pin at each end of the yarn. These will be points A (near the top of the necklace) and E (near the bottom). Attach a safety pin at the lower central point on the rope. This will be where the wave will be its widest (point C). Attach the remaining two safety pins halfway between points A and C (point B) and points C and E (point D) **(photo d)**. Use these points as guides as you stitch to help you determine where the waves should grow or shrink.

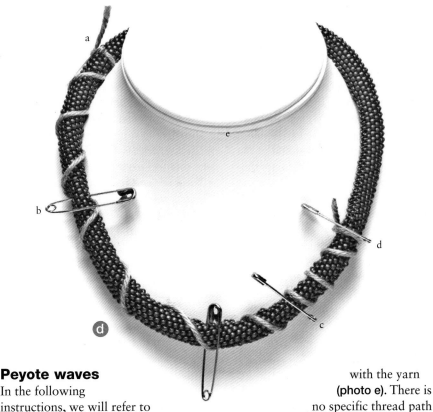

Peyote waves

In the following instructions, we will refer to the 9º seed beads in colors A–H as As, Bs, Cs, etc. These should not be confused with points A, B, C, D, or E on the rope, which will always be preceded by the label "point."

[1] Add a new thread to the beadwork near point A, and exit with your needle pointing toward points B–E. Following the yarn wrapped around the rope, sew As onto the rope, positioning the beads so the holes are approximately parallel with the yarn **(photo e)**. There is no specific thread path for this — simply sew them in place along the line of the yarn until you reach point E. Remove the yarn, but leave the pins in place.

[2] Working in the other direction, stitch a row of flat peyote stitch off the beads added in the previous step. Use mostly As with some Bs mixed in. Pick up two beads for some stitches in order to keep the spine of beadwork around the rope smooth and gap-free **(photo f)**. At the end of the row, sew through the next A in the rope.

[3] Continue in peyote stitch as follows, ending and adding thread as needed. The first few rows will extend past points A and E to create a gentle melding of the wave and the rope. Continue picking up two beads for some stitches, as in step 2.

e

f

g

h

i

Row 3: Turn by picking up a B and sewing through the last bead in each of the previous two rows. Work along the spine using Bs. When you get to a spot where you picked up two beads in the previous row, sew through the first bead, pick up a B, and sew through the next bead **(photo g)**. These increases help form the waves. To create a smooth transition to the rope, at the end of the row, pick up a B, and sew through the next bead in the rope **(photo h)**.

Row 4:
• Turn as in row 3, using a C **(photo i)**.
• Work approximately one rotation around the rope, using mostly Cs with some Ds and Fs mixed in.
• Switch to Bs until you are about three rotations from the other end.
• End with Cs, Ds, and Fs. Be sure to end the row with a C, and sew into the rope.

Row 5:
• Turn as in row 3, using an F.
• Work with Cs, Ds, and Es to point B.
• Continue with Bs and some Ds to point D.
• Use Cs with some Ds and Es until you reach the last rotation.
• End the row with Fs and Gs, making

sure you sew into the rope after the last stitch.

Row 6:
• Turn as in row 3, using a G.
• Work one rotation with Es, Fs, and Gs.
• Continue with Es and Fs, adding in Cs and Ds for one rotation.
• Use Cs with some Ds for one rotation.
• Use Bs with some Ds to point B.
• Use Cs with Ds and Es until you are one rotation from the end.
• Work the end rotation with Es, Fs, and Gs, making sure you sew into the rope after the last stitch.

Row 7: Sew through the first several stitches in row 6. Work as in row 6, but stop a few stitches from the end so that the end of the row remains narrow.

Rows 8–35: Continue working from one end of the spine to the other, making each subsequent row several stitches shorter on each end than the previous row. Keep these ideas in mind as you work:
• You will be creating "stripes" of color that blend together. Colors B, C, and F are the dominant colors. Use color D primarily in the shift from B to C. Use color E primarily in the shift from C to F. Color G is used along the outer edge of the color F stripe.

• The stripes of color will be narrower at the ends (just one or two rows per color) and wider in the middle (about 9–11 rows per dominant color).
• Offset the points at which you change colors so that the colors blend.
• The fullest portion of the wave is between points B and D. You should expect points B and D to have about 23–25 rows. Point C should have about 35–37 rows.
• The distance between points A and C is much longer than between points C and E, so the shift from narrow to wide from A to C takes a lot longer than the shift from wide to narrow from C to E.
• When increasing, take advantage of irregular bead sizes. First, pick up two skinny beads in place of a wide one to begin an increase. In the next row, use another skinny bead between the increase beads. This will help create a smooth, even expansion of beadwork.

Rows 36–37: Work two rows using Gs and Hs along the entire length of the wave. Use the color H 6º seed beads in the last row only, mixing them in with the G and H 9ºs.

[4] Remove the pins.

ODD-COUNT HERRINGBONE STITCH

Zig zag scallops

Choose a monochromatic color palette for a sophisticated look.

Freshwater pearls dangle from the points of this clever necklace

designed by **Sheryl Yanagi**

Work up two pliable odd-count herringbone strips with right-angle chevrons, and intertwine them for an elegant twist on a classic technique.

stepbystep

Odd half

Odd-count herringbone strip
[1] On 4 yd. (3.7 m) of thread or Fireline, work in ladder stitch (Basics) with 11º seed beads to make a ladder that is three beads long, leaving a 10-in. (25 cm) tail. Exit an end bead of the ladder.
[2] To work the next row: Pick up two 11ºs, and work a herringbone stitch (Basics and **figure 1, a–b**). Pick up an 11º, and sew down through the center 11º of the new row and up through the first 11º added in the row **(b–c)**.
[3] Repeat step 2 to work a strip that is 6 in. (15 cm) long (about 82 rows).

Points
[1] Pick up a 4 x 6 mm pearl and an 11º, skip the 11º, and sew back through the pearl and the next two 11ºs in the

column your thread exited at the start of this step. Sew up through two 11ºs in the center column and down through the first 11º in the following column **(figure 2)**.
[2] Pick up two 11ºs, and sew through the second and first 11ºs in the column your thread exited at the start of this step **(figure 3, a–b)**. Sew through the two 11ºs just added and the third and fourth 11ºs in the column **(b–c)**.
[3] Pick up an 11º, and sew through the adjacent 11º of the new row, the third and fourth 11ºs in the column, and the 11º just picked up **(figure 4)**.
[4] Using the 11ºs added in steps 2 and 3 as a base, work as in step 2 of "Odd-count herringbone strip" to make a strip that is 25 rows long.
[5] Repeat steps 1–4 to work an odd number of points (there are five points in the dark brown necklace and seven in the light brown necklace), but make the

strip after the last pearl only 15 rows long instead of 25 rows long. Don't end the thread or tail.

Even half
Work as in "Odd half" with the following changes: Work 10 more rows in step 3 of "Odd-count herringbone strip" and work one less point. (There are four points in the dark brown necklace and six points in the light brown necklace.)

Assembly
[1] Arrange the necklace halves so the longer strips of odd-count herringbone are pointing in opposite directions.
[2] Wrap the two center sections together, taking care of the following:
• Align the points of the even half between the points of the odd half.
• Make sure the herringbone strips are flat, not twisted.
• The points should all face the bottom of the necklace.
• Always overlap in the same direction by bringing the bottom strip to the top.

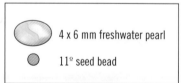

4 x 6 mm freshwater pearl

11º seed bead

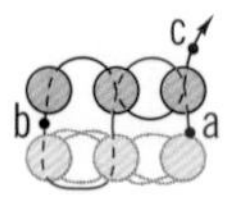

FIGURE 1

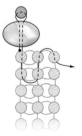

FIGURE 2

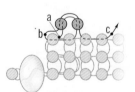

FIGURE 3

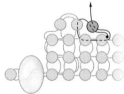

FIGURE 4

[3] Using a working thread, sew the short strip of one half to the long strip of the other half where they meet, following the existing thread path **(figure 5)**. End the thread. Repeat to attach the remaining short and long strips.

[4] Using a tail on one end of the necklace, sew through the beadwork to exit the center column. Pick up two 11ºs, a 4 x 6 mm pearl, and an 11º. Skip the last 11º, and sew back through the beads just added and the center column. Retrace the thread path, and end the thread (Basics).

[5] Using the tail on the other end of the necklace, sew through the beadwork to exit the center column. Pick up enough 11ºs to fit around the 4 x 6 mm pearl, and add an extra 11º. Sew back through the first 11º added to form a loop, then sew through the center column. Retrace the thread path, and end the thread.

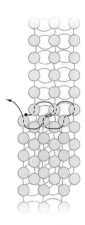

FIGURE 5

materials

necklace 17–20½ in. (43–52.1 cm)

- **10–14** 4 x 6 mm freshwater pearls
- 15–20 g 11º seed beads (dark brown necklace: Toho 703, matte cabernet; light brown necklace: Miyuki 2035, frosted mauve olive rose)
- nylon beading thread, size D, or Fireline 6 lb. test
- beading needles, #12

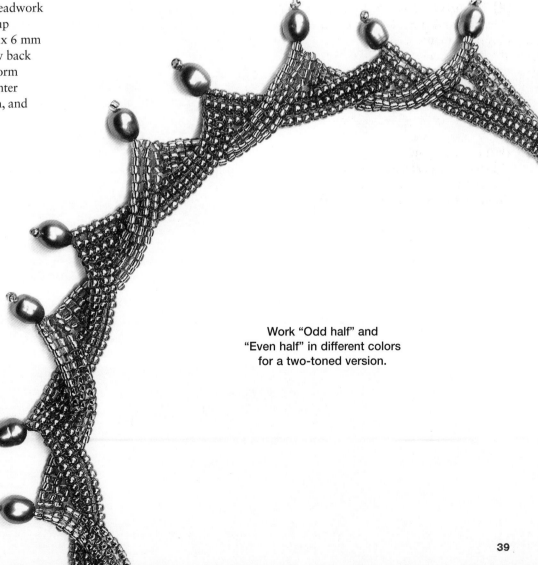

Work "Odd half" and
"Even half" in different colors
for a two-toned version.

Herringbone highway

Lanes of herringbone stitch pave the way for accents of pearls and fire-polished beads

designed by **Aryd'ell Hotelling**

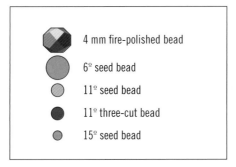

4 mm fire-polished bead

6° seed bead

11° seed bead

11° three-cut bead

15° seed bead

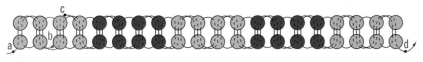

FIGURE 1

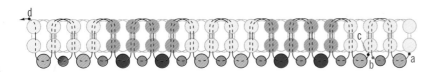

FIGURE 2

materials

blue-and-copper bracelet
7½ in. (19.1 cm)

- **48** 4 mm glass or crystal pearls (white)
- **24** 4 mm round fire-polished beads (Montana AB)
- **5 g** 6° seed beads (matte metallic copper)
- **5 g** 11° seed beads (Miyuki 0229, bronze-lined aqua)
- **3 g** 11° Czech three-cut seed beads (light cobalt)
- **2 g** 15° seed beads (matte metallic gold)
- **2** 8 mm snaps, or **2** 10 mm accent beads, for closure
- Fireline 4 lb. or 6 lb. test
- beading needles, #10 or #12

blue-and-brass bracelet colors:

- 4 mm glass or crystal pearls (blue-gray)
- 4 mm round fire-polished beads (Montana AB)
- 6° seed beads (Miyuki 457, dark bronze metallic)
- 11° seed beads (Miyuki 0229, bronze-lined aqua)
- 11° Czech three-cut seed beads (light cobalt)
- 15° seed beads (Miyuki 457, dark bronze metallic)

purple-and-gold bracelet colors:

- 4 mm glass or crystal pearls (white)
- 4 mm round fire-polished beads (amethyst)
- 6° seed beads (Toho 22B, silver-lined gold)
- 11° Czech seed beads (transparent amethyst luster)
- 11° cylinder beads (DB080, pale violet-lined crystal luster)
- 15° seed beads (Toho 22B, silver-lined gold)

Skipped stitches in a herringbone bracelet result in lines of negative space. Use larger seed beads and accent beads to bridge the gaps for a look that's both stylish and structural.

stepbystep

Herringbone band

[1] On a comfortable length of Fireline, pick up four 11° seed beads, leaving a 30-in. (76 cm) tail. Sew through all the beads again, and form them into two stacks of two beads **(figure 1, a–b)**.
[2] Working in ladder stitch (Basics), make a two-bead ladder: Pick up two 11°s, and sew through the previous stack of beads and the two beads just added to form a new stack **(b–c)**. Repeat to add one more stack of 11°s, four stacks of three-cut seed beads, four stacks of 11°s, four stacks of three-cuts, and four stacks of 11°s **(c–d)**. This forms the first two rows of the bracelet.
[3] With your thread exiting the bottom of the ladder, work an edging: Pick up an 11°, and sew up through the next stack of 11°s and down through the following stack **(figure 2, a–b)**. Pick up a 15° seed bead, and sew up through the previous stack and down through the next stack **(b–c)**. Repeat across the ladder, adding 11°s between the stacks of 11°s, adding three-cuts between the stacks of three-cuts, and alternating with 15°s **(c–d)**.
[4] With your thread exiting the top of the ladder, begin working the bracelet in flat herringbone stitch (Basics):
Rows 3–6: Work four rows of herringbone following the established bead pattern. To turn at the end of each row, sew down through the last bead in the previous row, pick up a 15°, and sew up through the last bead added in the new row.

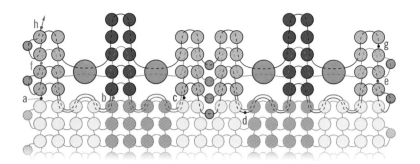

FIGURE 3

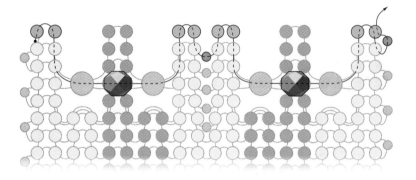

FIGURE 4

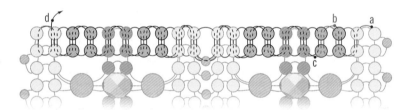

FIGURE 5

Row 7: Work a herringbone stitch with two 11ºs, then sew through the next stitch in row 6 without adding any beads, exiting the following three-cut **(figure 3, a–b)**. Work a stitch with two three-cuts, then sew through the next stitch in row 6 without adding any beads, exiting the following 11º **(b–c)**. Work a stitch with two 11ºs, pick up a 15º, sew through the next 11º, and work another stitch with two 11ºs **(c–d)**. Work the second half of the row as a mirror image of the first, and turn **(d–e)**.

Row 8: Repeat row 7, sewing through the beadwork to skip the same stitches in row 6 **(e–f)**.

Row 9: Picking up the appropriate beads per stitch, work a herringbone stitch on each stack of beads, but pick up a 6º seed bead between the stacks over the skipped stitches. Pick up a 15º between the two center stitches as before, and turn at the end of the row **(f–g)**.

Row 10: In row 11, you will add a 4 mm embellishment bead over the stack of three-cuts, which means you won't have an opportunity to work the three-cut stitches. To compensate, you'll add four beads for each three-cut stitch in this row: Work a herringbone stitch with two 11ºs, sew through the next 6º, and sew up through the following three-cut. Work a stitch with four three-cuts, then sew through the next 6º and 11º. Work the two center stitches as before, work the second half of the row as a mirror image of the first, and turn **(g–h)**.

Row 11: Work a herringbone stitch with two 11ºs, but sew down through two 11ºs instead of one. Sew through the next 6º, pick up a 4 mm fire-polished bead, sew through the following 6º, and sew up through the next two 11ºs. Work the two center stitches as before, work the second half of the row as a mirror image of the first, and turn **(figure 4)**.

[5] Repeat rows 9–11 to the desired length, but in the appropriate repeats of row 11, substitute a 4 mm pearl for the fire-polished bead to create a pattern of one row accented with fire-polished beads followed by two rows accented with pearls. Keep in mind that if you choose to use snaps for the closure, the ends of the band will over-

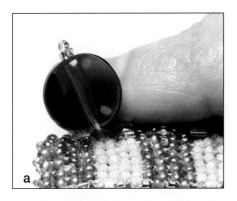

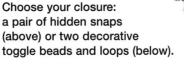

Choose your closure:
a pair of hidden snaps
(above) or two decorative
toggle beads and loops (below).

lap ½ in. (1.3 cm). End and add thread (Basics) as necessary. End on row 11.

[6] Sew down through the next two 11ºs. Working in ladder stitch, pick up two 11ºs, and sew through the previous two 11ºs and the 11ºs just added (**figure 5, a–b**). Pick up two 11ºs, and sew through the previous two 11ºs and the 11ºs just added (**b–c**). Work a ladder stitch thread path through the next two three-cuts and the previous two 11ºs without adding any new beads. Continue working a two-bead ladder across the top row, making sure to work a ladder stitch thread path through the center two stitches and the 15º between them (**c–d**).

Closure

Follow the appropriate steps below to add a snap closure or a double toggle.

Snaps

[1] Sew through the beadwork to exit an end 11º in the ladder you just stitched. Repeat step 3 of "Herringbone band" to add an edging.

[2] Sew through the beadwork to exit a stack of three-cuts on the back of this end of the bracelet. Sew one half of a snap to the three-cuts so that the snap is positioned between two pairs of 6ºs

near the end of the bracelet. Repeat to attach half of the second snap to the other stack of three-cuts on this end of the bracelet. End the working thread.

[3] With the tail, sew the other halves of the snaps to the front of the starting end of the bracelet, positioning them to correspond with the snap halves attached in step 2. End the tail.

Double toggle

[1] With the tail, sew through the beadwork to exit a three-cut in row 5 just below the stack of three-cuts that spans the entire bracelet. Pick up an 11º, a 10 mm bead, and three 15ºs. Skip the 15ºs, sew back through the 10 mm and the 11º, and sew through the next three-cut in the band (**photo a**). Retrace the thread path through the connection. Repeat this step to make another toggle, and end the tail.

[2] On the other end, with the working thread, sew through the beadwork to exit the top of the second stack of As from the edge. Pick up an odd number of alternating 11ºs and 15ºs to fit around a 10 mm bead (about 25), beginning and ending with an 11º. Sew down through a few beads in the next full stack of three-cuts (**photo b**).

DESIGN NOTES:
• In row 9, use firm tension to snug the 6ºs between the stacks of 11ºs and three-cuts. This will cause the sides of the band to taper in, but the remainder of the band will match this width. The wider starting end will be used for the closure.
• When working the purple/gold version of the bracelet, I substituted 11º cylinder beads for the three-cuts. The cylinder beads were not quite as tall as my 11º seed beads, so the cylinder stacks did not "grow" as fast as the seed bead stacks. To compensate, I culled my 11ºs to find the thinnest beads (to make these stacks "grow" slower) and occasionally picked up four beads for the cylinder stitches in the repeats of row 9 (to help the cylinder stacks "catch up" to the 11º stacks).

[3] Sew through the beadwork to exit the first 11º added in the loop. Working in peyote stitch (Basics), pick up a 15º, and sew through the next 11º in the loop. Repeat around the loop, sewing through the last 11º in the loop and into the beadwork (**photo c**).

[4] Repeat steps 2 and 3 to make a second peyote loop.

[5] Work as in step 3 of "Herringbone band" to add an edging between the peyote loops. End the working thread.

Buttoned up style

Highlight beautiful buttons in your beadwork

designed by **Hiroe Takagi**

Put your collection of shank and two-hole buttons to work in this necklace.

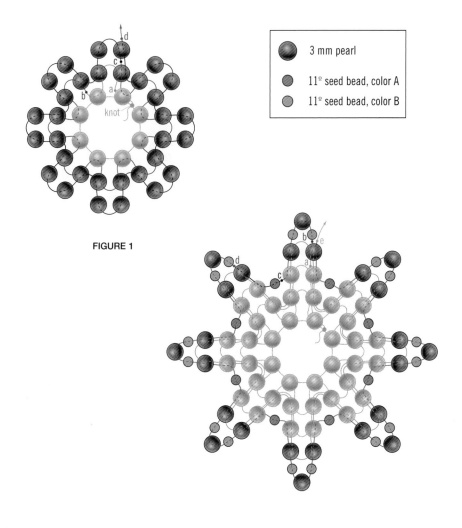

FIGURE 1

Legend:
- 3 mm pearl
- 11º seed bead, color A
- 11º seed bead, color B

FIGURE 2

materials
necklace 16 in. (41 cm)
- **4** 15 mm shank buttons
- **15** 15 mm two-hole buttons
- **12** 11.5 mm two-hole buttons
- **2** 13 x 19 mm oval glass accent beads
- glass pearls (maroon)
  8 12 mm
  12 8 mm
  196 3 mm
- **4** 13 x 20 mm metal leaf stampings*
- **3** 7 x 15 mm metal leaf stampings*
- **5–8 g** 11º seed beads, color A
  (Toho 330, gold-lustered rust)
- **3–5 g** 11º seed beads, color B
  (Toho 221, bronze)
- nylon beading thread, size D,
  or Fireline 6 lb. test
- beading needles, #10

Two layers of herringbone petals take shape around a central button for a cute flower component with vintage appeal. Join a few flowers with two-hole buttons, glass pearls, and metal leaves to create a necklace with classic style.

stepbystep

Two-layer flowers

Top layer

[1] On 2 yd. (1.8 m) of thread or Fireline, pick up eight 3 mm glass pearls, leaving an 8-in. (20 cm) tail. Tie the beads into a ring with a square knot (Basics), leaving a bit of slack between the beads. Sew through the first 3 mm in the ring.

[2] Pick up two 3 mms, and sew through the next 3 mm in the ring **(figure 1, a–b)**. Repeat this step around the ring, and step up through the first 3 mm added in this step **(b–c)**.

[3] Keeping your tension relatively loose, work the top layer of the flower

in tubular herringbone stitch (Basics) as follows, stepping up after each round:

Round 3: Work eight stitches with two 3 mms per stitch **(c–d)**.

Round 4: Work eight stitches with two 3 mms per stitch, but sew down and up through two 3 mms at a time **(figure 2, a–b)**.

Round 5: Pick up a color B 11º seed bead, a 3 mm, and a B, and sew down through the next two 3 mms **(b–c)**. Pick up a color A 11º seed bead, and sew up through the top two 3 mms in the next column **(c–d)**. Repeat these two stitches to complete the round **(d–e)**. After adding the last A, sew through the beadwork to exit a 3 mm added in round 2 **(figure 3, point a)**.

These shank buttons are a set, but imagine the possibilities of using mismatched buttons!

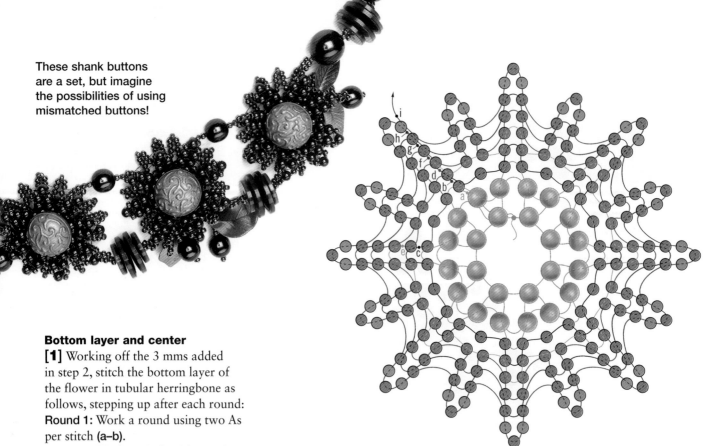

FIGURE 3

Bottom layer and center

[1] Working off the 3 mms added in step 2, stitch the bottom layer of the flower in tubular herringbone as follows, stepping up after each round:
Round 1: Work a round using two As per stitch (a–b).
Round 2: Work a stitch with two As, pick up an A, and sew up through the first A in the next stitch of the previous round (b–c). Repeat these two stitches to complete the round (c–d).
Round 3: Work a stitch with two As, pick up two As, and sew up through the first A in the next stitch of the previous round (d–e). Repeat these two stitches to complete the round (e–f).
Round 4: Using the increase pairs of As added in round 3 as the base for every other stitch, work a round with 16 stitches using two As per stitch (f–g).
Round 5: Work a round with 16 stitches using two As per stitch (g–h).
Round 6: Work 16 stitches using a B, an A, and a B for each stitch (h–i).

[2] Sew through the beadwork to exit a 3 mm in the center ring with the needle pointing up from the top layer.

[3] Sew through the shank of a button, then sew back through the center opening of the flower. Sew through one hole of a 15 mm two-hole button, pick up three As, sew through the other hole of the button, and sew through the center of the flower again (figure 4). Retrace the thread path a couple of times, and end the working thread and tail (Basics).

[4] Make a total of three two-layer flowers.

Necklace

[1] Add 1 yd. (.9 m) of thread (Basics) to one of the flowers, and exit an A at the tip of a bottom layer petal.

[2] Pick up a B, an 8 mm pearl, and a B, and sew through the A at the tip of a bottom layer petal on another flower (figure 5, a–b). Sew back through the three new beads and the petal your thread exited at the start of this step, and sew through the next four bottom layer petals as shown (b–c).

[3] Pick up two Bs, an A, a B, an 11.5 mm two-hole button, two 15 mm two-hole buttons, an 11.5 mm button, a B, an A, and two Bs. Skip three petals from the top connection with the other flower, and sew through the A at the tip of the next petal (c–d).

[4] Pick up two Bs, and sew back through the next A. Pick up a B, and sew back through the remaining holes of all four buttons. Pick up a B, and sew through the next A. Pick up two Bs, and sew through the tip A again (d–e). End the thread.

[5] Repeat steps 1–4 to connect the third flower to the previous two (f–g),

leaving three petals between the top and bottom connections.

[6] Add 1 yd. (.9 m) of thread to one of the side flowers, exiting the tip of the fourth petal from the top connection. Pick up four Bs, sew through the A at the tip of the flower petal again, and continue through the first two Bs just added. Pick up beads and buttons as shown (h–i). Sew through the last eight Bs and the clasp button again (i–j).

[7] Sew back through the next nine beads, exiting the first B after the nearest 12 mm pearl (j–k). Pick up a B, sew through the next group of buttons, pick up a B, skip a B, and sew through the following nine beads (k–l). Pick up a B, sew through the next group of buttons, pick up a B, skip a B, and sew through the following five beads (l–m). End the thread.

[8] Repeat steps 6 and 7 on the other side of the necklace, but instead of picking up eight Bs and a clasp button at the end of step 6, make a loop of Bs to fit around the button. Retrace the thread path through the loop before sewing back through this side of the necklace.

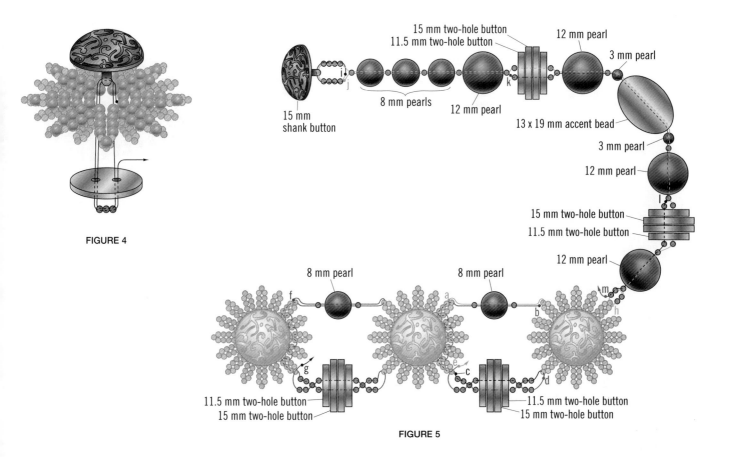

FIGURE 4

15 mm two-hole button

11.5 mm two-hole button

12 mm pearl

3 mm pearl

15 mm
shank button

8 mm pearls

12 mm pearl

13 x 19 mm accent bead

3 mm pearl

12 mm pearl

15 mm two-hole button

11.5 mm two-hole button

12 mm pearl

8 mm pearl

8 mm pearl

11.5 mm two-hole button

15 mm two-hole button

11.5 mm two-hole button

15 mm two-hole button

FIGURE 5

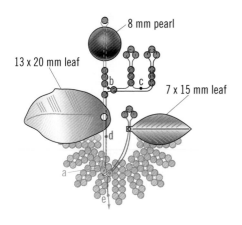

8 mm pearl

13 x 20 mm leaf

7 x 15 mm leaf

FIGURE 6

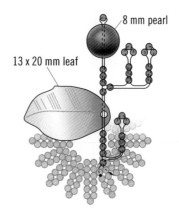

8 mm pearl

13 x 20 mm leaf

FIGURE 7

Fringe

[1] Add 1 yd. (.9 m) of thread to the middle flower, exiting an A in a petal that is adjacent to the center petal on the bottom layer **(figure 6, point a)**.
[2] Pick up a 13 x 20 mm leaf, four As, an 8 mm pearl, and a B, and sew back through the 8 mm and the next three As **(a–b)**.
[3] Pick up four As and three Bs, skip the Bs, and sew back through the last three As **(b–c)**. Pick up three As and

three Bs, skip the Bs, and sew back through the last three As, the two As added previously that you haven't sewn back through, and the leaf **(c–d)**.
[4] Sew back through the A your thread exited at the start of this fringe, and continue through the adjacent bead to exit the next column. Pick up a 7 x 15 mm leaf and three Bs. Skip the Bs, and sew back through the leaf and into the beadwork **(d–e)**.

[5] Sew through the beadwork to exit the petal on the other side of the center petal on the bottom layer, and add another fringe as shown in **figure 7**. End the thread.
[6] Add 1 yd. (.9 m) of thread to one of the side flowers, exiting the sixth petal from the bottom connection point. Work as in steps 2–4 to add a single fringe. End the thread. Repeat this step on the other side flower.

Herringbone
in a
hurry

Work up a three-strand bracelet with accelerated herringbone stitch

designed by **Maggie Roschyk**

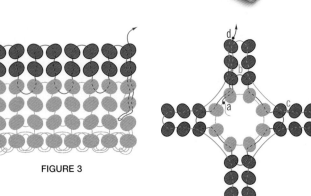

Learn the basic instructions for accelerated flat and tubular herringbone before applying it in a beautiful three-strand bracelet.

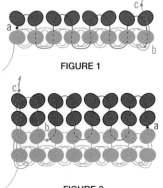

FIGURE 1

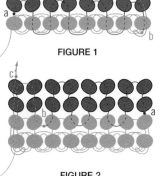

FIGURE 2

FIGURE 3

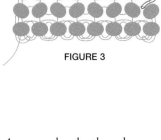

FIGURE 4

Accelerated herringbone
Flat sample

[1] On a comfortable length of thread, make a ladder (Basics) of eight 11º seed beads, leaving a 6-in. (15 cm) tail. Zigzag back through the ladder so the working thread and tail are exiting opposite ends of the first bead.

[2] Work a row of regular flat herringbone stitch using 11ºs (Basics and **figure 1, a–b**). To step up at the end of the row, sew under the bottom thread bridge between the last two beads in the ladder, and sew back through the next two edge 11ºs **(b–c)**.

[3] Work a row of accelerated

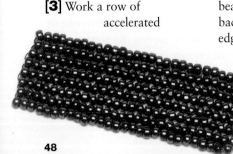

herringbone: Pick up four 11ºs per stitch instead of two, stopping short of the last stitch **(figure 2, a–b)**.

[4] To work the last stitch and step up at the end of an accelerated row, sew up through the next 11º in the previous row. Pick up four 11ºs, sew down through two beads instead of one, sew under the bottom thread bridge between the first two beads in the ladder, and sew back through the next four edge 11ºs **(b–c)**.

[5] To work subsequent rows: Continue adding rows as in steps 3 and 4, but in step

4 sew under the thread bridge between the last two beads in the previous row instead of the bottom thread bridge of the ladder **(figure 3)**. Add rows until you feel comfortable with the technique, ending and adding thread (Basics) as needed.

Tubular sample

[1] On a comfortable length of thread, pick up eight 11ºs, leaving a 6-in. (15 cm) tail. Tie the beads into a ring with a square knot (Basics), leaving a little space between the beads. Sew through the first 11º in the ring.

[2] Pick up two 11ºs, and sew through the next two

11ºs in the ring. Repeat around the ring, and step up through the first 11º added in this round **(figure 4, a–b)**.

[3] Work a round of accelerated tubular herringbone: Pick up four 11ºs, sew down through the next 11º, and sew up through the following 11º in the previous round **(b–c)**. Repeat to complete the round, and step up through the first two 11ºs picked up in the first stitch of this round **(c–d)**. Continue adding rounds until you feel comfortable with the technique, ending and adding thread as needed.

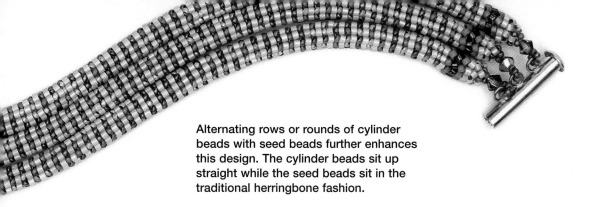

Alternating rows or rounds of cylinder beads with seed beads further enhances this design. The cylinder beads sit up straight while the seed beads sit in the traditional herringbone fashion.

stepbystep

[1] On a comfortable length of Fireline, pick up a repeating pattern of a color A 11º cylinder bead and a 15º seed bead four times, leaving a 12-in. (30 cm) tail. Sew through all the beads again to form a ring, and exit an A (figure 5, a–b).

[2] Pick up two As, and sew through the next A in the ring. Repeat around the ring, and step up through the first A picked up in this round (b–c).

[3] Work four rounds of tubular herringbone (Basics): a round of As (c–d), a round of color B 11º cylinder beads (d–e), a round of color C 11º cylinder beads (e–f), and a round of Bs (f–g).

[4] Work a round of accelerated herringbone stitch: Pick up an A, two 15ºs, and an A. Sew down through the next B, and sew up through the following B in the previous round. Repeat to complete the round, and step up through the first A and 15º picked up in this round (g–h).

[5] Pick up an A, two 15ºs, and an A. Sew down through the next 15º, and sew up through the following 15º in the previous round. Repeat to complete the round, and step up through the first A and 15º picked up in this round.

[6] Repeat step 5 61 times for a total of 126 rounds of alternating As and 15ºs, ending and adding thread (Basics) as needed.

[7] Work six rounds of tubular herringbone in the following colors: A, B, C, B, A, A. Step up through the first A picked up in the last round.

[8] Work a round of tubular herringbone, but pick up only one A per stitch. Step up through the first A picked up in this round.

[9] Pick up a 15º, and sew through the next A in the previous round. Repeat to complete the round. Retrace the thread path of the 15ºs and As twice, and exit a 15º.

[10] Pick up a 15º, a 4 mm bicone crystal, five 15ºs, and one loop of half of the clasp. Skip the last five 15ºs, and sew back through the 4 mm. Pick up a 15º, and sew through the 15º opposite the one your thread exited at the start of this step. Sew through the beadwork to retrace the thread path of the clasp connection, and end the working thread. With the tail, repeat to attach the corresponding loop of the other half of the clasp. End the tail.

[11] Make two more tubular herringbone ropes, and attach them to the remaining loops of the clasp.

materials

flat and tubular accelerated herringbone samples
- 3–4 g 11º seed beads
- nylon beading thread, size D
- beading needles, #10 or #12

bracelet 8 in. (20 cm)
- 6 4 mm bicone crystals (Swarovski, medium vitrail)
- 11º cylinder beads
  8–9 g color A (DB1458, silver-lined light honey opal)
  96 color B (DB371, matte opaque golden olive luster)
  48 color C (DB463, galvanized dark magenta)
- 4–5 g 15º seed beads (F463l, matte metallic mustard)
- 3-strand clasp
- Fireline 6 lb. test
- beading needles, #12

DESIGN NOTE: If your stitching tension is loose, the herringbone tubes will flatten out. To correct this, cut three pieces of ⅛-in. (3 mm) tubing, and insert one into each tube before closing up the end.

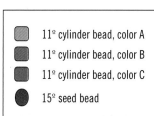

▨	11º cylinder bead, color A
▨	11º cylinder bead, color B
▨	11º cylinder bead, color C
●	15º seed bead

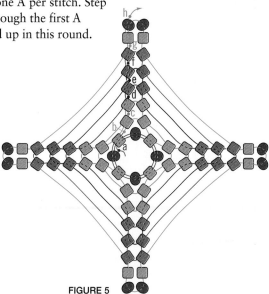

FIGURE 5

49

Tila token

Two-hole Tila beads lend stability to this delicate beaded band

designed by **Marcia Balonis**

Suspend Tila beads between delicate rows of herringbone stitch in this surprisingly sturdy bracelet.

stepbystep

Herringbone band

[1] On 2 yd. (1.8 m) of Fireline, pick up two color A 11º cylinder beads and two color B 11º cylinder beads, leaving a 12-in. (30 cm) tail. Sew through all the beads again, and form them into two stacks of two beads each **(figure 1, a–b)**.

[2] Working in two-bead ladder stitch (Basics), pick up two Bs, and sew through the previous stack of beads and the two Bs just added to form a new stack **(b–c)**. Continue working in two-bead ladder stitch to add two stacks of As, two stacks of Bs, and a stack of As **(c–d)**. This forms the first two rows of the bracelet.

[3] With the thread exiting the bottom of the first row, pick up a 15º seed bead, and sew up through the last bead in the second row **(d–e)** so you are in position to start the next row.

[4] Rows 3 and 4: Work in flat herringbone stitch (Basics) following the established bead pattern. To turn, sew down through the last bead in the previous row, pick up a 15º, and sew up through the last bead added in the new row.

Row 5: Work a herringbone stitch with an A and a B, and then sew through the next two stitches without adding

FIGURE 1

any beads, exiting the last B in the previous row **(figure 2, a–b)**. Work a stitch with a B and an A, and turn **(b–c)**.

Row 6: Work a herringbone stitch with an A and a B, but sew down through two Bs instead of one. Sew through the next two stitches without adding any beads, and then sew up through the

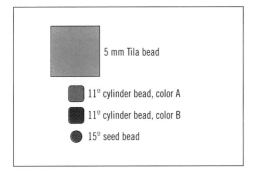

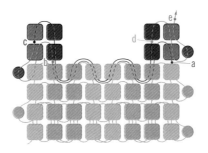

FIGURE 2

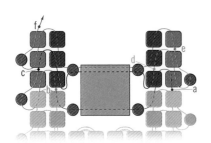

FIGURE 3

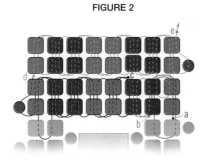

FIGURE 4

materials

green bracelet 6½ in. (16.5 cm)
- **27** 5 mm Tila beads (Miyuki 468, metallic malachite green iris)
- 3–4 g 11º Japanese cylinder beads in each of **2** colors:
  A (Miyuki 1051, matte metallic bronze gold iris)
  B (Miyuki 0128, amethyst gold iris)
- 2–3 g 15º seed beads (Miyuki 313, cranberry gold luster)
- clasp
- **2** 6 mm jump rings
- Fireline 6 lb. test
- beading needles, #11
- **2** pairs of pliers

gold iris bracelet colors:
- 5 mm Tila beads (Miyuki 457, bronze)
- 11º cylinder beads
  A (Miyuki 0133, opaque golden olive luster)
  B (Miyuki 0011, metallic olive)
- 15º seed beads (Miyuki 1897, opaque golden olive luster)

bronze bracelet colors:
- 5 mm Tila beads (Miyuki 2035, matte khaki iris)
- 11º cylinder beads
  A (Miyuki 0024, metallic green)
  B (Miyuki 0103, transparent pale red)
- 15º seed beads (Miyuki 2238, lined topaz/yellow)

next two Bs in the last stack (c–d). Work a herringbone stitch using a B and an A, and turn (d–e).

Row 7: Work a herringbone stitch with an A and a B, pick up a 15º, a 5 mm Tila bead, and a 15º, and sew through the top B in the last stack (figure 3, a–b). Work a herringbone stitch with a B and an A, and turn (b–c).

Row 8: Work a herringbone stitch with an A and a B, pick up a 15º, and sew through the available hole of the Tila bead added in the previous row. Pick up a 15º, and sew through the top B in the following stack (c–d). Work a herringbone stitch with a B and an A, and turn (d–e).

Row 9: Work a herringbone stitch with an A and a B, and sew through the 15º added in the previous row, the same hole of the Tila bead, the next 15º, and the top B in the last stack. Work a herringbone stitch with a B and an A, and turn (e–f).

[5] Repeat rows 7–9 to within one Tila bead of the desired length.

[6] To add the last Tila bead, repeat rows 7 and 8.

[7] Working in two-bead ladder stitch, pick up two As and two Bs, sew through the previous B and A, and sew through the two As and Bs just added (figure 4, a–b). Pick up two Bs, and sew through the previous two Bs and the Bs just added (b–c). Continue working in two-bead ladder stitch to add two stacks of As, two stacks of Bs, and a stack of As. Join the last two stacks to the B and A in the herringbone stack below by following a three-bead ladder stitch thread path and adding a 15º turn bead (c–d).

[8] Work a row of two-bead ladder stitch following the established pattern, attach the last two stacks as in step 7, and add a 15º to make the turn (d–e) so your thread is exiting the top of

the final stack. The two center stacks added in this row will be connected to the previous row when you attach the clasp. Do not end the working thread or tail.

Clasp

[1] With the working thread, sew through the beadwork to exit the top of the third stack of beads from the edge. Pick up seven 15ºs, skip the next two stacks, and sew through the end four beads in the following stack. Zigzag through the previous stacks to exit the top of the third stack, retrace the thread path through the seven-bead loop, and end the thread (Basics).

[2] Open a 6 mm jump ring (Basics), and attach the seven-bead loop to half of the clasp.

[3] Repeat steps 1 and 2 on the remaining end of the bracelet.

DESIGN NOTE:
For a wider bracelet, make two herringbone bands. On one band, pick up 2 mm crystals or 11º seed beads between the 15ºs along one edge. Lay the second band beside this edge so that the 15ºs straddle the 2 mms or 11ºs. Sew through the 15ºs on this band and the 2 mms or 11ºs on the other.

Pretty pearls

Diagonal right-angle weave aligns tiny pearls in neat rows, creating elegant wear-anywhere accessories

designed by **Diane Whiting**

Coordinate your colors with custom multistrand clasps from Alacarte Clasps. Match Swarovski baguette crystals to your pearls for a high-fashion finish that doubles as a focal in this classic accessory.

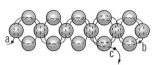

FIGURE 1

FIGURE 2

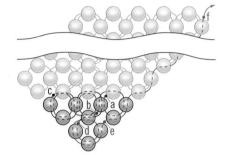

FIGURE 3

materials

bracelet 7⅜ in. (19 cm)
- **300–324** 3 mm crystal pearls (Swarovski, white, light gold, or platinum)
- 3-strand clasp
- Fireline 6 lb. test, or nylon beading thread, size D
- beading needles, #12

DESIGN NOTE:

If you want to try diagonal right-angle weave before picking up a bunch of pearls, use seed beads or peanut beads instead. Once you get the hang of the stitch, switch to pearls, or finish up the sample strip for a casual version.

stepbystep

[1] On a comfortable length of Fireline or thread, pick up four 3 mm pearls, leaving a 12-in. (30 cm) tail. Working in right-angle weave (Basics), make a strip five stitches long (**figure 1, a–b**). Zigzag back through the last two stitches, exiting the bottom pearl of the second-to-last stitch (**b–c**). This will offset the start of the second row, creating a decrease along this edge as the next row of pearls is added.

[2] Work a row of right-angle weave, using three pearls for the first stitch (**figure 2, a–b**), two pearls for each of the next three stitches (**b–c**), and three pearls for the last stitch (**c–d**). The last stitch is an increase stitch along this edge, creating the diagonal pattern. Zigzag back through the next three stitches, exiting the bottom pearl in the second stitch of this row (**d–e**).

[3] Repeat step 2 until you reach the desired length, ending and adding thread (Basics) as needed, and measuring from the highest points on each end.

[4] Exiting the second stitch of the end row, work one stitch using three pearls (**figure 3, a–b**) and two stitches using two pearls (**b–c**). Zigzag through the last two stitches, exiting the bottom pearl in the second stitch of this row (**c–d**).

[5] Work one stitch using three pearls, and sew through all the pearls added in this stitch (**d–e**).

[6] Using even tension, sew through the pearls along one edge of the bracelet (**e–f**) to anchor them. If your tension is too tight, the edge may curve, causing the stitches in the band to buckle. Smooth out the band on your work surface so it lies flat and the edges are straight.

[7] Repeat steps 4 and 5 on this end, then work as in step 6 along the remaining edge.

[8] Exit the first pearl in the end row. Sew through the first loop of half of the clasp and the next two pearls in the end row. Repeat to attach the remaining loops, and retrace the thread path. End the working thread. Using the tail, repeat this step on the other end of the bracelet.

Crystal
caps

Weave a lovely crystal topper for a large pearl or gemstone, and then enclose the bead within a seed bead cage

designed by **Amy Johnson**

	3 mm bicone crystal
	11º seed bead
	15º seed bead

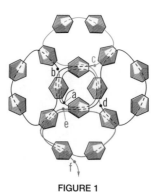

FIGURE 1

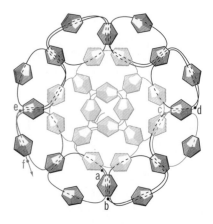

FIGURE 2

stepbystep

Crystal cap and seed bead cage

[1] On 2 yd. (1.8 m) of Fireline, pick up four 3 mm bicone crystals, and tie them into a ring with a square knot (Basics), leaving a 10-in. (25 cm) tail. Sew through the first 3 mm in the ring **(figure 1, a–b)**.

[2] To begin round 1, pick up four 3 mms, and sew through the 3 mm your thread exited at the start of this step and the next 3 mm in the original ring **(b–c)**.

[3] Pick up three 3 mms, and sew through the nearest 3 mm in the previous stitch, the 3 mm your thread exited at the start of this step, and the next 3 mm in the original ring **(c–d)**. Repeat this step once **(d–e)**.

[4] Sew through the nearest 3 mm in the first stitch, pick up two 3 mms, and sew through the nearest 3 mm in the previous stitch, the 3 mm your thread exited at the start of this step, the nearest 3 mm in the first stitch, and the first 3 mm picked up in this step **(e–f)**.

[5] To begin round 2, pick up three 3 mms, and sew through the 3 mm your thread exited at the start of this step and the first 3 mm picked up in this stitch **(figure 2, a–b)**.

[6] Pick up two 3 mms, and sew back through the next edge 3 mm in the previous round, the 3 mm your thread exited at the start of this step, the two 3 mms picked up in this step, and the next edge 3 mm **(b–c)**.

[7] Pick up two 3 mms, and sew through the nearest 3 mm in the previous stitch, the 3 mm your thread exited at the start of this step, and the first 3 mm picked up in this step **(c–d)**.

[8] Repeat steps 6 and 7 two times **(d–e)**.

[9] Pick up a 3 mm, and sew through the nearest 3 mm in the first stitch of this round, the next edge 3 mm in the previous round, the 3 mm your thread exited at the start of this step, and the 3 mm picked up in this step **(e–f)**.

[10] Using the tail, sew through the next 3 mm in the original ring. Pick up a 15º seed bead, and sew through the next 3 mm in the ring. Repeat this stitch to complete the round, and then sew through three 3 mms from a stitch in round 1. Pick up a 15º, and sew through the next two outer 3 mms in the next stitch of round 1. Repeat to complete the round, and end the tail (Basics).

[11] With the working thread, pick up an 11º seed bead, and sew through the next 3 mm along the outer edge of round 2. Repeat this stitch to complete

You can use any 12 mm round bead in this project. If necessary, adjust the number of 15ºs in step 12 to change the size of the seed bead cages.

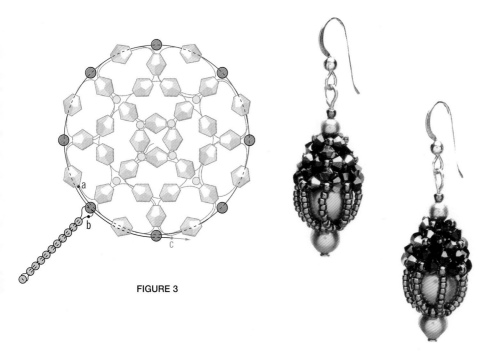

FIGURE 3

the round, and then sew through the first 11º **(figure 3, a–b)**.

[12] Pick up 11 15ºs. Skip the last 15º, and sew back through the next 10 15ºs, the 11º your thread exited at the start of this step, and the next 3 mm and 11º along the outer edge of round 2 **(b–c)**. Repeat this step to complete the round, and then sew through one of the spokes of 15ºs, exiting the end 15º. Don't end the working thread.

[13] Make a second crystal cap and cage.

Assembly

[1] On a head pin, string a 6 mm pearl, a 12 mm pearl or gemstone bead, a 6 mm pearl, a crystal cap with the spokes of the cage facing the 12 mm, a 4 mm pearl, and an 11º. Make a plain loop (Basics).

[2] With the working thread, pick up a 15º, and sew through the end 15º of the next spoke. Repeat this stitch to complete the round, creating a ring between the 12 mm and the 6 mm at the bottom of the head pin **(photo)**. Retrace the thread path, and end the working thread.

[3] Open the loop of an earring finding (Basics), and attach the plain loop.

[4] Assemble the second earring.

materials

copper earrings, 2 in. (5 cm)

- crystal pearls (Swarovski, bright gold)
  2 12 mm
  4 6 mm
  2 4 mm
- **64** 3 mm bicone crystals (Swarovski, crystal copper)
- **18** 11º seed beads (Miyuki 318L, raspberry gold luster)
- **1 g** 15º seed beads (Miyuki 318L, raspberry gold luster)
- **2** 2-in. (5 cm) head pins, 22-gauge (gold)
- pair of earring findings (gold)
- Fireline 6 lb. test
- beading needles, #12 or #13
- chainnose pliers
- roundnose pliers
- wire cutters

pink/green earring colors:

- 12 mm round gemstone beads (rhodonite)
- 4 and 6 mm crystal pearls (Swarovski, light green)
- 3 mm bicone crystals (Swarovski, vintage pink AB 2X)
- 11º seed beads (Miyuki P475, light rose permanent galvanized)
- 15º seed beads (F460l, olivine bronze matte metallic iris)

black/gold earring colors:

- 12 mm, 6mm, and 4mm crystal pearls (Swarovski, bright gold)
- 3 mm bicone crystals (Swarovski, jet AB)
- 11º seed beads (Toho 457L, metallic light bronze)
- 15º seed beads (Toho 457L, metallic light bronze)

Cocktail cuff

What a combination! Take a classic pearl cuff and embellish it with sparkling margaritas to create this glamorous bracelet

designed by **Jane Danley Cruz**

The origin of pearl bracelets can be traced back to China. Today bracelets are more popular than ever and are enjoyed as a wardrobe staple.

FIGURE 1

FIGURE 2

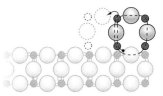

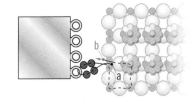

6 mm crystal margarita

4 mm pearl

11º seed bead

15º seed bead

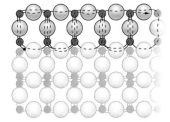

FIGURE 3

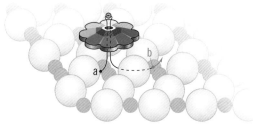

FIGURE 4

FIGURE 5

Stitch this fetching pearl band and nestle margaritas within the right-angle weave stitches for an alluring I-could-have-danced-all-night accessory.

stepbystep

Pearl base

[1] On a comfortable length of Fireline, pick up a repeating pattern of an 11º seed bead and a 4 mm pearl four times, leaving a 6-in. (15 cm) tail. Sew through all the beads again to form a ring, and exit an 11º. Form the ring into a square.

[2] Working in right-angle weave (Basics), pick up a 4 mm, an 11º, a 4 mm, an 11º, and a 4 mm, sew through the last three beads your thread exited in the previous stitch (**figure 1, a–b**), and continue through the first four beads just added (**b–c**).

[3] Repeat step 2 for the desired length. My 6¾-in. (17.1 cm) bracelet is 27 right-angle weave stitches long.

[4] With your thread exiting the last 11º, 4 mm, and 11º in the end stitch, sew through the next 4 mm in the stitch.

[5] Pick up a repeating pattern of an 11º and a 4 mm three times, and then pick up an 11º. Sew through the 4 mm your thread exited at the start of this step and the first three beads added in this stitch (**figure 2**). Continue working in right-angle weave to create a second row of right-angle weave.

[6] Repeat steps 4 and 5 to create a third row of right-angle weave (**figure 3**), ending and adding thread (Basics) as needed.

Embellishment

[1] Add 2 yd. (1.8 m) of thread to the base, exiting an inside 4 mm at one end of the first row of right-angle weave (**figure 4, point a**). Pick up a 6 mm margarita and a 15º seed bead, skip the 15º, and sew back through the margarita and the 4 mm in the next right-angle weave stitch (**a–b**). Repeat to the end of the row.

[2] Sew through the end 11º, 4 mm, and 11º, and continue through the next inside 4 mm. Continue to add a second row of margaritas and 15ºs as in step 1, and end the thread.

Clasp

[1] Add 9 in. (23 cm) of thread to one end of the base, exiting the second 11º in the end right-angle weave stitch of the first row (**figure 5, point a**).

[2] Pick up two 11ºs, a loop of the clasp, and two 11ºs, and sew through all the beads in the end right-angle weave stitch (**a–b**). Retrace the thread path through the loop of beads and the clasp.

[3] Sew through the next end 11º, and repeat step 2 to attach the next loop of the clasp.

[4] Sew through the next end 4 mm and 11º, and repeat steps 2 and 3. End the thread.

[5] Repeat steps 1–4 on the other end of the base.

materials

bracelet 6¾ in. (17.1 cm)

- **52** 6 mm margaritas (Swarovski, crystal light vitrail unfoiled)
- **192** 4 mm round pearls (Swarovski, platinum)
- **3–4 g** 11º seed beads (Miyuki 461, metallic chocolate)
- **1–2 g** 15º seed beads (Toho 711, nickel-plated silver)
- 4-strand box clasp (Eclectica, 262-641-0961)
- Fireline 6 lb. test
- beading needles, #13

DESIGN NOTE:

You can embellish this bracelet with margarita thrones as well.

Crystal tapestry

Use bicone crystals to give this piece the look of cloth with a sparkling floral motif

designed by **Ludmila Raitzin**

Send sparkles in every direction while wearing this colorful crystal cuff.

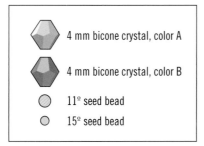

	4 mm bicone crystal, color A
	4 mm bicone crystal, color B
	11º seed bead
	15º seed bead

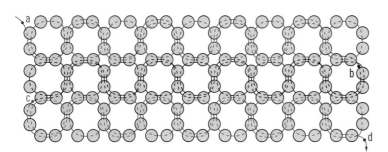

FIGURE 1

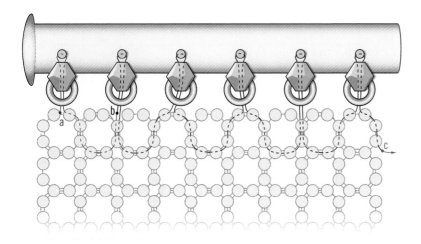

FIGURE 2

materials
bracelet 8 in. (20 cm)
- 4 mm bicone crystals (Swarovski)
  78 color A (chrysolite)
  107 color B (erinite)
  55 color C (light topaz)
  64 color D (sun)
  68 color E (light Siam)
- 20 g 11º seed beads (silver-lined gold)
- 12 15º seed beads (light green)
- 6-strand slide clasp
- Fireline 6 lb. test
- beading needles, #12

To capture the bright, cheery colors of summer flowers, start with a base of right-angle weave. Then, follow the pattern to embellish the base with bold crystal colors. The weight of the crystals lends a luxurious, fabric-like drape to this bracelet.

stepbystep

Right-angle weave base
[1] On a comfortable length of Fireline, pick up eight 11º seed beads, leaving a 12-in. (30 cm) tail. Stitch right-angle weave (Basics) with this modification: Make a strip of nine stitches using eight 11ºs for the first stitch and six 11ºs for each subsequent stitch **(figure 1, a–b)**.

Each "side" of every stitch will have two beads (instead of one, as in traditional right-angle weave).
[2] Add a row (Basics), using six 11ºs for the first stitch and four 11ºs for each subsequent stitch **(b–c)**.
[3] Repeat step 2 **(c–d)** until you have 40 rows, ending and adding thread (Basics) as needed. Exit between two 11ºs in an end stitch.

Clasp
[1] Sew through a loop of the clasp, and then pick up a color A 4 mm bicone crystal and a 15º seed bead. Skip the 15º, and sew back through the A, the loop of the clasp, and the next several 11ºs in the end row to exit near the next loop of the clasp **(figure 2, a–b)**.
[2] Repeat step 1 to connect the remaining loops of the clasp **(b–c)**. Retrace the thread path to secure the join, and end the working thread.
[3] Using the tail, repeat steps 1 and 2 on the other end of the bracelet.

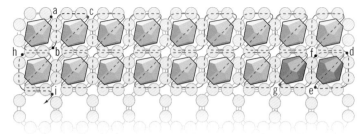

FIGURE 3

4 mm bicone crystals

Color A, chrysolite

Color B, erinite

Color C, light topaz

Color D, sun

Color E, light Siam

Crystal embellishment

[1] Add a comfortable length of doubled Fireline to an end row, exiting two end 11°s in a corner stitch with your thread pointing toward the opposite edge of the base (**figure 3, point a**). This will be referred to as row 1 of the base.

[2] To embellish row 1: Pick up an A, and sew through the two 11°s opposite the 11°s your thread exited at the start of this step in the same direction (**a–b**). Sew through the next two 11°s in row 1 of the base, and then continue through the next two end 11°s in the following stitch (**b–c**). Repeat to complete the row using As (**c–d**). Sew through the next four 11°s in row 2 of the base (**d–e**).

[3] To embellish row 2: Pick up a color B 4 mm bicone crystal, and sew through the two 11°s opposite the 11°s your thread exited at the start of this step (**e–f**). Sew through the next four 11°s in row 2 (**f–g**). Repeat to complete the row using a B for the next stitch and As for the remaining stitches (**g–h**). Sew through the next four 11°s to position your thread to begin row 3 (**h–i**).

[4] Work rows 3–40 using 4 mm bicone crystals in colors A–E, picking up one bead per stitch, and ending and adding doubled thread as needed. Make sure when you add thread that your new thread exits the same spot you left off. Refer to the **pattern** as needed:

Row 3: Five As, one B, one A, and two Bs.
Row 4: Six Bs and three As.
Row 5: Two Bs, one A, and six Bs.
Row 6: Nine Bs.
Row 7: Five Bs, two Cs, and two Bs.
Row 8: One B, three Cs, one B, one C, and three Bs.
Row 9: Two Bs, five Cs, one B, and one C.
Row 10: One B, one C, two Ds, one C, one D, two Cs, and one B.
Row 11: One B, one C, one D, one C, three Ds, one B, and one C.
Row 12: Three Cs, four Ds, and two Cs.

Row 13: One C, six Ds, one B, one C.
Row 14: One B, two Ds, one E, one D, one C, and three Ds.
Row 15: One E, four Ds, one E, one C, and two Ds.
Row 16: One B, one E, one D, two Es, one D, and three Es.
Row 17: One E, one D, three Es, one D, and three Es.
Row 18: Eight Es and one D.
Row 19: One D and eight Es.
Row 20: One B, one E, one D, three Es, one D, and two Es.
Row 21: Three Es, one D, two Cs, and three Es.
Row 22: One B, three Es, one C, and four Es.
Row 23: Nine Es.
Row 24: One B, two Es, one D, two Es, two Ds, and one E.
Row 25: Four Ds, one E, one D, one E, one C, and one B.
Row 26: Two Bs, one E, and six Ds.
Row 27: Three Ds, one C, four Ds, and one B.
Row 28: Two Bs, one C, one B, one C, three Ds, and one C.
Row 29: Four Cs, one D, one B, one D, and two Bs.
Row 30: Two Bs, five Cs, one B, and one A.
Row 31: One A, two Bs, five Cs, and one B.
Row 32: Two Bs, four Cs, one B, and two As.
Row 33: One A, four Bs, one C, and three Bs.
Row 34: One B, one A, and seven Bs.
Row 35: Three Bs, one A, and five Bs.
Row 36: Three Bs, one A, one B, three As, and one B.
Row 37: One B, five As, and three Bs.
Row 38: Two Bs and seven As.
Row 39: Eight As and one B.
Row 40: Nine As.

[5] End any remaining threads.

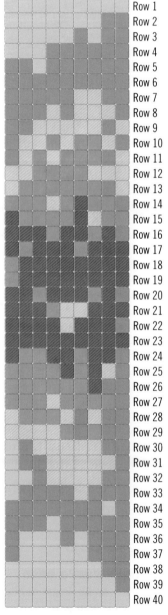

Row 1
Row 2
Row 3
Row 4
Row 5
Row 6
Row 7
Row 8
Row 9
Row 10
Row 11
Row 12
Row 13
Row 14
Row 15
Row 16
Row 17
Row 18
Row 19
Row 20
Row 21
Row 22
Row 23
Row 24
Row 25
Row 26
Row 27
Row 28
Row 29
Row 30
Row 31
Row 32
Row 33
Row 34
Row 35
Row 36
Row 37
Row 38
Row 39
Row 40

PATTERN

CUBIC RIGHT-ANGLE WEAVE
Power trio

Embellish a supple
spine of cubic
right-angle weave
with sparkling
seed beads

designed by **Isabella Lam**

Stitch three or four of
these fun bracelets
to wear together.

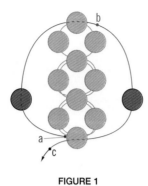

FIGURE 1

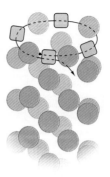

FIGURE 2

Legend:

- 8º seed bead
- 11º cylinder bead
- 15º seed bead

Get ready to rock and roll! In rock music, a power trio features guitar, bass, and drums for maximum musical impact. This bracelet uses three types of beads to much the same effect.

stepbystep

Rope

[1] On a comfortable length of Fireline, work a strip of three right-angle weave stitches (Basics) using 8º seed beads and leaving a 6-in. (15 cm) tail. Join the first and last stitches to form a ring: Exit an end 8º in the last stitch. Pick up an 8º, sew through the end 8º in the first stitch (**figure 1, a–b**), pick up an 8º, and sew through the end 8º in the last stitch (**b–c**). Sew through the four 8ºs on the top and bottom of the cube to make it more stable.

[2] Continue working in cubic right-angle weave, working off of the four top 8ºs in the previous cube: Exit a top 8º, pick up three 8ºs, and sew through the top 8º your thread just exited and the first 8º just picked up. For the next stitch, pick up two 8ºs, sew through the next top 8º, the side 8º in the previous stitch, and the two 8ºs just picked up. For the third stitch, sew through the next top 8º, and pick up two 8ºs. Sew through the side 8º in the previous stitch, the third top 8º, and the first 8º just picked up. For the fourth stitch, pick up an 8º, and sew through the side 8º in the first stitch, the fourth top 8º, the side 8º in the previous stitch, and the 8º just picked up. To complete the cube, sew through the four new top 8ºs to stabilize the structure.

[3] Repeat step 2 to make a rope the desired length, ending and adding thread (Basics) as necessary. When the rope is completed, end the working thread and tail.

DESIGN NOTE:

To go from rocker to glamour girl, substitute 2 mm round crystals for the cylinder beads.

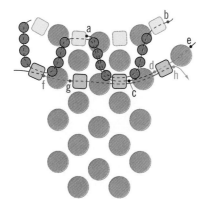

FIGURE 3

Embellishment

[1] Add 2 yd. (1.8 m) of Fireline to one end of the rope, exiting an end 8º. Pick up an 11º cylinder bead, and sew through the next end 8º in the same round of the rope. Repeat this stitch three more times, and step up through the first cylinder picked up in this step **(figure 2)**.

[2] Pick up four 15º seed beads, a cylinder, and four 15ºs. Skip the next cylinder added in the previous round, and sew through the following cylinder **(figure 3, a–b)**. Repeat this stitch, and step up through the first four 15ºs and cylinder picked up at the start of this step **(b–c)**.

[3] Sew through the adjacent 8º in the next round of the rope that is parallel to the hole in the cylinder your thread is exiting **(c–d)**. Pick up a cylinder, and sew through the next 8º in the same round **(d–e)**, the center cylinder in the next stitch of the previous step **(e–f)**, and the next 8º in the same round of the rope **(f–g)**. Pick up a cylinder, and sew through the next 8º in the same

round of the rope, the center cylinder added in the next stitch of the previous step, the following 8º in the same round of the rope, and the first cylinder picked up in this step **(g–h)**. This will ensure that the embellishment stitches line up.

[4] Repeat steps 2 and 3 for the length of the rope, and end the thread.

Clasp

[1] Add 12 in. (30 cm) of thread to one end of the rope, and pick up an end cap, an 8º, three 15ºs, half of the clasp, and three 15ºs. Sew back through the 8º and the end cap, and continue into the rope. Retrace the thread path several times to secure, and end the thread.

[2] Repeat step 1 on the other end of the rope.

materials

pink bracelet 8 in. (20 cm)
- 7–8 g 8º seed beads (Toho 2107, milky electric pink)
- 2–3 g 11º cylinder beads (Miyuki DBC0310, matte black)
- 2–3 g 15º seed beads (Toho 711, nickel-plated silver)
- 2 10 x 11 mm end caps (silver)
- clasp
- Fireline 6 lb. test
- beading needles, #11

blue bracelet colors:
- 8º seed beads (Toho 511F, metallic frosted Mediterranean blue)
- 11º cylinder beads (Miyuki DB0218, medium blue opaque luster)
- 15º seed beads (Toho 711, nickel-plated silver)

gold bracelet colors:
- 8º seed beads (Miyuki 551, gilt-lined opal)
- 11º cylinder beads (Miyuki DB0027, metallic dark green iris cut)
- 15º seed beads (Miyuki 1421, dyed silver-lined golden olive)

purple bracelet colors:
- 8º seed beads (Toho 928, color-lined purple/rosaline AB)
- 11º cylinder beads (Miyuki DB0027, metallic dark green iris cut)
- 15º seed beads (Miyuki 551, gilt-lined opal)

pearl bracelet colors:
- 8º seed beads (Toho 592, antique ivory pearl Ceylon)
- 11º cylinder beads (Miyuki DB0042, silver-lined gold)
- 15º seed beads (Miyuki 313, cranberry gold luster)

CUBIC RIGHT-ANGLE WEAVE

Creating connections

Shape rows of cubic right-angle weave with three simple connecting techniques

designed by **Alla Maslennikova**

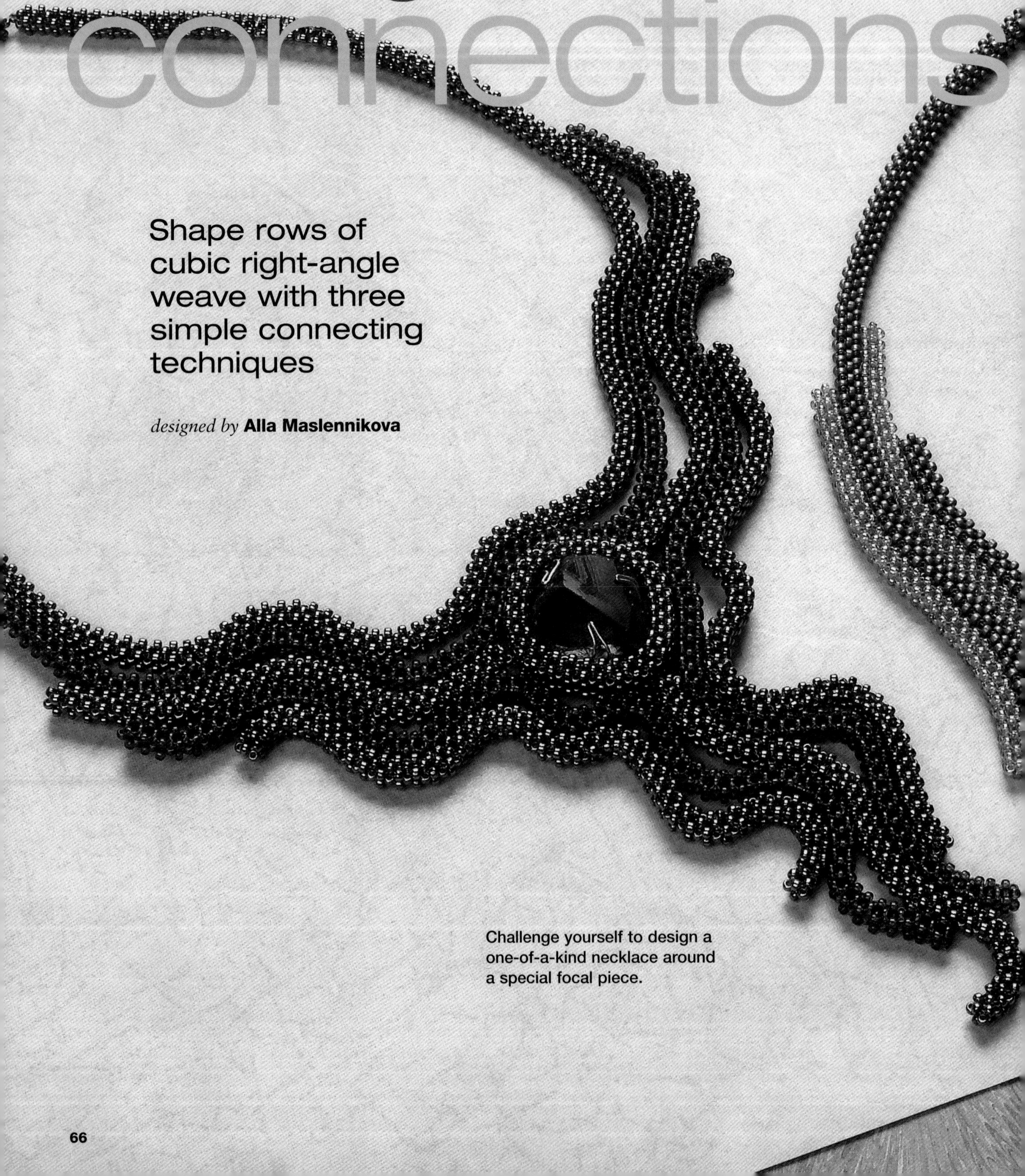

Challenge yourself to design a one-of-a-kind necklace around a special focal piece.

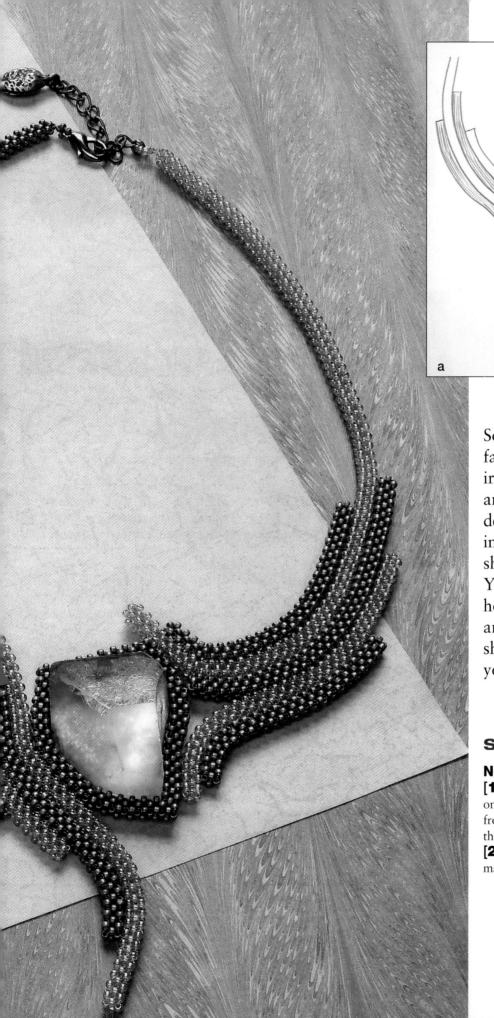

a

Sometimes you'll find a
fabulous focal piece with
irregular edges or sharp
angles. Sketching out your
design ideas will help you
incorporate these tricky
shapes into your beadwork.
You'll be delighted to see
how rows of cubic right-
angle weave can be easily
shaped into almost anything
you can dream up!

stepbystep

Necklace design

[1] Outline the shape of your focal piece
on paper. Make a second outline 4 mm
from the first outline for the width of
the cubic right-angle weave bezel.
[2] Sketch your design around the focal,
making 4 mm strips as desired (photo a).

materials

yellow/gray necklace 15–17 in. (38–43 cm)

- 1–2-in. (2.5–5 cm) stone, crystal, or glass focal piece
- 20–50 g 15º seed beads in each of **2** colors: A (190F, matte nickel), B (1889, golden olive goldluster)
- clasp
- **2** 3–4 mm jump rings
- nylon beading thread, size D
- beading needles, #12 or #13
- E6000 adhesive
- Lacy's Stiff Stuff or Ultrasuede
- metal bezel with prongs (optional, beadsbydee.com)
- **2** pairs of pliers

brown necklace colors:

- 15º seed beads: A (457L, light bronze), B (134, smoky topaz)

gold necklace colors:

- 15º seed beads: A (1053, yellow gold galvanized), B (132, light topaz)

DESIGN NOTES:

- **You can use 11º seed beads to speed up the process of making cubic right-angle weave rows, but you may lose some design options, such as really tight curves.**
- **Metal bezels, like the ones below, are available in various shapes and sizes.**

b

c

d

e

f

Focal bezel

[1] Glue the focal to a piece of Lacy's Stiff Stuff or Ultrasuede, and let it dry. Trim the backing, leaving at least a 4 mm border around the edges **(photo b)**. If your focal is a regular shape or has a pointed back, you can use a metal bezel to set the stone first **(photo c)**. If the bezel has holes in the base, you can use the holes to join the beaded bezel to the focal, or you can stitch the metal bezel to the backing.

[2] Using color A 15º seed beads, work a row of cubic right-angle weave (see "Cubic Right-Angle Weave," p. 195) the same length as one of the sides of the focal. If your focal is round or oval, make a row that wraps all the way around the circumference, leaving a little space between the end stitches to join them, then skip to step 4.

[3] To make sharp turns around the stone, work the next stitch off the edge beads as if you were starting a second row of cubic right-angle weave. Continue stitching to get to the next turn. If the angle of the turn is 90-degrees or sharper, work as if starting a new row, then continue stitching to get to the next turn **(photo d)**. If the turn is more than 90 degrees, continue adding stitches as

normal — the beadwork will curve around these softer angles **(photo e)**. Continue in this manner until you surround the focal, leaving space for one stitch to join the ends. Exit an end bead of the last stitch.

[4] Join the ends: Pick up an A, and sew through the corresponding A of the other end stitch. Pick up an A, and sew through the A your thread exited at the start of this step **(figure)**. Continue in cubic right-angle weave to finish the join.

[5] Exit an A at the bottom of the bezel, sew through the backing from front to back, then sew back through to the front, and continue through the A your thread just exited **(photo f)**. Sew through the beadwork to exit the next bottom A. Continue in this manner to attach the bottom As to the backing, and end the thread. Trim any excess backing, being careful not to cut the thread.

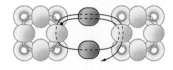

FIGURE

This technique produces beautiful results even without a focal piece.

In the photos below, the red lines indicate the number of stitches between the locking joins on two connected rows of cubic right-angle weave. The larger the difference between the number of joins on each row, the sharper the curve will be.

g

h

i

j

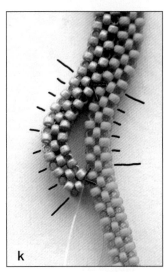

k

Rows of cubic right-angle weave

Working with comfortable lengths of thread, make the desired number of rows of cubic right-angle weave using color A and color B 15º seed beads, ending and adding thread (Basics) as needed. End all the threads.

Connecting techniques

Depending on your design, you'll be connecting rows of As and Bs using one or more of the joins below.
[1] Add 18 in. (46 cm) of thread to a row before making each join, and end the thread after the join is completed. Use your sketch as you work to make sure your rows line up as desired. Start connecting rows to each other and to one side of the focal bezel using the following join techniques:
• **Simple join:** This join merely connects two rows, but the rows can shift up and down if this is the only join used. Align two rows next to each other. Exit an edge bead of one row, sew through the corresponding bead in the other row, and sew through the edge bead of the first row again (photo g). Retrace the thread path a few times.

• **Locking join:** Work as in a simple join, but after retracing the thread path, sew through the adjacent corresponding edge bead of the second row on either side of the simple join (photo h). This will prevent the two rows from shifting.
• **Straight join:** Use simple and locking joins to make connections between two rows where the stitches in each row line up next to each other (photo i).
• **Curved join:** Use simple and locking joins to make connections between two rows, skipping a stitch in one of the rows, which will pull the other row into a curved shape by compensating for the skipped stitch (photo j).
• **Wavy join:** Use simple and locking joins to make connections between two rows, skipping more than one stitch in one of the rows, which will pull the other row into a more pronounced curve. The number of stitches you skip determines how wavy the join becomes, allowing you to add space between the rows as well (photo k).
[2] Use the same techniques to join rows to each other and to the other side of the focal bezel.

Clasp
[1] To attach a clasp, add a thread to a row on one end of the necklace, and exit an end bead. Pick up five As or Bs depending on the color of the row, and sew through the opposite end bead. Sew back through the beads just added and through the bead your thread exited at the start of this step. Retrace the thread path, and end the thread. Repeat on the other end of the necklace.
[2] Open a jump ring (Basics), and attach a loop of seed beads and half of the clasp. Repeat on the other end.

A chain used in place of a jump ring on one end of the necklace allows you to adjust the length and add a decorative accent if desired.

CUBIC RIGHT-ANGLE WEAVE

Standing
ovation

Combine several bead styles to take the
guesswork out of this daring cubic right-angle
weave design

designed by **Anna Elizabeth Draeger**

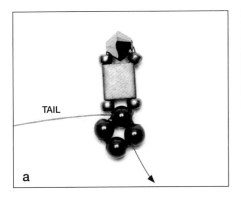

TAIL

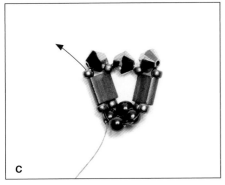

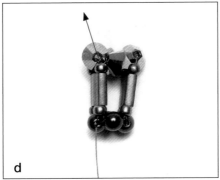

a

b

c

d

materials

topaz AB bangle
inner diameter 7⅝ in. (19 cm)

- **144** 4 mm bicone crystals
  (Swarovski, topaz AB)
- **144** 3 mm crystal pearls
  (Swarovski, deep brown)
- **48** 6 mm two-hole tile beads
  (Czech, opaque yellow Picasso)
- 3–4 g 10º cylinder beads
  (Miyuki DBM0254, bronze luster)
- 2–3 g 11º seed beads
  (Miyuki 9361, yellow-lined aqua AB)
- 2–3 g 15º seed beads
  (Miyuki 458, metallic brown iris)
- Fireline 6 lb. test
- beading needles, #12

light gray opal AB bangle colors:
- 4 mm bicone crystals
  (Swarovski, topaz AB 2X)
- 3 mm crystal pearls
  (Swarovski, light green)
- 5 mm Tila beads (Miyuki 462,
  metallic gold iris)
- 10º cylinder beads
  (Miyuki 0254, bronze luster)
- 11º seed beads (Miyuki 462D, gold iris)
- 11º cylinder beads, substituted for 15º
  seed beads (Miyuki 029, metallic purple
  gold iris)

zigzag bangle colors:
- **180** 4 mm bicone crystals
  (Swarovski, metallic light gold)
- **180** 3 mm crystal pearls
  (Swarovski, deep brown)
- **60** 5 mm Tila beads
  (Miyuki 2008, matte metallic patina iris)
- 10º cylinder beads
  (Miyuki DBM0254, bronze luster)
- 11º seed beads
  (Miyuki 9361, yellow-lined aqua AB)
- 15º seed beads
  (Miyuki 458, metallic brown iris)

Nothing turns heads like the flash of Swarovski Elements, and these fashionable bangles sport a solid ring of those eye-catching crystals along its outer edge. The spoke-like structure provided by Miyuki Tila beads or Czech two-hole tile beads elevates the design, while the inner ring of pearls provides a comfortable base layer that makes this bracelet easy to wear.

stepbystep

[1] On a comfortable length of Fireline, pick up four 3 mm pearls, leaving a 6-in. (15 cm) tail. Sew through all the pearls again to form a ring, and sew through the first pearl once more so the working thread and tail are exiting opposite ends of the first pearl.

[2] Make a spoke: Pick up an 11º seed bead, sew through one hole of a 6 mm two-hole tile bead or a 5 mm Tila bead, and pick up an 11º, a 4 mm bicone crystal, and an 11º. Sew down through the remaining hole of the same tile bead, pick up an 11º, and sew through the pearl your thread exited at the start of this step and the next pearl in the ring **(photo a)**.

[3] Pick up an 11º, sew through one hole of a new tile bead, and pick up an 11º and a 4 mm. Sew down through the adjacent 11º, tile bead, and 11º in the previous spoke, and then sew through the pearl your thread exited at the start of this step and the following pearl in the ring **(photo b)**.

[4] Pick up an 11º, sew up through the remaining hole of the tile bead just added, and pick up an 11º and a 4 mm. Sew down through the 11º, the corresponding hole of the same tile bead, and the next 11º in the new spoke, and then sew through the pearl your thread exited at the start of this step and the following pearl in the ring. Sew up through the nearest 11º, tile bead, and 11º in the previous spoke **(photo c)**.

[5] Pick up a 4 mm, and sew down through the adjacent 11º, tile bead, and 11º in the new spoke. Retrace the thread path through the next four beads **(photo d)**.

e

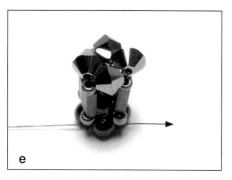

f

g

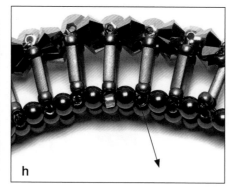

h

[6] Sew through the ring of 4 mms to complete the first cubic right-angle weave unit. Sew through the beads in the new spoke, and exit the pearl opposite the one your tail is exiting (photo e).

[7] Pick up three pearls, and sew through the pearl your thread exited at the start of this step and the next pearl in the new ring (photo f).

[8] Repeat steps 3–7 until you reach the desired length, ending and adding thread (Basics) as needed. The beadwork must fit around the widest part of your hand minus the length of one stitch. Depending on your stitching tension, the beadwork may snug up a bit in step 12. To avoid making the bangle too small, work one

extra stitch if you usually have loose stitching tension.

[9] Repeat steps 3–6.

[10] Pick up a pearl, and sew through the end pearl of the first pearl ring. Pick up a pearl, and sew through the end pearl of the last pearl ring (photo g). Retrace the thread path to secure the join, and sew up through an 11º, tile bead, and 11º in the last spoke added.

[11] Pick up a 4 mm, and sew through the 11º, tile bead, and 11º in the first spoke. Retrace the thread path, and sew through the beadwork to add the last 4 mm to the top of the bangle. Retrace the thread path, and end the working thread and tail.

[12] Add 2 yd. (1.8 m) of Fireline to the base layer of pearls, exiting an edge pearl on one side of the bangle. Pick up a 15º seed bead, and sew through the next pearl along this edge (photo h). Repeat to complete the round. Sew through the beadwork to exit an edge pearl on the other side of the bangle, and repeat to add a 15º between all the pearls along this edge. End the threads. Repeat this step to add a 10º cylinder between all the 4 mms along each outside edge of the bangle.

Working the zigzag design is a little trickier than the straight bangle, but the result is stunning!

DESIGN NOTES:

- To make a zigzag design, work four cubic right-angle weave units in one direction as in steps 3–6, and then change direction by sewing through an adjacent pearl in the ring before making the next base ring of pearls. Work three units each time you change direction.
- If you are concerned about sizing your bangle or would like to add a clasp to the end units, skip steps 10 and 11 until you've completed the remaining steps. Then, go back to steps 10 and 11 to join the end stitches, or make a seed bead ring on each end to attach a clasp.
- I've made two other variations of this bangle using seed beads instead of pearls: 11º seed beads in one and 10º cylinder beads in another. This brought the units closer together, which prompted me to use 3 mm bicone crystals in place of the 4 mms. If you substitute beads, you may need more tile beads and crystals.

MODIFIED SQUARE STITCH

HOLLYWOOD squared

Sporting all the glamour of the golden age of Hollywood, this captivating cuff is a style essential

designed by **Donna Sutton**

A statement bracelet is a great way to dress up any outfit.

materials

black-and-silver bracelet

6¾ in. (17.1 cm)

- **10** SS29 Xilion 2-hole crystal settings, silver plated (Swarovski 17704, crystal)
- **12 g** 5 mm Tila beads (Miyuki 401F, matte black)
- **25** 4 mm bicone crystals (Swarovski, crystal)
- **25** 3 mm bicone crystals (Swarovski, crystal)
- **60** 2 mm round crystals (Swarovski, crystal)
- **8–10 g** 11º cylinder beads (Miyuki DB010, matte black)
- **8–10 g** 15º seed beads (Miyuki 1559, sparkling dark gray-lined crystal)
- **1¼ in. (3.2 cm)** French (bullion) wire
- **5-strand clasp**
- Fireline 6 lb. test
- beading needles, #12

burgundy-and-opal bracelet colors:

- SS29 Xilion 2-hole crystal settings, gold plated (Swarovski 17704, white opal)
- 5 mm Tila beads (Miyuki 2005, matte metallic dark raspberry iris)
- 11º seed beads, in place of the 2 mm round crystals (Toho 421, gold-lustered transparent pink)
- 11º cylinder beads (Miyuki DB1051, matte metallic bronze gold iris)
- 15º seed beads (Miyuki 1428, silver-lined wine)

Stitch your way to a dazzling Tila bead cuff studded with seed beads and two-hole crystal settings.

The base of this bracelet is constructed using modified square stitch, securing new rows of beads to previous rows of beads rather than stitching one bead to one bead as in traditional square stitch (Basics).

stepbystep

Tila bead base

[1] On a comfortable length of Fireline, attach a stop bead (Basics), leaving a 6-in. (15 cm) tail. Pick up a repeating pattern of a 5 mm Tila bead and an 11º cylinder bead four times. Pick up a Tila bead, and sew through the second hole of the same Tila bead (**figure 1, a–b**).

[2] Pick up five cylinders, skip the next Tila bead, and sew through the second hole of the following Tila bead (**b–c**). Repeat this stitch once to complete the row (**c–d**). Sew through the first hole of the end Tila bead and all the beads added in step 1 (**d–e**). Make sure the Tila beads with an available hole are flipped as shown.

[3] Pick up a Tila bead and a cylinder, and sew through the second hole of the next Tila bead. Pick up a cylinder, a Tila bead, and a cylinder, and sew through the second hole of the following Tila bead (**figure 2, a–b**). Pick up a cylinder and a Tila bead. Working in modified square stitch, sew through the nearest hole of the adjacent Tila

bead, all the beads in the previous row (**b–c**), and all the beads added in this row (**c–d**). Snug up the beads.

[4] Sew through the second hole of the end Tila bead. Pick up a cylinder, a Tila bead, and a cylinder, and sew through the second hole of the next Tila bead. Repeat this stitch once to complete the row (**d–e**).

[5] Pick up a Tila bead and a cylinder, and sew through the second hole of the next Tila bead. Pick up a cylinder, a Tila bead, and a cylinder, and sew through the second hole of the following Tila bead (**figure 3, a–b**). Pick up a cylinder and a Tila bead. Sew through the nearest hole of the adjacent Tila bead (**b–c**), all the beads in the previous row, and all the beads added in this row (**c–d**).

[6] Repeat steps 4 and 5 twice (**d–e**).

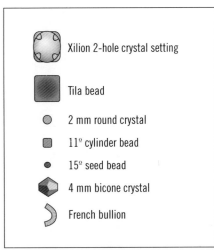

	Xilion 2-hole crystal setting
	Tila bead
	2 mm round crystal
	11º cylinder bead
	15º seed bead
	4 mm bicone crystal
	French bullion

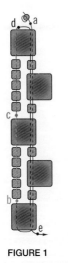

FIGURE 1

FIGURE 2

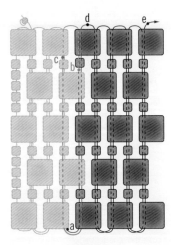

FIGURE 3

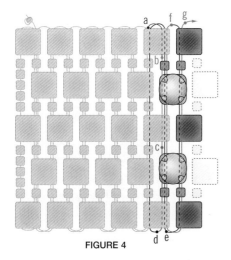

FIGURE 4

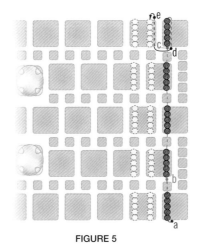

FIGURE 5

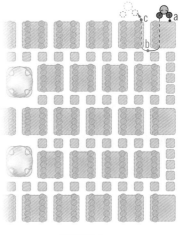

FIGURE 6

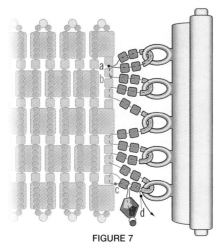

FIGURE 7

[7] Sew through the second hole of the end Tila bead (figure 4, a–b). Pick up a cylinder and a two-hole crystal setting, making sure to sew through the appropriate hole so that the crystal is facing up, and then sew through the second hole of the next Tila bead (b–c). Pick up a crystal setting (making sure the crystal is facing up) and a cylinder, and sew through the second hole of the following Tila bead (c–d). Sew through the first hole of the end Tila bead, all the beads in the previous row, and all the beads added in this row (d–e).

[8] Pick up a Tila bead and a cylinder, and sew through the second hole of the

next crystal setting. Pick up a Tila bead, and sew through the second hole of the following crystal setting. Pick up a cylinder and a Tila bead (e–f). Sew through the nearest hole of the adjacent Tila bead, all the beads in the previous row, and all the beads added in this row (f–g).

[9] Repeat steps 4–8 four times, ending and adding thread (Basics) as needed.

[10] Repeat steps 4 and 5 four times, and then sew through the second hole of the end Tila bead.

[11] Pick up five cylinders, and sew through the second hole of the next Tila bead. Repeat this stitch once. Sew through the nearest hole of the adjacent Tila bead, all the beads in the previous row, and all the beads added in this row. Remove the stop bead, and end the threads.

Embellishing the base

[1] Add a comfortable length of Fireline to the base, exiting an inner hole of an end Tila bead with the thread pointing away from the edge of the beadwork (figure 5, point a).

[2] Pick up five 15º seed beads, skip the next Tila bead, and sew through the following cylinder (a–b). Repeat this stitch three times (b–c). Pick up five 15ºs, and sew back through the corresponding hole of the end Tila bead (c–d). Sew through the nearest hole of the adjacent Tila bead with your thread pointing away from this edge of the beadwork (d–e).

[3] Work as in step 2 for the length of the base, ending and adding thread as needed. When you come to a row with a crystal setting, sew through

the setting and the cylinder adjacent to the next Tila bead, and continue embellishing with 15ºs.

[4] With the thread exiting the outer hole of an end Tila bead (figure 6, point a), pick up a 15º, a 2 mm round crystal, and a 15º, and sew through the other hole of the same Tila bead (a–b). Sew through the nearest hole of the adjacent Tila bead with your thread pointing away from this edge of the beadwork (b–c). Repeat this step for the length of the base to create a picot edging.

[5] At the end of the base, weave through the beadwork to exit the outer hole of the end Tila bead on the opposite edge. Repeat step 4, and end the thread.

Clasp

[1] Add a comfortable length of Fireline to the base, exiting the first cylinder after an end Tila bead.

[2] Pick up two cylinders, ⅛ in. (3 mm) of French wire, a loop of the clasp, and two cylinders, and sew through the next cylinder in the base (figure 7, a–b). Repeat this step to attach all five loops of the clasp, skipping the Tila bead at the center of this row (b–c).

[3] To embellish the clasp connection, sew through the beadwork to exit one of the two cylinders connecting the clasp to the base. Pick up a 4 mm bicone crystal and a 15º, skip the 15º, and sew back through the 4 mm and the next cylinder connecting the clasp to the base (c–d). Repeat this step as desired, alternating 4 mms and 3 mms to achieve the desired effect. End the thread.

[4] Repeat steps 1–3 on the remaining end of the bracelet.

DESIGN NOTES:

- Substitute 11º seed beads from your stash for the 2 mm round crystals.
- Eliminate the bicone clasp fringe for a more casual cuff.

Metallic masonry

For easy shaping, nothing beats brick stitch

designed by **Lorraine Coetzee**

Contrasting colors really make this bracelet sizzle. If you prefer more muted tones, consider using a monochromatic color scheme.

Following the maxim "use the right tool for the right job" promotes happy results in beading. For this bracelet with shaped edges, the right tool — brick stitch — makes this complicated-looking pattern easy to achieve.

step by step

Bracelet band

[1] Thread a needle on a comfortable length of nylon thread or monofilament. Referring to the **pattern**, work the center row in ladder stitch (Basics) using the appropriate color 11º cylinder beads and leaving a 6-in. (15 cm) tail.

[2] Working off the ladder, stitch the next 41 rows in brick stitch (Basics), increasing or decreasing at the edges (Basics) as indicated. End and add thread (Basics) as needed.

[3] You'll need to work a two-bead increase in row 43: Begin the row with a regular increase (a B and a D), and sew down through the B **(figure 1)**. Pick up

a B, and sew through the previous B and D again **(figure 2, a–b)**. Work the next 13 stitches as usual **(b–c)**. Pick up a B, and sew through the previous B again **(c–d)**.

[4] To work the two-bead increase in the next row, pick up two Ds, sew under the end thread bridge in the previous row, and sew back through the second D **(figure 3, a–b)**. Work an increase with a B off the same thread bridge, and then stitch another B to the first increase B **(b–c)**. Zigzag back through the previous two Ds **(figure 4, a–b)**. Work the next 15 stitches as usual **(b–c)**. Pick up a B, and sew through the previous B again **(c–d)**.

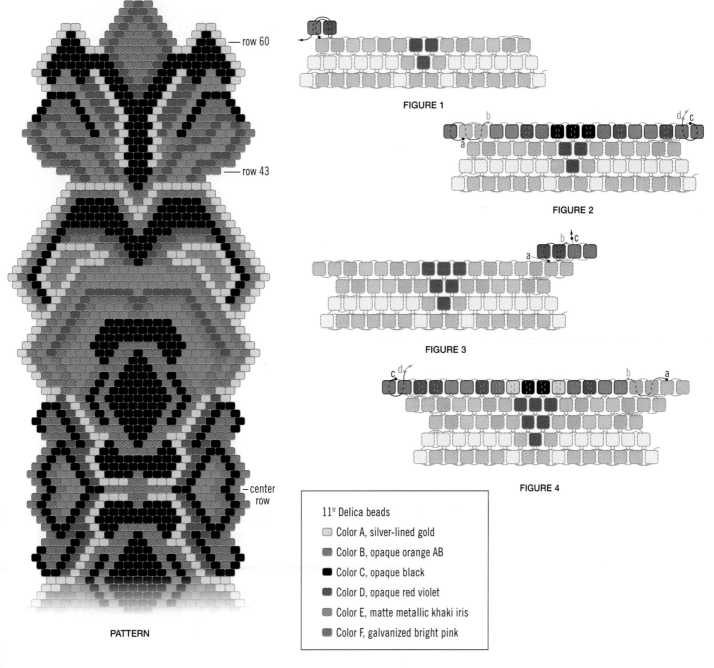

— row 60

— row 43

FIGURE 1

FIGURE 2

FIGURE 3

—center row

FIGURE 4

PATTERN

11º Delica beads

☐ Color A, silver-lined gold

▨ Color B, opaque orange AB

■ Color C, opaque black

▨ Color D, opaque red violet

▨ Color E, matte metallic khaki iris

▨ Color F, galvanized bright pink

materials

purple/orange bracelet 7½ in. (19.1 cm)

- 11º cylinder beads (Miyuki Delicas)
  3 g color A (DB0042, silver-lined gold)
  3 g color B (DB0161, opaque orange AB)
  4 g color C (DB0010, opaque black)
  2 g color D (DB1379, opaque red violet)
  3 g color E (DB0380, matte metallic khaki iris)
  1 g color F (DB0425, galvanized bright pink)
- 1 g 15º seed beads (Toho 4, silver-lined gold)
- nylon beading thread, size D
- clear monofilament, 6 lb. test (.010 in.) (optional)
- beading needles, #12

brown bracelet colors (shown in step-by-step photos):

- 11º cylinder beads (Miyuki Delicas)
  color A (DB0331, matte 24k gold plated)
  color B (DB0653, opaque pumpkin)
  color C (DB0254, bronze luster)
  color D (DB0126, cinnamon rainbow gold luster)
  color E (DB1731, beige-lined opal AB)
  color F (DB0065, lined topaz AB)
- 15º seed beads (Toho 221, bronze)

---

[5] Beginning in row 60, you will need to work partial rows to create the three end peaks. Work one peak, skip a bead in row 59, stitch the second peak, skip a bead in row 59, and stitch the third peak. End the working thread and tail.
[6] After completing the first end of the pattern, add a new thread to the center row, and work the remaining 64 rows as a mirror image of the first end. End and add thread as needed, and end the thread when you complete the pattern.

Toggle clasp

[1] For the toggle ring: On 2 ft. (61 cm) of nylon thread, center 28 15º seed beads. Tie them into a ring with a square knot (Basics), leaving an 8-in. (20 cm) tail, and sew through the first 15º again. Work one round of tubular peyote stitch (Basics) using 15ºs for a total of three rounds. Work three rounds using Es. With the tail, work two rounds using Es, and then zip up (Basics) the edges to form a tubular ring. Exit an E in the middle round of Es.
[2] Pick up an F, a 15º, and a D, and sew through the next E in the outer round. Repeat this stitch to complete the round, and step up through the first F and 15º picked up in this round.
[3] Pick up an F, and sew through an edge F at one end of the bracelet band. Sew through the adjacent D and back through the new F and the 15º in the toggle ring (photo a). Pick up an F, and sew through the other edge F at the same end of the band. Sew through the adjacent D and back through the new F (photo b) and the 15º in the toggle ring. Retrace the thread path to secure the connection, and end the thread.
[4] For the toggle bar: On 2 ft. (61 cm) of nylon thread, attach a stop bead (Basics), leaving an 8-in. (20 cm) tail. Pick up 16 As. Work two rows of flat

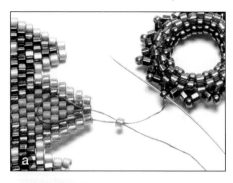

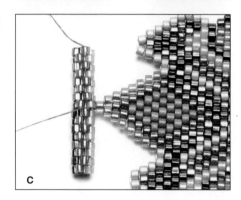

even-count peyote stitch (Basics) using Fs, two rows with Es, and two rows with Ds. Zip up the ends to form a tube, and exit near the middle of the tube.
[5] Attach the toggle bar: Pick up two Fs, and sew through an edge F. Sew through the beadwork to come up through the other edge F, pick up an F, and sew back through the first F picked up in this step and into the toggle bar (photo c). Retrace the thread path, and end the thread.

DESIGN NOTES:

- Even if you normally use Fireline or WildFire, we strongly recommend using nylon thread or monofilament for this bracelet. Brick stitch is a relatively stiff stitch, and if you use a thread without any give, you won't be able to curve the bracelet around your wrist.
- For a longer bracelet, consider stringing a few accent beads between the end of the band and the clasp. For a shorter bracelet, omit the toggle clasp, and overlap the ends, using a snap to close one end over the other.

SPIRAL ROPE

Double duty

The 6º seed beads along the edges give this supple bracelet cuff-like characteristics when worn.

This reversible bracelet offers lots of options to play with color & pattern

designed by **Ellen Tihane**

- 4 5–6 mm accent beads (hematite)
- 2 4 mm bicone crystals (Swarovski, jet)
- 12 g 6º seed beads (Czech, olive AB)
- 11º seed beads
  4–5 g color A (Miyuki 308, cobalt gold luster)
  4–5 g color B (Czech, aluminum)
  2 g color C (Czech, aluminum)
  8 g color D (Toho 458A, metallic brown iris)
- 3-strand slide clasp
- Fireline 6 lb. test
- beading needles, #11
- bobbin

blue four-rope bracelet colors:
- 6º seed beads (Czech, navy AB)
- 11º seed beads
  color A (Czech, aluminum)
  color B (Toho 82, navy blue iris metallic)
  color C (Toho 85, dark purple iris metallic matte)
  color D (Toho 558, galvanized platinum gold)

bronze four-rope bracelet colors:
- 6º seed beads (Toho 221, bronze)
- 11º seed beads
  color A (Toho 458A, metallic brown iris)
  color B (Toho 329A, gold-lustered African sunset)
  color C (Toho 99F, frosted gold-lined black matte)
  color D (Toho 509, higher metallic purple green iris)

stepbystep

Two-rope bracelet
First spiral rope

[1] On 4 yd. (3.7 m) of Fireline, center two 6º seed beads, and wrap half of the thread around a bobbin. With the remaining half of the thread, pick up a color A 11º seed bead, a color B 11º seed bead, an A, a color C 11º seed bead, and three color D 11º seed beads. Sew through the two 6ºs again, forming a loop of 11ºs around the 6ºs **(figure 1)**. Move the loop to the left of the 6ºs.

[2] Pick up a 6º, an A, a B, an A, a C, and three Ds, and sew through the previous 6º and the new 6º added in this stitch. Move the new loop to the left **(figure 2)**; each new loop will rest on top of the previous loop.

[3] Repeat step 2 for the desired length of the rope, keeping an even but not tight tension. Retrace the thread path of the last stitch, and tie a couple of half-hitch knots (Basics), but do not trim the thread.

Second spiral rope

For clarity, the side of the rope with the As and Bs visible will be called the front, and the side with the Ds visible will be called the back.

[1] Twist the first spiral rope so the 6ºs line up along the left edge and the As and Bs are visible from the front **(photo a)**.

[2] Unwind the other half of the thread from the bobbin. Sew through the first loop, sew around the thread bridge between two 6ºs, and sew back through four 11ºs in the loop to exit the C **(figure 3)**.

[3] Pick up three Ds, two 6ºs, an A, a B, and an A, sew down through the C in the first loop of the first spiral rope, and continue through the Ds and 6ºs just picked up **(figure 4)**.

[4] Pick up a 6º, an A, a B, and an A, and sew down through the C in the next loop of the first rope **(figure 5, a–b)**, with your needle pointing toward the loop made in the previous step and exiting behind the previous loop to the back of your work. Pick up three Ds, and sew up through the top 6º from the previous stitch and the new 6º added in this stitch **(b–c)**. The three Ds of this stitch will not be visible from the front.

[5] Repeat step 4 for the length of the first rope, keeping an even but not tight tension.

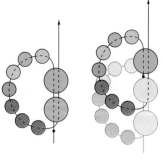

FIGURE 1   **FIGURE 2**

⬤	6º seed bead
◐	11º seed bead, color A
◑	11º seed bead, color B
◕	11º seed bead, color C
◔	11º seed bead, color D

[6] When you complete the second spiral rope, you will have an A, a B, and an A showing at the end of the band on the back side. To tidy this up, pick up three Ds, sew down through the last C in the band, pick up three Ds, and sew up through the last 6º in the second spiral rope **(photo b)**. The Ds will lie on top of the A, B, and A. Sew through the beadwork to exit the corresponding 6º in the first spiral rope, with your needle pointing away from

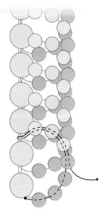

FIGURE 3

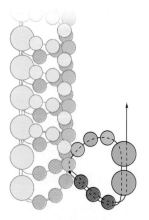

FIGURE 4

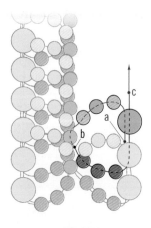

FIGURE 5

the beadwork. Pick up three Ds, sew down through the last C in the band, pick up three Ds, and sew up through the last 6º in the first spiral rope (photo c).

Clasp

[1] With the thread exiting an end 6º in the band, pick up a 5–6 mm accent bead and an end loop of the clasp. Sew back through the accent bead and the first several 6ºs in the band. Sew through the beadwork to exit the end 6º, and retrace the thread path.

[2] Sew through the beadwork to exit the last C, and pick up a 4 mm bicone crystal and a loop of the clasp. Sew back through the 4 mm and the beadwork to exit the end 6º in the other edge of the band.

[3] Repeat step 1 to add an accent bead and the final loop of the clasp. End the threads (Basics).

[4] Add thread (Basics) to the other end of the band, and repeat steps 1–3.

Four-rope (or more!) bracelet

To make a wider bracelet with four ropes: Work loops of 11ºs off of the 6ºs along the right edge of the bracelet, as in "First spiral rope." Then work as in "Second spiral rope." Add as many spiral ropes as you desire, but in order for the pattern to be consistent, you will need to begin each additional rope on the same end and always work off the right edge of the bracelet. You will also have to adjust the clasp attachment accordingly. A multi-loop slide clasp is a good option. Just find one that fits the final width of your bracelet, and attach it with jump rings (Basics), as in the bracelets on p. 79.

DESIGN NOTES:

- **Even but not tight tension is the key to success in this bracelet. If you stitch very tight, like me, loosen up but stay consistent.**
- **The colors listed are merely a guide. You can also experiment with more than four colors and change up the order of them, as shown in this bracelet.**

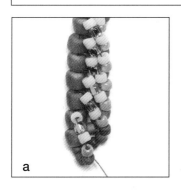

a

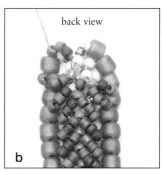

back view

b

back view

c

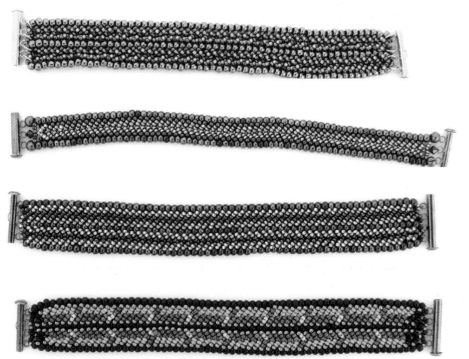

81

Hogarth
crystal
curve

A beading fluke turned into a twist of fate and a super-sparkly necklace

designed by **Wendy Lueder**

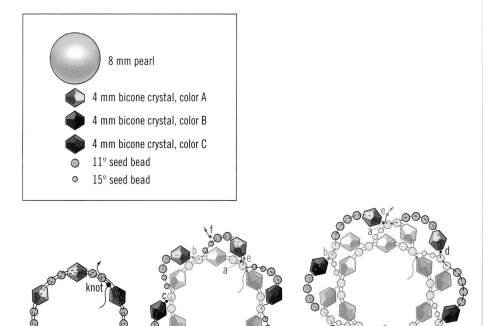

Legend

- 8 mm pearl
- 4 mm bicone crystal, color A
- 4 mm bicone crystal, color B
- 4 mm bicone crystal, color C
- 11º seed bead
- 15º seed bead

FIGURE 1   FIGURE 2   FIGURE 3

materials

necklace (p. 82) 18 in. (46 cm)

- **17** 8 mm glass pearls (cream)
- 4 mm bicone crystals
  102 color A (Thunder Polish, sun AB)
  103 color B (Thunder Polish, ruby jade AB)
  103 color C (Thunder Polish, red AB)
- 24 g 11º seed beads (Toho PF471, galvanized gold)*
- 6 g 15º seed beads (Toho 471, galvanized gold)*
- magnetic clasp
- 2 wire guards
- Fireline 6 lb. test
- beading needles, #12

bracelet (p. 85) 7½ in. (19.1 cm)

- **3** 8 mm crystal pearls (Swarovski, white)
- 4 mm bicone crystals
  37 color A (Swarovski, light emerald)
  37 color B (Swarovski, tanzanite)
  36 color C (Swarovski, medium sapphire)
- 8 g 11º seed beads (nickel-plated brass; Eclectica, 262-641-0965)*
- 2 g 15º seed beads (nickel-plated brass; Eclectica, 262-641-0965)*
- toggle clasp
- Fireline 6 lb. test
- beading needles, #12

The grams given are for galvanized seed beads, which are heavier than non-galvanized beads. If using non-galvanized beads, you may need fewer grams.

I was creating a Russian spiral rope when I noticed that the beads made a pleasing flat spiral just before I pulled the thread tight to form the tube. As I connected multiple flat spirals for a necklace, a pattern of Hogarth Curves — gentle S-shapes common in floral arrangements — emerged at the intersection of the spirals.

stepbystep

Flat spiral

Ring of beads

On 40 in. (1 m) of Fireline, pick up the following beads, leaving a 10-in. (25 cm) tail: a pattern of two 11º seed beads and a color A 4 mm bicone crystal twice, a pattern of two 11ºs and a color B 4 mm bicone crystal twice, and a pattern of two 11ºs and a color C 4 mm bicone crystal twice. Tie the beads into a ring with a square knot (Basics). Sew through all the beads in the ring again, and continue through the first 11º picked up **(figure 1)**.

Round 1

[1] Pick up an A, two 11ºs, and two 15º seed beads. Skip the next 11º and 4 mm in the ring, and sew through the following 11º **(figure 2, a–b)**. Repeat this step once **(b–c)**.
[2] Repeat step 1 substituting Bs for the As **(c–d)**, and then repeat step 1 substituting Cs for the As **(d–e)**. Retrace the thread path through this round, and step up through the first A and two 11ºs added in step 1 **(e–f)**.

Round 2

[1] Pick up an A and four 11ºs, skip the next 4 mm added in the previous round, and sew through the following two 11ºs **(figure 3, a–b)**.
[2] Repeat step 1 twice substituting Bs for the As **(b–c)**, and then repeat step 1 twice substituting Cs for the As **(c–d)**. Repeat step 1 once more using an A **(d–e)**. Retrace the thread path through the round, and end the working thread **(Basics)** but not the tail.

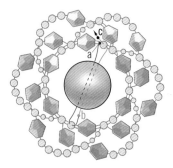

FIGURE 4

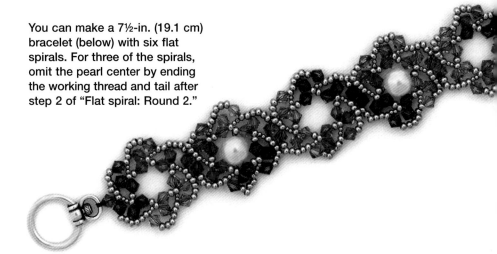

You can make a 7½-in. (19.1 cm) bracelet (below) with six flat spirals. For three of the spirals, omit the pearl center by ending the working thread and tail after step 2 of "Flat spiral: Round 2."

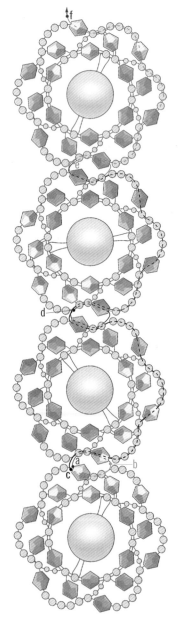

FIGURE 5

Pearl center

[1] With the tail, sew through the first two 11ºs in the initial ring of beads, exiting at **figure 4, point a**.

[2] Add the pearl center using tight tension to avoid thread showing: Pick up an 8 mm pearl, and sew through the 11º opposite the 11º your thread is exiting **(a–b)**. Sew back through the pearl and the 11º on the first side of the ring **(b–c)**. Retrace the thread path, and end the tail.

Necklace

[1] Make a total of 17 flat spirals.

[2] Add 2 yd. (1.8 m) of Fireline (Basics) to a flat spiral, and exit the 11º before the first C in round 2. Pick up a C, and sew through one side of a wire guard, half of the clasp, and the other side of the wire guard. Sew back through the C and the 11º your thread exited at the start of this step **(photo)**. Retrace the thread path through the

clasp connection, and then sew through round 2 of the spiral in the same direction it was worked to exit the second A added in round 2, opposite the clasp connection **(figure 5, point a)**.

[3] Place a new flat spiral next to the first, and arrange them as shown in **figure 5** so that the second A in round 2 of the first spiral aligns with the first A in round 2 of the new spiral. Sew through the adjacent two 11ºs and A in the new spiral **(a–b)**, and then sew through the adjacent two 11ºs and A in the first spiral **(b–c)**. Retrace the thread path through the connection, and sew through round 2 of the new spiral in the same direction it was worked to exit the second B in round 2, opposite the connection **(c–d)**.

[4] Place a new flat spiral next to the spiral just attached, aligning the first B in round 2 of the new spiral with the B your thread is exiting. Attach the spirals as in step 3, and sew through round 2 of the new spiral in the same direction it was worked to exit the second C in round 2, opposite the connection **(d–e)**.

[5] Place a new flat spiral next to the spiral just attached, aligning the first C in round 2 of the new spiral with the C your thread is exiting. Attach the spirals as in step 3, and sew through round 2 of the new spiral in the same direction it was worked to exit the second A in round 2, opposite the connection **(e–f)**.

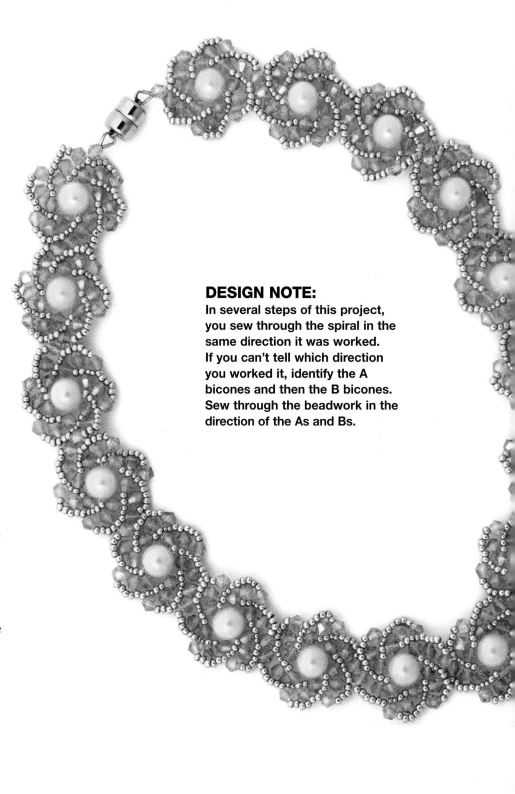

[6] Repeat steps 3, 4, and 5 to attach a total of nine flat spirals in a straight line. After connecting the ninth spiral and sewing through round 2 to exit the C opposite the connection, continue through the next six 11°s and 4 mm to exit the first A in round 2. This modified connection point will create the V-shape at the center of the necklace.

[7] Attach the eight remaining flat spirals in a straight line, making sure that you're always attaching the first A, B, or C in round 2 of the first spiral to the second A, B, or C in round 2 of the new spiral. After connecting the last spiral and sewing through round 2 to exit the B opposite the connection, continue through the next 11°.

[8] Pick up a B, and sew through one side of a wire guard, half of the clasp, and the other side of the wire guard. Sew back through the B and the 11° your thread exited at the start of this step. Retrace the thread path through the clasp connection, and end the thread.

DESIGN NOTE:
To increase or decrease the length of the necklace by 2 in. (5 cm), add or omit one flat spiral on each side.

DESIGN NOTE:
In several steps of this project, you sew through the spiral in the same direction it was worked. If you can't tell which direction you worked it, identify the A bicones and then the B bicones. Sew through the beadwork in the direction of the As and Bs.

RUSSIAN SPIRAL

Springy
spiral bangles

Beading wire lends structure
to a favorite spiral stitch

designed by **Sara Oehler**

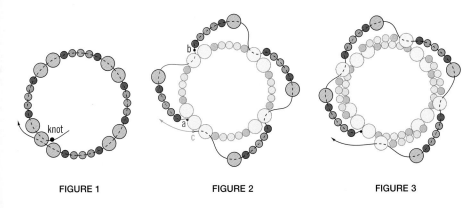

FIGURE 1   FIGURE 2   FIGURE 3

Russian spiral normally produces a soft drape, but substituting beading wire for regular thread gives this stitch an unexpected springy feel while allowing it to hold its shape. This provides the structure needed for a big, bold bangle!

○ 8º seed bead
● 15º seed bead, color A
○ 15º seed bead, color B
○ 15º seed bead, color C

step by step

[1] Tie an overhand knot (Basics) at the very end of 2–4 yd. (1.8–3.7 m) of beading wire. Tie a second knot if desired. String a pattern of two 8º seed beads, a color A 15º seed bead, a color B 15º seed bead, a color C 15º seed bead, a B, and an A. Repeat this pattern three more times, and then string an 8º. Go through the first 8º picked up to form a ring (figure 1).
[2] String an A, a B, a C, a B, an A, and an 8º. Skip the next six beads in the ring, and sew through the following 8º (figure 2, a–b). Repeat this step three more times to complete the round (b–c).
[3] String an A, a B, a C, a B, an A, and an 8º. Skip the next five 15ºs in the previous round, and go through the following 8º. Repeat this step three times to complete the round (figure 3).
[4] Repeat step 3 until you reach your desired length, ending and adding wire as needed. To end a wire: Exiting an 8º after completing a round, tie an overhand knot or two as close to the 8º as possible (photo a), and trim the wire close to the knot. To add a new wire:

Tie an overhand knot or two at the very end of another 2–4 yd. (1.8–3.7 m) of wire, and go through the same 8º in which you ended the previous wire. Tuck the knots into the center of the tube as you continue to repeat step 3.
[5] Join the ends: After completing a round, align the first and last rounds so that the bead patterns match up.
[6] String an A, a B, a C, a B, and an A, but instead of picking up a new 8º, go through the corresponding 8º in the first round of the tube. Skip the next five 15ºs in the last round, and go through the following 8º in the last round (photo b). Repeat this step to complete the join, always picking up 15ºs and going through the existing 8ºs in the first and last rounds.
[7] Tie an overhand knot or two as close as possible to the 8º your thread exited at the start of this step, and thread the end of the wire through the space between two 15º stitches, exiting the other side of the tube. Tug gently on the wire to bring the knot to the inside of the tube, and carefully trim the remaining wire.

materials

turquoise bangle
2¼-in. (5.7 cm) inner diameter
7¼-in. (18.4 cm) inner circumference
- 2–3 g 8º seed beads (Toho 55F, opaque frosted turquoise)
- 15º seed beads
  4–5 g color A (Miyuki 2005, matte metallic raspberry iris)
  4–5 g color B (Toho 304, burgundy gold luster)
  2–3 g color C (Toho 959, pink-lined pink)
- 5–7 yd. (4.6–6.4 m) flexible beading wire, .014 (Soft Flex, copper)
- wire cutters

green bangle colors:
- 8º Japanese seed beads (matte light olive; fusionbeads.com)
- 15º seed beads
  color A (Toho 508, higher metallic olivine)
  color B (matte transparent emerald AB; fusionbeads.com)
  color C (Miyuki 551, gilt-lined white opal)

DESIGN NOTE:

If desired, start with a longer length of beading wire to avoid having to tie knots throughout the bangle. Center the first ring of beads on the wire, and then work with one end at a time, switching to the other end when you run out. Use 5 yd. (4.6 m) of wire to make a 6-in. (15 cm) inner-circumference bangle.

a

b

Russian
wraparound

Bugles chase spinning
seed bead bands in an
easy rope technique

designed by **Carolyn Cave**

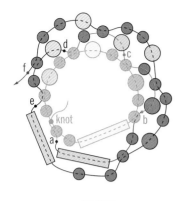

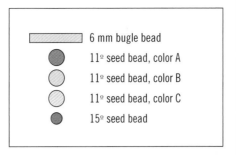

FIGURE

6 mm bugle bead	
11º seed bead, color A	
11º seed bead, color B	
11º seed bead, color C	
15º seed bead	

materials

blue bangle 2½ in. (6.4 cm) inside diameter
- 5–7 g 6 mm bugle beads (teal)
- 3 g 11º seed beads in each of **3** colors:
  A (dark blue), B (sky blue), C (blue-green)
- 5 g 15º seed beads (Miyuki 332, fancy
  forest green)
- 3-in. (7.6 cm) inside-diameter macramé ring
- Fireline 6 lb. test
- beading needles, #10 or #12
- bias seam binding (optional)
- sewing thread (to match binding, optional)
- sewing needle (optional)

red necklace 18–20 in. (46–51 cm)
- 10–12 g 6 mm bugle beads (red)
- **2** 3 mm bugle beads (red)
- 5 g 11º seed beads in each of **3** colors:
  A (ruby), B (amethyst), C (raspberry)
- 7 g 15º seed beads (Miyuki 298,
  transparent rainbow burgundy)
- clasp
- **2** 7–9 mm diameter cones or bead caps
- 4 mm black rubber tubing
- Fireline 6 lb. test
- beading needles, #10 or #12

pink bracelet colors:
- 6 mm bugle beads (Miyuki BGL2-001,
  silver-lined crystal)
- 3 mm bugle beads (Miyuki BGL1-001,
  silver-lined crystal)
- 11º seed beads
  color A (Miyuki 11-596, opaque tea
  rose luster)
  color B (Miyuki 11-1, silver-lined crystal)
  color C (Miyuki 11-155F, matte
  transparent pale pink)
- 15º seed beads (Toho 15R741,
  copper-lined alabaster)
- 4 mm transparent vinyl tubing

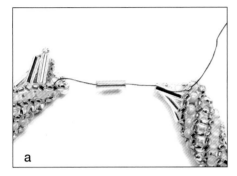

a

b

Russian spiral takes netting on a roller coaster ride, producing a flexible corkscrew rope perfect for a necklace or bracelet. Use some unexpected elements for the core, like a macramé ring or tubing from the hardware store.

stepbystep

Bangle

[1] If desired, wrap bias seam binding around the macramé ring to make the ring 4 mm thick all the way around. Overlap the ends of the binding slightly, then trim the excess. Using a sewing needle and thread, sew the ends of the binding together.

[2] On a comfortable length of Fireline, pick up two 15º seed beads, a 6 mm bugle bead, two 15ºs, a color A 11º seed bead, two 15ºs, a color B 11º seed bead, two 15ºs, a color C 11º seed bead, and two 15ºs, leaving a 6-in. (15 cm) tail. Tie the beads into a ring around the macramé ring with a square knot (Basics). Sew through the first 15º again.

[3] Pick up a bugle and two 15ºs, and sew through the first 15º after the bugle in the previous round (figure, a–b). Pick

up an A and two 15ºs, and sew through the first 15º after the A in the previous round (b–c). Pick up a B and two 15ºs, and sew through the first 15º after the B in the previous round (c–d). Pick up a C and two 15ºs, and sew through the first 15º after the C in the previous round (d–e).

[4] Continue as in step 3 (e–f) to form the spiral rope around the macramé ring, ending and adding thread (Basics) as needed. Stop when there is 3–4 mm between the ends of the spiral rope, ending with a C stitch.

[5] Twist the spiral rope as necessary so the bead pattern on both ends of the rope lines up.

[6] To begin connecting the ends, pick up a bugle, and sew through the 15º just before the A in the first round (photo a). Pick up a 15º, and sew through the 15º just after the bugle added in the last round (photo b).

CORE OPTIONS:

- The macramé ring or tubing may show through the beads in the Russian spiral, especially between the bugles. To make the ring or tubing as inconspicuous as possible, consider these tips:
  - For the bangle, you can wrap the macramé ring in bias seam binding. Select a color that matches the bugles.
  - For the necklace, use black or colored rubber tubing if using dark beads and transparent vinyl tubing if using light beads. You can also color transparent vinyl tubing with permanent marker to match your beads.

- For a flexible bangle, omit the macramé ring, as in photos a–d.

- If you prefer a bracelet with a clasp, like the pink version, follow the steps for "Necklace," cutting the tubing and working the rope to the desired bracelet length.

DESIGN NOTE:

The blue bangle uses bugle beads that are 2 mm in diameter, whereas the pink version uses 1.5 mm diameter bugles. The blue bangle also uses Czech 11º seed beads, which are thinner than the Japanese 11ºs used for the pink version. As a result, the blue bangle has smaller gaps between the bugles, though gaps will not detract from the overall look of the piece.

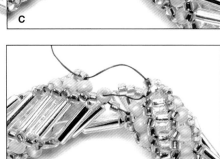

[7] Pick up an A, and sew through the 15º just before the B in the first round (photo c). Pick up a 15º, and sew through the 15º just after the A in the last round (photo d). Your thread should form a zigzag between the two ends.
[8] Pick up a B, and sew through the 15º just before the C in the first round. Pick up a 15º, and sew through the 15º just after the B in the last round.
[9] Pick up a C, and sew through the 15º just before the bugle in the first round. Pick up a 15º, and sew through the 15º just after the C in the last round.
[10] Sew through the next bugle and 15º, and retrace the thread path through the connecting round. End the working thread and tail.

Necklace

[1] Determine the desired finished length of your necklace, and subtract the length of the clasp and each cone or bead cap. Cut a piece of rubber or vinyl tubing to that length.
[2] Work step 2 of "Bangle," but leave a 10-in. (25 cm) tail, and tie the beads around one end of the tubing.
[3] Work step 3 of "Bangle," and repeat for the length of the tubing, ending and adding thread (Basics) as needed. End with a bugle stitch.
[4] Pick up a color A 11º seed bead and a 15º seed bead, and sew through the first 15º after the A in the previous round. Pick up a B and a 15º, and sew

through the first 15º after the B in the previous round. Pick up a C and a 15º, and sew through the first 15º after the C in the previous round. Pick up a 3 mm bugle bead and a 15º, and sew through the 15º after the 6 mm bugle in the previous round.
[5] Sew through the new A, B, C, and 15º after the 3 mm bugle, pulling tight to taper the end of the rope. Sew through the beads again, exiting the 15º.
[6] Pick up a cone or bead cap, nine 15ºs, and half of the clasp. Sew back through the first 15º picked up and the cone or bead cap, and sew through the top A on the tapered end (photo e). Retrace the thread path through the clasp connection, and sew through the top B on the tapered end. Retrace the thread path once more, and sew through the top C on the tapered end. End the working thread.
[7] Repeat steps 4–6 on the other end of the necklace, keeping in mind that you will be stitching the last round in the opposite direction and picking up 11ºs in reverse order.

Fluffy beads

Embellish a beaded bead with rings of crystals for a light and airy sphere with sparkly appeal

designed by **Laura Shea**

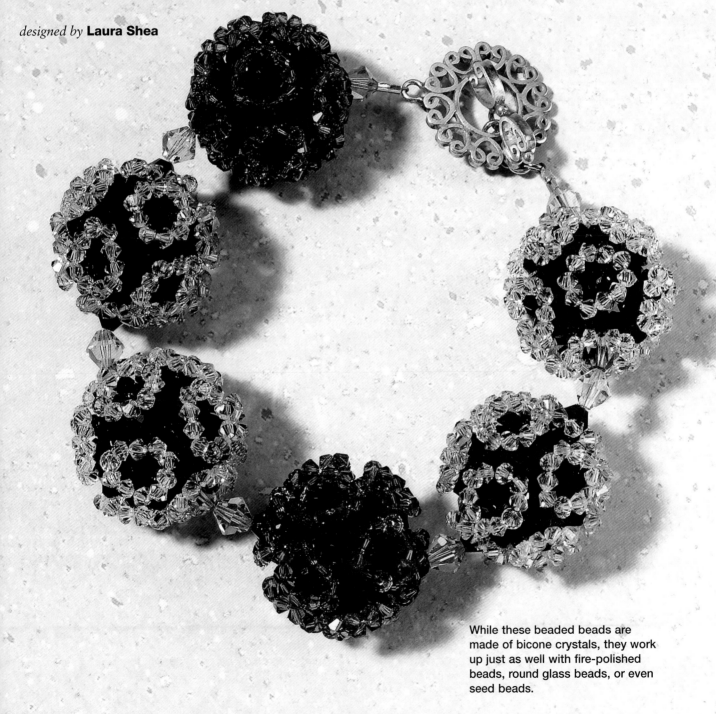

While these beaded beads are made of bicone crystals, they work up just as well with fire-polished beads, round glass beads, or even seed beads.

materials

beaded bead 1 in. (2.5 cm)

- 3 mm bicone or round crystals or fire-polished beads
  60 color A
  90 color B
  120 color C
- monofilament 6 lb. test
- beading needles, #12 (optional)
- chainnose or flatnose pliers (optional)

DESIGN NOTES:

- **To make this bracelet, use Swarovski garnet for colors A and B and three different hues for color C (light peach, rosaline, and Indian pink). Make two beads with each color.**
- **To make sure you pick up the right beads for each stitch, try this: Remove the backing from a large Avery clear mailing label, and place it sticky-side up on figure 5. Place all of the beads on the label. Pick each bead up off the label as you work the beaded bead.**

⬡	3 mm bead, color A
⬡	3 mm bead, color B
⬡	3 mm bead, color C

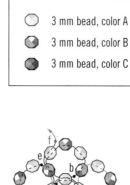

FIGURE 1

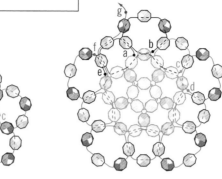

FIGURE 2

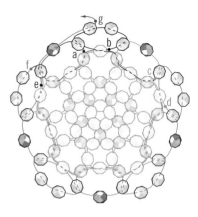

FIGURE 3

The base of each bead in the bracelet on p. 91 is stitched in a single color of crystals. The figures and instructions use two colors because the contrast makes it easier to see the structure of the bead and how it goes together. If you're new to beaded beads, work the base with two colors first. Once you're comfortable with the pattern, go ahead and stitch the base with a single color. The embellishment is worked with the base color and a contrasting color.

stepbystep

Base bead

[1] Thread a needle on 1 yd. (.9 m) of monofilament. You can make this bead without a needle, but it will take longer than if you use one. To get a needle on the monofilament, first flatten the end with flatnose or chainnose pliers.

[2] The first round consists of a single stitch: Pick up five color A 3 mm beads, leaving a 6-in. (15 cm) tail. Sew through the first bead again to form a ring (**figure 1, a–b**).

[3] Round 2 consists of five stitches:

Stitch 1: Pick up five beads (B, A, B, A, B), and sew through the bead your thread exited at the start of this stitch and the next bead in the ring (**b–c**).

Stitch 2: Pick up four beads (B, A, B, A), and sew through the adjacent B in the previous stitch, the bead your thread just exited in the ring, and the next bead in the ring (**c–d**).

Stitches 3–4: Repeat stitch 2 twice, and sew through the adjacent B in stitch 1 (**d–e**).

Stitch 5: Pick up three beads (A, B, A), and sew through the adjacent B in the previous stitch, the A in the initial ring, the adjacent B in stitch 1, and the following A in stitch 1 (**e–f**).

[4] Round 3 consists of 10 stitches:

Stitch 1: Pick up three beads (A, A, A), and sew through the two adjacent As in stitches 5 and 1 in the previous round, then continue through the next B (**figure 2, a–b**).

Stitch 2: Pick up four beads (A, B, A, B), and sew through the adjacent A from the previous stitch, the B your thread exited at the start of this step, and the next two As in the previous round (**b–c**).

Stitch 3: Pick up two beads (A, A), and sew through the adjacent A from the previous stitch, the two As your thread exited at the start of this stitch, and the following B (**c–d**).

Stitches 4–9: Repeat stitches 2 and 3 three times (**d–e**), then sew through the adjacent A in stitch 1 (**e–f**).

Stitch 10: Pick up three beads (B, A, B), and sew through the adjacent A in the previous stitch, the B and A your thread exited at the start of this step, and the next A and B in stitches 1 and 2 of this round (**f–g**).

[5] Round 4 consists of 10 stitches:

Stitch 1: Pick up three beads (A, B, A), and sew through the adjacent B in the previous stitch, the next A and B your thread exited at the start of this stitch, and the next A in the previous round (**figure 3, a–b**).

Stitch 2: Pick up three beads (A, A, A), and sew through the adjacent A in the previous stitch, and the next A, B, A, and B in the previous round (**b–c**).

Stitch 3: Pick up two beads (A, B), and sew through the adjacent A in the previous

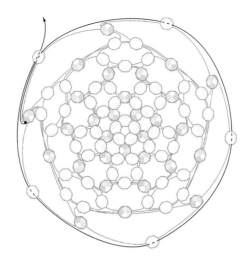

FIGURE 4

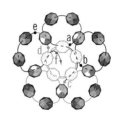

FIGURE 5

FIGURE 6

stitch, the B, A, and B your thread exited at the start of this step, and the following A **(c–d)**.

Stitches 4–9: Repeat stitches 2 and 3 three times **(d–e)**, then sew through the adjacent A in stitch 1 **(e–f)**.

Stitch 10: Pick up two beads (A, A), and sew through the adjacent A in the previous stitch, the two As your thread exited at the start of this stitch, and the next B and A in stitches 1 and 2 of this round **(f–g)**.

[6] Round 5 consists of five stitches:

Stitch 1: Pick up three beads (B, A, B), and sew through the adjacent A in the previous stitch, the B and A your thread exited at the

start of this step, and the next A, B, and A in the previous round **(figure 4, a–b)**.

Stitch 2: Pick up two beads (B, A), and sew through the adjacent B from the previous stitch, the A, B, and A your thread exited at the start of this stitch, and the next A, B, and A in the previous round **(b–c)**.

Stitches 3–4: Repeat stitch 2 twice **(c–d)**, then sew through the adjacent B of stitch 1 **(d–e)**.

Stitch 5: Pick up a bead (A), and sew through the adjacent B in the previous stitch and the A, B, A, and B your thread exited at the start of this stitch **(e–f)**.

[7] Sew through the A from each stitch in round 5 to

finish the base bead **(figure 5)**. End the working thread and tail (Basics), making sure any knots do not block the holes in the As.

Embellishment

The embellishment round is added to the rings of As. If you used a single color in the base, notice that the base has both five-bead and six-bead rings. You'll embellish the five-bead rings.

[1] Add 3 yd. (2.7 m) of monofilament (Basics) in the base, and exit an A. Pick up a B, two color C 3 mm beads, and a B, and sew through the A your thread exited at the start of this stitch and the next A in the base ring **(figure 6, a–b)**.

[2] Pick up a B and two Cs, and sew through the adjacent B in the previous stitch, the A your thread exited at the start of this stitch, and the following A in the base ring **(b–c)**.

[3] Repeat step 2 twice **(c–d)**, then sew through the adjacent B from step 1 **(d–e)**.

[4] Pick up two Cs, and sew through the adjacent B from the previous stitch and the A in the base ring **(e–f)**.

[5] Sew through the base to exit an A in the next five-bead ring.

[6] Work as in steps 1–5 to embellish the remaining five-bead rings on the base. End the thread.

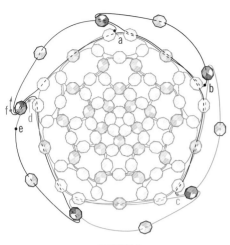

Whether you go for low or high contrast, these sizable beaded beads make a statement.

Beads and geometry

If you've been beading a while, you may recognize the base of this beaded bead as a truncated icosadodecahedron, or as Laura calls it, an Archimedes bead. Laura named it after the form known as an Archimedean solid, or a polyhedron made up of two or more regular polygons.

A bead chain runs through it

Weave seed beads and crystals through colored chain for a supple bracelet

designed by
Connie Whittaker

Let the chain guide your color choices in this inspired design.

94

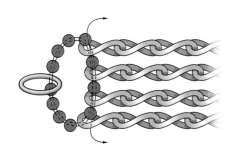

FIGURE 1

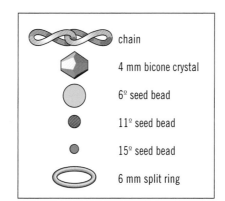

chain

4 mm bicone crystal

6º seed bead

11º seed bead

15º seed bead

6 mm split ring

FIGURE 2

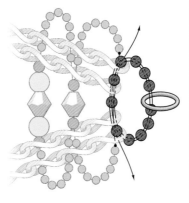

FIGURE 3

FIGURE 4

materials

pink bracelet 8¼ in. (21 cm)

- **38** 4 mm bicone crystals (Swarovski, rosewater opal AB)
- **72** 6º seed beads (06-94216, Duracoat galvanized dark seafoam)
- **1–2 g** 11º seed beads (11-561, galvanized green teal)
- **3–5 g** 15º seed beads (15-509C, metallic purple green iris)
- lobster claw clasp
- 30–32 in. (76–81 cm) 5 x 7.5 mm twist aluminum chain (pink; Midwest Beads, midwestbeads.com)
- **2** 6 mm split rings
- Fireline 6 lb. test
- beading needles, #12
- **2** pairs of pliers

silver bracelet colors:

- 4 mm bicone crystals (Swarovski, olivine AB)
- 6º seed beads (06-265C, rainbow metallic purple-lined crystal)
- 11º seed beads (11R85, metallic plum iris)
- 15º seed beads (15-F463W, matte metallic black purple iris)
- chain (silver white)

turquoise bracelet colors:

- 4 mm bicone crystals (Thunder Polish, green light)
- 6º and 11º seed beads (6- and 11-94202, Duracoat gold)
- 15º seed beads (15-509C, metallic purple green iris)
- chain (light blue)

DESIGN NOTE:
Substitute any 4 mm round beads or pearls for the 6º seed beads.

stepbystep

[1] Count 40 links of chain (about 7½ in./19.1 cm). Open the next link as if it were a jump ring (Basics), remove the link, and set the measured chain aside. Repeat three times to make a total of four 40-link chains.

[2] Thread a needle on each end of 3 yd. (2.7 m) of Fireline, and center an end link of all four chains, 11 11ºs seed beads, and a split ring. With one needle, sew through all the beads, end chain links, and split ring to form a ring, then continue through the end links and the next four 11ºs. Position the four 11ºs inside the end links (figure 1).

[3] With one needle, pick up nine 15º seed beads, and sew through the next link of two adjacent chains, keeping the links parallel. Repeat with the other needle (figure 2, a–b and aa–bb).

[4] With one needle, pick up an 11º, a 4 mm bicone crystal, and an 11º, and sew through the corresponding links of the next two chains. Cross the other needle through the beads just picked up, and sew through the corresponding links of the next two chains (b–c and bb–cc).

[5] Repeat step 3.

[6] With one needle, pick up an 11º, a 6º seed bead, a 4 mm, a 6º, and an 11º, and sew through the corresponding links of the next two chains. Cross the other needle through the beads just picked up, and sew through the corresponding links of the next two chains (figure 3).

[7] Repeat steps 3 and 6

until there are two links left at the end of each chain.

[8] Repeat steps 3 and 4.

[9] Repeat step 3.

[10] With one needle, pick up 11 11ºs and a split ring, and sew through the first four 11ºs again. Cross the other needle through all the beads and split ring just picked up, and sew through the first four 11ºs again (figure 4). With each needle, retrace the thread path through the bracelet, and end the threads (Basics).

[11] Attach a lobster claw clasp to one split ring.

Enchanted
gazebo

Make open-air beaded beads with bugles, pearls, and crystals for a classy, vintage look

designed by **Laura Landrum**

Make beaded beads
in monochromatic or
complementary colors.

DESIGN NOTE:

Play with design: Make a necklace with the alternating sequence of beaded beads and 12 mm pearls for the whole piece, or make just one or three beaded beads for the necklace or bracelet.

materials

one beaded bead ⅝ in. (1.6 cm)

- **5** 12 mm twisted bugle beads
- **20** 4 mm bicone crystals
- **10** 4 mm crystal pearls
- **10** 11º seed beads
- **30** 15º seed beads
- **5** 5 x 1.5 mm daisy spacers
- Fireline 6 lb. test
- beading needles, #10 or #12

bracelet 8¼ in. (21 cm)

- **25** 12 mm twisted bugle beads (Matsuno, transparent rainbow gold)
- **5** 12 mm crystal pearls (Swarovski, bronze)
- **10** 7 x 4 mm fire-polished rondelles (gold)
- **100** 4 mm bicone crystals (Swarovski, peridot satin)
- **50** 4 mm crystal pearls (Swarovski, bronze)
- **10** 3 mm round beads (gold)
- **1–3 g** 11º seed beads (Miyuki 1, silver-lined gold)
- **1–3 g** 15º seed beads (Toho 222, dark bronze)
- **25** 5 x 1.5 mm daisy spacers (copper)
- **10** 10 mm bead caps (gold)
- **10** 8 mm bead caps (gold)
- elastic beading cord, 1 mm
- G-S Hypo Cement

necklace 20 in. (51 cm)

- **25** 12 mm twisted bugle beads (Miyuki 2035, matte metallic khaki iris)
- crystal pearls (Swarovski, brown)
  6 12 mm
  6 6 mm
  6 5 mm
  50 4 mm
- **18** 7 x 4 mm fire-polished rondelles (black diamond)
- **106** 4 mm bicone crystals (Thunder Polish, silver champagne)
- **38** 3 mm round beads (Czech, crystal shadow AB)
- **1–3 g** 11º seed beads (Toho 279, rainbow light topaz gray lined)
- **1–3 g** 15º seed beads (Toho 994, gold-lined rainbow crystal)
- **37** 5 x 1.5 mm daisy spacers (gunmetal)
- **12** 10 mm bead caps (brass)
- **10** 8 mm bead caps (antiqued silver)
- clasp
- **2** crimp beads
- **2** wire guards
- flexible beading wire, .014–.015
- crimping pliers
- wire cutters

stepbystep

Beaded bead

[1] Thread a needle on each end of 1½ yd. (1.4 m) of Fireline, and center a 12 mm twisted bugle bead.

[2] With each needle, pick up a 4 mm pearl. With one needle, pick up a bugle, and cross the other needle through it **(figure 1)**.

[3] Repeat step 2 until you have a total of five bugles **(figure 2)**.

[4] With each needle, pick up a 4 mm pearl, and cross both needles through the first bugle picked up in step 1 to form a ring.

[5] With each needle, pick up a 15º seed bead and a 4 mm bicone crystal. With one needle, pick up a 15º, a 5 x 1.5 mm daisy spacer, and a 15º. Cross the other needle through the last three beads just picked up **(figure 3, a–b and aa–bb)**.

FIGURE 1

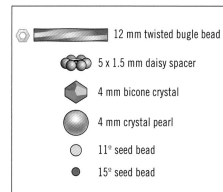

12 mm twisted bugle bead

5 x 1.5 mm daisy spacer

4 mm bicone crystal

4 mm crystal pearl

11º seed bead

15º seed bead

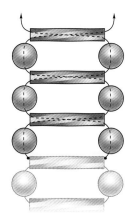

FIGURE 2

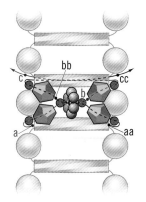

FIGURE 3

FIGURE 4

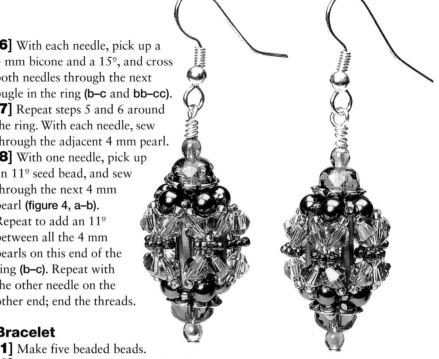

pair of earrings 1½ in. (3.8 cm)

- **10** 12 mm twisted bugle beads (Miyuki 2035, matte metallic khaki iris)
- **4** 7 x 4 mm fire-polished rondelles (black diamond)
- **40** 4 mm bicone crystals (Thunder Polish, silver champagne)
- **20** 4 mm crystal pearls (Swarovski, brown)
- **4** 3 mm round beads (Czech, crystal shadow AB)
- **1** g 11º seed beads (Toho 279, rainbow light topaz gray lined)
- **1** g 15º seed beads (Toho 994, gold-lined rainbow crystal)
- **10** 5 x 1.5 mm daisy spacers (gunmetal)
- **4** 8 mm bead caps (antiqued silver)
- **2** 2½-in. (6.4 cm) head pins
- pair of earring findings
- chainnose pliers
- roundnose pliers
- wire cutters

[6] With each needle, pick up a 4 mm bicone and a 15º, and cross both needles through the next bugle in the ring (**b–c** and **bb–cc**). **[7]** Repeat steps 5 and 6 around the ring. With each needle, sew through the adjacent 4 mm pearl. **[8]** With one needle, pick up an 11º seed bead, and sew through the next 4 mm pearl (**figure 4, a–b**). Repeat to add an 11º between all the 4 mm pearls on this end of the ring (**b–c**). Repeat with the other needle on the other end; end the threads.

Bracelet
[1] Make five beaded beads.
[2] On 10 in. (25 cm) of elastic beading cord, string: a 7 x 4 mm rondelle, an 8 mm bead cap from inside to outside, a beaded bead, an 8 mm bead cap from outside to inside, a rondelle, a 3 mm round bead, a 10 mm bead cap from outside to inside, a 12 mm pearl, a 10 mm bead cap from inside to outside, and a 3 mm round bead. Repeat this sequence four times for a total of five beaded beads and five 12 mm pearls.
[3] Using appropriate tension, tie the ends of the cord with a square knot (Basics). Dot the knot with glue, and let dry. Trim the excess cord, and pull the knot into an adjacent bead to hide it.

Necklace
[1] Make five beaded beads.
[2] Center a beaded bead on 24 in. (61 cm) of beading wire.
[3] On each side of the center beaded bead, string: an 8 mm bead cap from outside to inside, a 7 x 4 mm rondelle, a 3 mm round bead, a 10 mm bead cap from outside to inside, a 12 mm pearl, a 10 mm bead cap from inside to outside, a 3 mm round bead, a rondelle, an 8 mm bead cap from inside to outside, and a beaded bead. Repeat this pattern once, and then string: an 8 mm bead cap from outside to inside, a rondelle, a 3 mm, a 10 mm bead cap from outside to inside, a 12 mm pearl, and a 10 mm

bead cap from inside to outside.
[4] On each end of the wire, string: a 3 mm, a rondelle, a 3 mm, a daisy spacer, an 8 mm pearl, and a daisy spacer. Repeat this pattern twice, and then string a 3 mm, a rondelle, and a 3 mm.
[5] On each end of the wire, string: a 5 mm pearl, a 3 mm, a 4 mm bicone crystal, and a 3 mm. Repeat this pattern twice.
[6] On each end of the wire, string a crimp bead, one side of a wire guard, and half of the clasp. Guide the wire through the other side of the wire guard, and go back through the crimp bead, making sure the clasp half is centered in the wire guard. Test the necklace for fit, and add or remove beads as desired. Crimp the crimp beads (Basics), and trim the excess wire.

Earrings
[1] Make two beaded beads.
[2] On a head pin, string: a 3 mm round bead, a 7 x 4 mm rondelle, an 8 mm bead cap from inside to outside, a beaded bead, an 8 mm bead cap from outside to inside, a rondelle, and a 3 mm. Make a wrapped loop (Basics). Open the loop of an earring finding (Basics), and attach the wrapped loop.
[3] Make a second earring.

CROSSWEAVE TECHNIQUE

Spring fling

Stitch a vernal garland to wear year-round

designed by **May Brisebois**

materials

pink necklace 17½ in. (44.5 cm)

- **10** 11 x 5.5 mm faceted briolette pendants (Swarovski, fern green)
- **45** 6 mm round gemstone beads (terra jasper)
- **67** 4 mm round beads, color A (cats-eye glass beads, pink)
- **10** 4 mm round pearls, color B (Swarovski, powder rose)
- **2–3** g 11º seed beads (Toho 186, color-lined raspberry crystal)
- lobster claw clasp with soldered jump ring (silver)
- Fireline 6 lb. test
- beading needles, #12

lavender necklace colors:

- 7 x 5 mm CZ briolette teardrops (olivine green)
- 4 mm round beads in each of **2** colors: A (fiber-optic glass beads, purple), B (glass pearls, cream)
- 4 mm round glass pearls (antique gold)
- 11º seed beads (Toho 1300, transparent alexandrite)

turquoise necklace colors:

- 10 mm top-drilled gemstone drops (lemon jade; Eclectica, 262-641-0961)
- 6 mm round beads (Czech, dark peach)
- 4 mm round beads (Czech, dark turquoise)
- 11º seed beads (Miyuki 051, galvanized silver)

Combine fiber-optic glass and gemstone beads with crystal briolettes to make a lovely necklace reminiscent of cherry blossoms. Make one in any color palette to show off the shades of your favorite flower.

step by step

Blossoms

[1] Thread a needle on each end of 24 in. (61 cm) of Fireline. With one needle, pick up five 11º seed beads, and center them on the thread. Cross the other needle through the last 11º picked up to form a ring (**figure 1**).

[2] Work in crossweave technique as follows: With the right-hand needle, pick up a color A 4 mm round bead, an 11º, a 6 mm round bead, an 11º, and an A (**figure 2, a–b**). With the left-hand needle, cross through the last two beads picked up (**aa–bb**).

[3] With the left-hand needle, sew through the next 11º in the center ring (**b–c**). With the right-hand needle, pick up a 6 mm, an 11º, and an A (**bb–cc**). Cross the left-hand needle through the last two beads picked up (**c–d**).

[4] With the left-hand needle, sew through the next 11º in the center ring (**cc–dd**). With the right-hand needle, pick up a 6 mm, an 11º, and an A (**d–e**). Cross the left-hand needle through the last two beads picked up (**dd–ee**).

[5] Repeat step 3 (**e–f** and **ee–ff**).

[6] With the right-hand needle, pick up a 6 mm (**f–g**). With the left-hand needle, sew through the next 11º in the center ring, the adjacent A and 11º added in step 2, and the 6 mm just added (**ff–gg**). Snug up the beads so the beadwork cups around the edge, and end the threads (Basics).

[7] Make a total of nine blossoms.

Centerpiece

[1] Position the blossoms on your work surface as shown in **figure 3**. Thread a needle on each end of 2 yd. (1.8 m) of

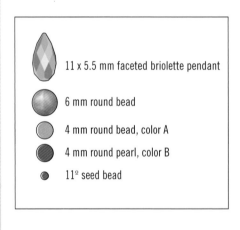

11 x 5.5 mm faceted briolette pendant

6 mm round bead

4 mm round bead, color A

4 mm round pearl, color B

11º seed bead

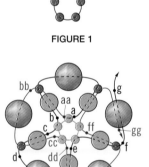

FIGURE 1

FIGURE 2

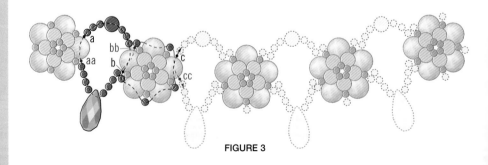

FIGURE 3

Use bright center beads, neutral blossom beads, and gemstone drops for an earthy look, as in my turquoise necklace. You can use chain for the neck straps for a Southwestern feel.

DESIGN NOTES:
- In the purple necklace, I used 4 mm pearls in place of the 6 mm beads to create more delicate blossoms.
- Instead of stitching beaded neck straps, end the threads after step 5 of "Centerpiece," and experiment with attaching a chain or ribbon to each side of the centerpiece.

Fireline, and center the thread in a 6 mm in a blossom on one end (**a** and **aa**).

[2] With the top needle, pick up three 11ºs, a color B 4 mm glass pearl, and three 11ºs. With the bottom needle, pick up four 11ºs, a briolette, and four 11ºs. Cross both needles through a 6 mm in the next blossom (**a–b** and **aa–bb**).

[3] With the bottom needle, pick up an 11º, and sew through the next 6 mm around the perimeter. Repeat twice (**b–c**). With the top needle, pick up an 11º, and sew through the next 6 mm around the perimeter of the blossom. Repeat once (**bb–cc**). Both needles

will be exiting opposite sides of the same 6 mm.

[4] Repeat steps 2 and 3 to connect all nine blossoms.

[5] Repeat step 2 once, but cross both needles through a new A instead of a 6 mm in a blossom.

Neck straps
[1] With each needle, pick up seven 11ºs, and cross both needles through an A. Repeat for the desired length neck strap. For a 17½-in. (44.5 cm) necklace, there are 11 units in each neck strap.

[2] With each needle, pick up two 11ºs, and cross through half of the clasp and the 11ºs added with the other needle. With each needle, retrace the thread path through the entire neck strap, crossing through the As to reinforce. End the threads.

[3] Thread a needle on each end of 1 yd. (.9 m) of Fireline, and center the thread in the 6 mm on the remaining end of the necklace. Repeat step 2 of "Centerpiece," but cross the needles through a new A instead of a 6 mm in a blossom. Repeat steps 1 and 2 of "Neck straps."

CROSSWEAVE TECHNIQUE

Captured

cosmos

Stitch a beaded
universe at the
center of a
chain-link star

designed by **Jenny Van**

Use crossweave technique to create a two-sided beaded bead as colorful and intricate as an interstellar cloud. Attach curved-link spokes interspersed with bicones and oval crystals for a perfectly proportionate pendant.

stepbystep

Beaded bead
Side 1, cluster 1
[1] Thread a needle on each end of 2 yd. (1.8 m) of Fireline. Center an 11º seed bead, a color A 4 mm bicone crystal, and a 4 mm pearl. With one needle, pick up an A, and cross the other needle through it (figure 1, a–b and aa–bb).
[2] With the left-hand needle, pick up an 11º and an A (b–c). With the right-hand needle, pick up a pearl, and cross through the A just picked up with the left-hand needle (bb–cc).
[3] With the right-hand needle, pick up a pearl (c–d). With the left-hand needle, pick up an 11º, sew through the first A added in step 1, and cross through the pearl just picked up with the right-hand needle (cc–dd).

Side 1, cluster 2
[1] With the left-hand needle, pick up a color B 4 mm bicone crystal, an 11º, and a B (figure 2, a–b). Cross the right-hand needle through the last B picked up (aa–bb).
[2] With the right-hand needle, pick up a pearl and a B (b–c). With the left-hand needle, pick up an 11º, and cross through the last B picked up (bb–cc).
[3] With the left-hand needle, pick up an 11º, sew through the first B added in step 1 of this cluster, and pick up a pearl (c–d). With the right-hand needle, cross through the pearl just picked up (cc–dd). Snug up the beads, pushing the pearls

to the back to make sure the As and Bs are on the same side of your work.

Side 1, cluster 3
Repeat cluster 2, substituting As for Bs.

Side 1, clusters 4 and 5
Repeat clusters 2 and 3.

Side 1, cluster 6
[1] Repeat steps 1 and 2 of cluster 2.
[2] Join the first and last stitch: With the left-hand needle, pick up an 11º, and sew through the first B added at the start of this cluster. Cross both needles through the adjacent pearl in cluster 1 to form a ring (figure 3, a–b and aa–bb).
[3] With both needles, sew through the beadwork, and cross through the outer edge pearl in cluster 1 (b–c and bb–cc).

Side 2, cluster 1
[1] Turn the beadwork over so the pearl base is facing up. With the right-hand needle, pick up an A, an 11º, and an A. Cross the left-hand needle through the last A picked up.
[2] With the left-hand needle, pick up a pearl and an A. With the right-hand needle, pick up an 11º, and cross through the last A picked up.
[3] With the left-hand needle, pick up a pearl. With the right-hand needle, pick up an 11º, sew through the first A added in step 1 of this cluster, and cross through the last pearl picked up.

materials

necklace with pendant
17½ in. (44.5 cm)
- **30** 6 x 4 mm oval beads (metallic green, beadsj.com)
- 4 mm bicone crystals
  18 color A (Swarovski, blue zircon)
  46 color B (Swarovski, topaz)
- **18** 4 mm glass pearls (mauve)
- **3–4 g** 11º seed beads (Toho 557, galvanized gold)
- **30** 16 x 1 mm curved chain links (gold, beadsj.com)
- clasp
- Fireline 6 lb. test
- beading needles, #12

necklace with centerpiece colors:
- 6 x 4 mm oval beads (metallic green)
- 4 mm bicone crystals:
  color A (Swarovski, light rose satin),
  color B (Swarovski, rose alabaster AB 2X)
- 4 mm glass pearls (mauve)
- 11º seed beads (Toho 557, galvanized gold)
- 16 x 1 mm curved chain links (gold, beadsj.com)

DESIGN NOTE:
Try substituting 15º seed beads for the 11ºs in the beaded bead.

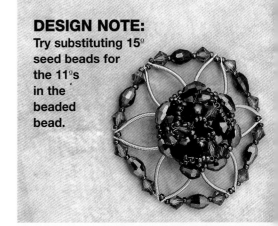

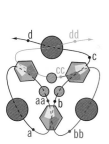

FIGURE 1

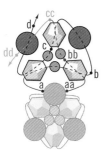

FIGURE 2

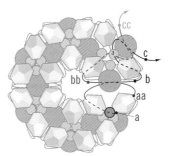

FIGURE 3

103

Side 2, cluster 2

[1] With the left-hand needle, pick up a B, an 11º, and a B. Cross the right-hand needle through the last B picked up.
[2] With the right-hand needle, sew through the adjacent pearl from side one of the beaded bead, and pick up a B. With the left-hand needle, pick up an 11º, and cross through the last B picked up.
[3] With the right-hand needle, pick up a pearl. With the left-hand needle, pick up an 11º, sew through the first B added in step 1 of this cluster, and cross through the last pearl picked up.

Side 2, cluster 3

[1] With the left-hand needle, pick up an A, an 11º, and an A. Cross the right-hand needle through the last A picked up.
[2] With the right-hand needle, sew through the adjacent pearl from side one of the beaded bead, and pick up an A. With the left-hand needle, pick up an 11º, and cross through the last A picked up.
[3] With the right-hand needle, pick up a pearl. With the left-hand needle, pick up an 11º, sew through the first A added in step 1 of this cluster, and cross through the last pearl picked up.

Side 2, clusters 4 and 5

Repeat clusters 2 and 3.

Side 2, cluster 6

[1] Repeat steps 1 and 2 of cluster 2.
[2] Join the first and last stitch: With the left-hand needle, pick up an 11º, and sew through the first B added in step 1 of this cluster. Cross both needles through the adjacent pearl from the first cluster on this side of the beaded bead.
[3] Sew through the beadwork, and cross both needles through a pearl along the outer edge of the beaded bead.

Embellishments

[1] With one needle, sew through the end loop of a curved link from front to back **(photo)** and an end loop of another curved link from back to front, and sew through the next pearl along the outer edge of the beaded bead **(figure 4, a–b)**. Pick up five 11ºs, and sew through the pearl again **(b–c)**. Repeat this step five times.
[2] With the other needle, retrace the thread path through the beads and links added in step 1, exiting next to the first thread. Tie the threads together with a square knot (Basics).
[3] With one needle, sew through the next three 11ºs **(figure 5, a–b)**. Pick up an 11º, a 6 x 4 mm oval bead, and an 11º, and sew through the center 11º in the next loop along the edge **(b–c)**. Repeat this stitch to complete the round, and retrace the thread path to reinforce. End this thread (Basics).
[4] With the other needle, sew through the beadwork to exit an A along the inner edge of the beaded bead. Pick up three 11ºs, and sew through the adjacent B along the inner edge **(figure 6, a–b)**. Pick

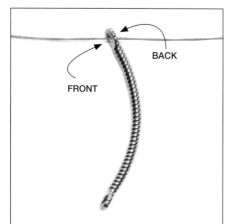

BACK

FRONT

6 x 4 mm oval bead

4 mm bicone crystal, color A

4 mm bicone crystal, color B

4 mm glass pearl

11º seed bead

6 x 1 mm curved chain link

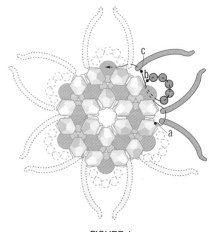

FIGURE 4

up three 11ºs, and sew through the next A toward the center of the beaded bead (b–c). The three 11ºs will lie diagonally across the surface of the beaded bead. Repeat these two stitches twice, and end the thread.

[5] Attach a stop bead (Basics) to the center of 2 yd. (1.8 m) of Fireline. With one needle, sew through a remaining end loop of a curved link from front to back (figure 7, a–b).

[6] Pick up an 11º, an A, an 11º, a 6 x 4 mm oval bead, an 11º, an A, and an 11º, and sew through the remaining end loop of the next curved link (b–c). Pick up an 11º, and sew through the remaining end loop of the following curved link. Repeat this step to complete the round (c–d), exiting an 11º between two chain links.

Necklace with pendant

[1] With the working thread from a completed beaded bead, sew through the next end loop and 11º.

[2] Pick up an 11º, the end loop of a curved link from back to front, four 11ºs, a 6 x 4 mm oval bead, and four 11ºs, and sew through the other end loop of the curved link from front to back.

[3] Pick up an 11º, a B, an 11º, an end loop of a curved link from back to front, four 11ºs, a 6 x 4 mm oval bead, and four 11ºs, and then sew through the other end loop of the curved link from front to back.

[4] Repeat step 3 to create a chain half the length of the overall desired necklace length.

[5] Pick up nine 11ºs and half of the clasp, and sew back through the last 11º and end loop of the curved link added in the previous step. Retrace the thread path several times to secure, and end the thread.

[6] Remove the stop bead on the beaded bead. With this thread, sew through the last 11º added in step 5 of "Beaded bead: Embellishments," the end loop of the next curved link, and the next 11º. Repeat steps 2–5 to create the other half of the chain.

Necklace with five-bead centerpiece (p. 104)

[1] Make and embellish five beaded beads, but do not end the threads.

[2] To connect the beaded beads, thread a needle on each thread from a beaded bead, making sure the threads are exiting opposite sides of an 11º between two curved links. With each needle, pick up an 11º. Cross each needle through the corresponding 11º on another beaded bead. Retrace the thread path several times, and end the threads.

[3] Thread a needle on each thread of the second beaded bead added in the previous step. With both needles, sew through the beadwork to exit an 11º between two curved links on the opposite side of the previous join. Make the join as in step 2.

[4] To join the third beaded bead to the fourth, repeat step 2, referring to p. 104 for the position of the join.

[5] Repeat step 2 to join the fifth beaded bead.

[6] To create the chain on either end of the centerpiece, thread a needle on each end of 1 yd. (.9 m) of Fireline, and center the end loop of a curved link, the 11º, and an end loop of the next curved link in the outer ring of an end beaded bead across from the join. With each needle, pick up an 11º. With one needle, pick up an 11º, and cross the other needle through it.

[7] With the right-hand needle, pick up an end loop of a curved link from back to front, four 11ºs, a 6 x 4 mm oval bead, and four 11ºs, and sew through the other end loop of the curved link from front to back. With the left-hand needle, pick up an end loop of a curved link from back to front, four 11ºs, a 6 x 4 mm oval bead, and four 11ºs, and sew through the other end loop of the curved link from front to back.

[8] With one needle, pick up an 11º, and cross the other needle through it. With each needle, pick up an 11º. With one needle, pick up an 11º, and cross the other needle through it.

[9] Repeat steps 7 and 8 three times or to the desired length.

[10] Repeat step 5 of "Necklace with pendant."

[11] Repeat steps 6–10 for the other end of the necklace.

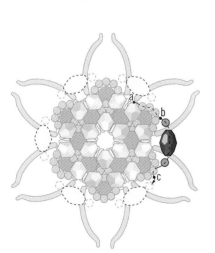

FIGURE 5

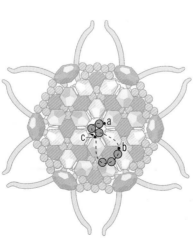

FIGURE 6

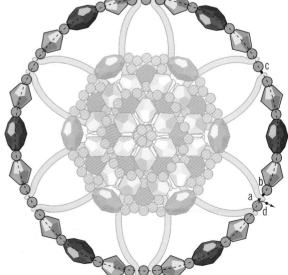

FIGURE 7

Elegant
dangles

Briolette dangles
nestled in a chain of
seed beads create a
beautiful, classic line

designed by **Anu Rao**

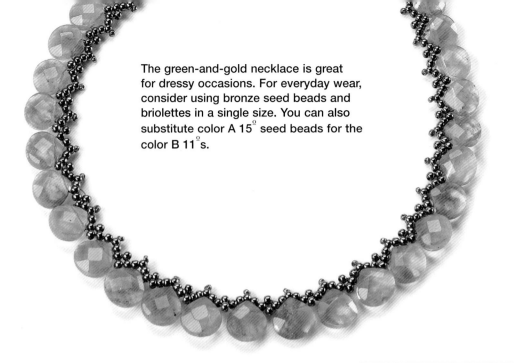

The green-and-gold necklace is great for dressy occasions. For everyday wear, consider using bronze seed beads and briolettes in a single size. You can also substitute color A 15° seed beads for the color B 11°s.

materials

necklace 16 in. (41 cm)

- **33** 9–18 mm gemstone briolettes, in graduated sizes if desired
- 11° seed beads
  5 g color A (Toho 557PF, permanent finish gold)
  1 g color B (Toho 7B, transparent emerald)
- clasp
- Fireline or WildFire beading thread, 6 lb. test
- beading needles, #12

DESIGN NOTE:
Make a matching pair of earrings with leftover briolettes: For each earring, center a briolette on 12 in. (30 cm) of thread, and pick up three 15°s, an 11°, and three 15°s. Sew through the briolette and the next three 15°s and 11° again. Pick up seven 15°s, and sew through the 11° again. Retrace the thread path through the entire earring, and end the thread. Attach the dangle to an earring finding.

If you are using briolettes in graduated sizes, first select the largest one for the center of the necklace; separate the rest into two groups of 16 that graduate symmetrically from small to large.

stepbystep

[1] Cut two 1-yd. (.9 m) pieces of Fireline or WildFire. Attach a needle and a stop bead (Basics) to each thread, leaving 6-in. (15 cm) tails. With one needle, pick up a color A 11° seed bead (figure, a–b). With the other needle, sew through the A in the opposite direction (aa–bb).
[2] Work a crossweave stitch: With one needle, pick up two As (b–c). With the other needle, pick up an A, and cross through the second A picked up with the first needle (bb–cc). Continue working crossweave stitches with As until the strip is about 3 in. (7.6 cm) long (c–d and cc–dd).
[3] With one needle, pick up two As and a color B 11° seed bead, sew back through the second A picked up, and pick up two As (d–e). With the other needle, pick up a briolette (if you are using

graduated sizes, pick up the smallest briolette from one side), and cross through the last A picked up with the other needle (dd–ee).
[4] Work a crossweave stitch with As as in step 2 (e–f and ee–ff).
[5] Repeat steps 3 and 4 (f–g and ff–gg) until all of the briolettes have been used (if you are using graduated sizes, add them from smallest to largest for the first half and then largest to smallest for the other half).
[6] Work crossweave stitches with As until the strap on this end is about 3 in. (7.6 cm) long. Remove the stop beads from the starting end, and test the necklace for fit. Adjust, if needed, by adding or removing an equal number of stitches on each end.
[7] With one needle at one end, pick up an A and half of the clasp. With the other needle on this end, pick up an A, and cross through the clasp half. With each thread, retrace the thread path through the clasp connection a few times, and end the threads (Basics). Repeat this step at the other end of the necklace.

gemstone briolette

11° seed bead, color A

11° seed bead, color B

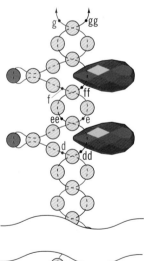

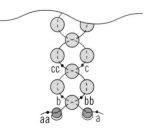

FIGURE

CUBIC CROSSWEAVE
TECHNIQUE

Classic contours

One three-dimensional technique makes many components in this regal necklace

designed by **Grace Nehls**

You can use any one of
these components separately
to create variations that
suit your style. For instance,
a shorter version of the focal
bar can be used as an
earring or pendant.

Intricate rings of cubic crossweave technique serve as bezels, a toggle clasp, and a curvy focal bar from which to suspend a pendant. Create a matching pair of earrings for an ensemble that is sure to please.

stepbystep

Bezeled rivolis

[1] Thread a needle on each end of 2½ yd. (2.3 m) of Fireline, and center three color A 15º seed beads. With one needle, pick up an A, and cross the other needle through it.

[2] With each needle, pick up an A. With one needle, pick up an A, and cross the other needle through it. Repeat this stitch once (figure 1).

[3] With each needle, pick up an A. Cross both needles through the end A in the first stitch (figure 2).

[4] With one needle, sew through a top A on the adjacent side (figure 3, a–b). Sew through the ring of four As on this side (b–c). Repeat with the other needle on the opposite side.

[5] Cross both needles through a bottom A on the adjacent side (figure 4). This completes the first cubic crossweave unit and positions the thread to

build subsequent units. There are six sides per unit, which all look the same. The A your threads exit after completing each unit determines the direction of the new unit.

[6] Continue working in cubic crossweave technique to build a subsequent unit off of a previous unit: With each needle, pick up an A. With one needle, pick up an A, and cross the other needle through it. Repeat this stitch once (figure 5). With each needle, pick up an A. Cross both needles through the top A in the previous unit opposite the bottom A your thread exited at the start of this step (figure 6). Repeat steps 4 and 5.

[7] Repeat step 6 to make a total of 21 cubic crossweave units.

[8] Join the end units: With each needle, pick up an A. Cross both needles through the corresponding A in the first unit, and sew through the adjacent As (figure 7). Cross both needles through the next A. With each needle, pick up an A. Cross

materials

necklace 17 in. (43 cm)
- 6 14 mm rivolis (Swarovski, purple haze)
- 20 8 mm pearls (Swarovski, cream)
- 6 6 mm pearls (Swarovski, cream)
- 8 4 mm pearls (Swarovski, cream)
- 10 3 mm pearls (Swarovski, cream)
- 2 4 mm bicone crystals (Swarovski, jet)
- 536 2 mm round crystals (Swarovski, jet)
- 7–8 g 15º seed beads, color A (Toho 221, bronze)
- 2–3 g 15º Charlottes, color C (Czech, black)
- 2–3 g 13º Charlottes, color B (Czech, cream)
- Fireline 4 or 6 lb. test
- beading needles, #12

pair of earrings 1¾ in. (4.4 cm)
- 2 8 mm pearls (Swarovski, cream)
- 2 4 mm pearls (Swarovski, cream)
- 2 3 mm pearls (Swarovski, cream)
- 2 4 mm bicone crystals (Swarovski, jet)
- 60 2 mm round crystals (Swarovski, jet)
- 1–2 g 15º seed beads, color A (Toho 221, bronze)
- 1–2 g 15º Charlottes, color C (Czech, black)
- 1–2 g 13º Charlottes, color B (Czech, cream)
- 2 3 mm soldered jump rings (optional)
- pair of earring findings
- Fireline 4 or 6 lb. test
- beading needles, #12
- 2 pairs of pliers (optional)

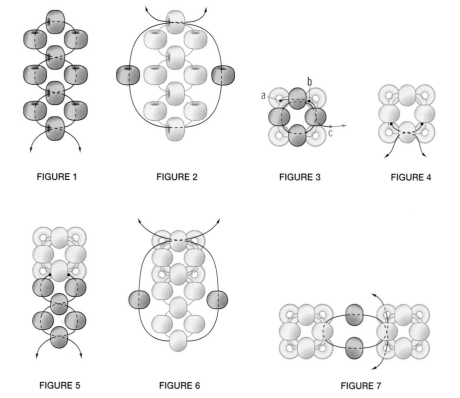

FIGURE 1   FIGURE 2   FIGURE 3   FIGURE 4

FIGURE 5   FIGURE 6   FIGURE 7

a

b

c

both needles through the corresponding A in the last unit. With each needle, sew through the side As to complete the join.

[9] With one needle, exit an A along the inner edge of one side of the bezel. This will become the back of the bezel. Pick up a color B 13º Charlotte, and sew through the next A along the inner edge. Repeat this stitch around the ring, and step up through the first B picked up in this round.

[10] Work a round of tubular peyote stitch (Basics) off the previous round using color C 15º Charlottes. Sew through the beadwork to exit an A along the outer edge of the same side of the bezel.

[11] Place a 14 mm rivoli into the ring with the back of the rivoli facing the rounds of beads just added. Gently push the rivoli into the bezel, allowing the front side of the bezel to surround the rivoli (photo a).

[12] Using the other needle, sew through the beadwork to exit an A along the inner edge of the front side of the bezel. Work a round as in step 9, and then sew through the beadwork to exit an A along the outer edge of the

DESIGN NOTES:
- For a budget-friendly option, substitute 11º seed beads for the 2 mm round crystals.
- Create a bracelet by using a bezeled rivoli centered between two pearl components. Make the toggle clasp, and add straps as in step 7 of "Assembly" to fit.
- If you prefer using one needle instead of two, work the bezels and other components in cubic right-angle weave instead of cubic crossweave.

front of the bezel.

[13] Work as in step 9 to embellish the outer edge using 2 mm round crystals. Using either thread, add 2 mms to the other outer edge. Retrace the thread path through the outer edges, but do not end the threads. You will use them to join the components later.

[14] Make a total of six bezeled rivolis.

Bezeled pearls

[1] Work as in steps 1–6 of "Bezeled rivolis," making a total of 14 cubic crossweave units.

[2] Join the end units as in step 8 of "Bezeled rivolis."

[3] With one needle, sew through the beadwork to exit an A in the center of the inner edge of the bezel. Pick up an 8 mm pearl, and sew through the center A opposite the A your thread just exited (photo b). Retrace the thread path to secure the pearl, and then sew through the beadwork to exit an A along the inner edge on one side of the bezel.

[4] With the same needle, pick up a C, and sew through the next A of the inner edge. Repeat this step to complete the round, and then retrace the thread path around the inner edge.

[5] With the same needle, sew through the beadwork to exit an A along the outer edge of the same side of the bezel. Work a round as in step 4, but use 2 mms instead of Cs. End this thread (Basics).

[6] Using the other needle, sew through the beadwork to exit an A along the inner edge of the remaining side of the bezel, and then repeat steps 4 and 5. End the thread.

[7] Make a total of four bezeled pearls.

Toggle ring

Work as in steps 1–13 of "Bezeled rivolis," omitting the rivoli added in step 11. End the threads.

Toggle bar

[1] Work as in steps 1–6 of "Bezeled rivolis," making a total of nine cubic crossweave units.

[2] Exit the end A on one end of the bar. Pick up a B, and sew through the next A along one edge of the bar. Repeat this stitch to the end of the row, exiting the A opposite the A your thread exited at the start of this step (photo c).

[3] Pick up a 2 mm, and sew through the next A along the opposite edge. Repeat this stitch to the end of the row (photo d), and end the thread.

[4] Using the remaining thread, repeat steps 2 and 3 on the opposite side of the toggle bar.

Focal bar

[1] Work as in steps 1–6 of "Bezeled rivolis," making a total of 41 cubic crossweave units.

[2] Sew through the beadwork to exit the second center A on one end of the focal bar. Pick up an 8 mm pearl, skip seven center As, and sew through the next center A (photo e). Retrace the thread path, and then sew through the next stitch in the bar, exiting the A opposite the A joining the pearl just added. Repeat this step, skipping seven center As for the next 8 mm, skipping six As for the center 8 mm, and skipping seven center As for the last two 8 mms. As you add the 8 mms, it will create the curves in the focal bar, and each 8 mm will sit on the inner side of each curve on alternate sides of the focal bar.

[3] Work as in steps 2 and 3 of "Toggle bar" to embellish both edges of one side of the bar, using Cs and 2 mms in the following pattern: nine stitches using Cs, eight stitches using 2 mms (photo f), eight stitches using Cs, eight stitches using 2 mms, and nine stitches using Cs. Embellish the other edge on this side, but pick up 2 mms opposite the Cs, and

d

e

f

pick up Cs opposite the 2 mms. Embellish the remaining edges on the other side of the bar, matching the beads used for the corresponding edges on the first side. End the threads.

Assembly

[1] With the remaining thread from a bezeled rivoli, exit a center A along the outer edge of the bezel.

[2] Pick up an A, an 8 mm, and an A, and sew through a corresponding center A on another bezel. Sew back through the beads just added and retrace the thread path several times. End this thread.

[3] Lay out two more bezeled rivolis next to the previous two to form a diamond shape, and using the remaining threads from one of the new bezels, exit a 2 mm on the front surface. Sew through a corresponding 2 mm along the outer edge of the adjacent bezel and the next 2 mm in the new bezel. Repeat to attach the 2 mms on the back surface of the bezels. Work in this manner to join the new bezel to the other bezel from step 2. Repeat this step to join the fourth bezel to the original two bezels.

[4] Sew through the beadwork to exit the center A along the outer edge at the top of the bezel in the diamond shape. Pick up an A, and sew through a corresponding A at the bottom of the center curve on the focal bar. Pick up an A, and sew through the center A of the bezel your thread exited at the start of this stitch. Retrace the thread path, and then repeat this join on the back of the bezel and focal bar.

[5] Position a bezeled rivoli between two bezeled pearls. Using the remaining threads from the bezeled rivoli, join

the three bezels using the technique explained in step 3. Repeat this step with the remaining bezeled rivoli and bezeled pearls.

[6] String the necklace: Lay out the focal bar and one rivoli-and-pearl unit. Add 12 in. (30 cm) of Fireline to the focal bar, exiting an end A on the top of the bar. Pick up a repeating pattern of an 8 mm pearl and an A four times, and then pick up an 8 mm pearl. Sew through a corresponding A on the outer edge of the rivoli-and-pearl unit, and sew back through all the beads just picked up. Sew through the A on the focal bar opposite the A your thread exited at the start of this step, and sew through the 8 mms and As just picked up and the corresponding A of the rivoli-and-pearl unit. End the thread.

[7] Add 12 in. (30 cm) of Fireline to the other end of the same rivoli-and-pearl unit, and exit the corresponding A along the outer edge opposite the join. Pick up a repeating pattern of a 6 mm pearl and an A three times, a 4 mm bicone crystal, a repeating pattern of an A and a 4 mm pearl four times, and a repeating pattern of an A and a 3 mm pearl five times. Sew through a center A along the outer edge of the toggle ring, and sew back through all the beads just picked up. Sew through the A in the rivoli-and-pearl unit opposite the A your thread exited at the start of this step, and retrace the thread path, sewing through the corresponding A on the toggle ring. End the thread.

[8] Repeat steps 5–7 on the other side of the necklace, but in step 7, add a repeating pattern of an A and a 2 mm four times, and then pick up an A. Sew

through two center As along the inner curve of the toggle bar, and complete step 7 to reinforce the join. End any remaining threads.

Earrings

[1] Make a bezeled pearl, but don't end the threads.

[2] Exit an A along the outer edge on one side of the bezel. Pick up a 4 mm pearl, an A, a 4 mm bicone, an A, a 3 mm pearl, and an A. Sew through a soldered jump ring or an earring finding, and sew back through all the beads just picked up. Retrace the thread path, but sew through a corresponding A along the outer edge on the other side of the bezel. Retrace the thread path once more, and end the threads (Basics).

[3] If you sewed the earring to a soldered jump ring, open the loop of an earring finding (Basics), and attach the soldered jump ring.

[4] Make a second earring.

Retro
daisies

Darling
daisy motifs
dance along a
netted base

designed by **Janice Chatham**

Crossweave technique produces an even,
fluid base for these pretty petals.

Build a base of lacy lattice with sparkling Charlottes, and then plot a path of colorful blooms. Two alternating colors make for a not-too-flower-child look, though a rainbow of fire-polished beads would do the trick, if that's your thing!

stepbystep

Base

[1] Thread a needle on each end of 1 yd. (.9 m) of Fireline, and center three color A 13º Charlottes. With one needle, pick up an A, and cross the other needle through it (**figure 1, a–b** and **aa–bb**).

[2] With each needle, pick up five As. With one needle, pick up an A, and cross the other needle through it (**b–c** and **bb–cc**).

[3] With each needle, pick up an A. With one needle, pick up an A, and cross the other needle through it (**c–d** and **cc–dd**).

[4] Repeat steps 2 and 3 16 times (**d–e** and **dd–ee**). End both threads (Basics).

[5] To begin the second row, repeat step 1 (**figure 2, a–b** and **aa–bb**).

[6] With one needle, pick up two As, sew through the center A of the first set of five As from the first row (**bb–cc**), and then pick up two As. With the other needle, pick up five As. With one needle, pick up an A, and cross the other needle through it (**b–c** and **cc–dd**).

[7] With each needle, pick up an A. With one needle, pick up an A, and cross the other needle through it (**c–d** and **dd–ee**).

[8] Repeat steps 6 and 7 16 times (**d–e** and **ee–ff**). End both threads.

[9] To work the third row, repeat step 1, and then repeat steps 6–8.

[10] Add 1 yd. (.9 m) of Fireline (Basics) to one end of the base, exiting the first center A along one edge of the base with your thread pointing toward the other end of the base (**figure 3, point a**).

materials

pink/green bracelet 6–7 in. (15–18 cm)

- **4** 4 mm round crystals in each of **2** colors: C (Swarovski, padparadscha AB), E (Swarovski, turquoise)
- **40** 3 mm round fire-polished beads in each of **2** colors: D (Czech, pink), F (Czech, lime green)
- **7–8** g 13º Charlotte seed beads, color A (Czech, nickel plated)
- **2–3** g 15º seed beads, color B (Toho 462A, pink gold iris)
- clasp
- **2** 4–6 mm jump rings
- Fireline 6 lb. test
- beading needles, #12
- **2** pairs of pliers

blue/gold bracelet colors:

- 4 mm round crystals, color C (Swarovski, air blue opal), color E (Swarovski, crystal vitrail medium)
- 3 mm round fire-polished beads, color D (Czech, metallic blue iris), color F (Czech, matte metallic gold)
- 13º Charlotte seed beads, color A (Czech, nickel plated)
- 15º seed beads, color B (Toho 462A, pink gold iris)

green/cream bracelet colors:

- 4 mm round crystals, color C (Swarovski, jet), color E (Swarovski, crystal vitrail medium)
- 3 mm round fire-polished beads, color D (Czech, green), color F (Czech, cream)
- 13º Charlotte seed beads, color A (Czech, antique gold)
- 15º seed beads, color B (Toho 462A, pink gold iris)

teal/red bracelet (p. 114) colors:

- 4 mm round crystals, color C (Swarovski, jet), color E (Swarovski, crystal vitrail medium)
- 3 mm round fire-polished beads, color D (Czech, teal), color F (Czech, red)
- 13º Charlotte seed beads, color A (Czech, nickel plated)
- 15º seed beads, color B (Toho 462A, pink gold iris)

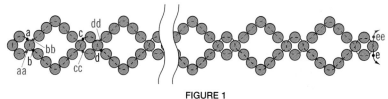

FIGURE 1

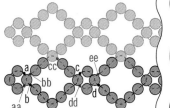
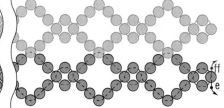

FIGURE 2

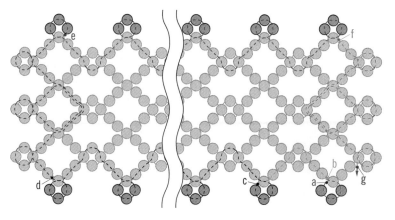

FIGURE 3

113

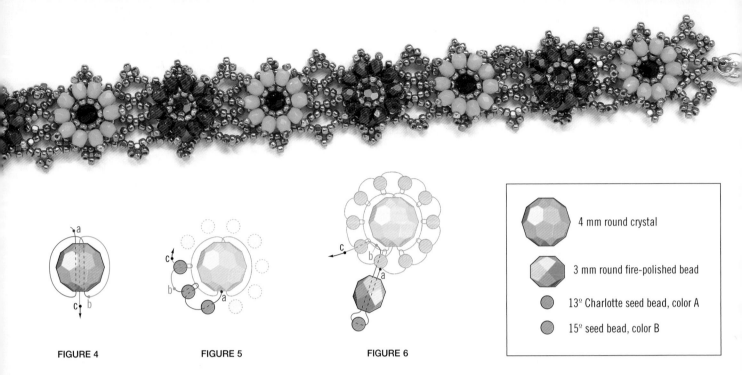

— FIGURE 4 | FIGURE 5 | FIGURE 6

4 mm round crystal

3 mm round fire-polished bead

13° Charlotte seed bead, color A

15° seed bead, color B

[11] To add a picot embellishment to the edge of the base, pick up three As, and sew through the A your thread exited at the start of this step (a–b). Sew through the next eight As along the edge of the base (b–c).

[12] Repeat step 11, completing the picot embellishment on the last center A on this edge (c–d). Sew through the end stitches to reinforce the end picots, and exit the first center A on the other edge of the base (d–e). Repeat step 11 along this edge (e–f), and then sew through the remaining end stitches (f–g). End the thread.

Daisies

[1] On 1 yd. (.9 m) of Fireline, pick up a color C 4 mm round crystal, leaving a 12-in. (30 cm) tail. Sew through the 4 mm again, creating a loop of thread around the outer edge of the bead (figure 4, a–b). Repeat to add a second loop of thread

(b–c). Retrace the thread path to create four loops of thread, and then position the pairs of loops on opposite sides of the 4 mm.

[2] Pick up two color B 15° seed beads, sew under the pair of loops on one side of the 4 mm, and sew back through the second B picked up (figure 5, a–b).

[3] Pick up a B, sew under the pair of loops next to the previous B, and then sew back through the B just picked up (b–c). Repeat this step around the 4 mm, sewing through the other pair of loops when you get to that side of the bead, until you have 10 Bs surrounding the 4 mm. To secure the first B added in this round, sew through the first B, sew under the pair of loops, and sew back through the first B again.

[4] To make the petals, pick up a color D 3 mm fire-polished bead and a B. Skip the B, and sew back through the 3 mm and the B in the ring (figure 6, a–b).

Sew through the next B in the ring (b–c). Repeat this step to add a petal to each B in the ring. End the working thread but not the tail.

[5] Make a total of eight daisies, four using Cs and Ds, and four using color E 4 mm round crystals and color F 3 mm fire-polished beads.

Assembly

[1] Using the tail from a daisy, sew through the second A your threads crossed through in the center row on one end of the base. Sew back through the 4 mm in the daisy, and then sew through the opposite A between the next set of stitches in the base. Retrace the thread path several times, and end the thread.

[2] Skip a set of stitches in the base, and repeat step 1 with the second color daisy. Repeat this step until all the daisies have been added to the base, alternating between the two colors.

[3] Open a jump ring (Basics), and attach half of the clasp to the center picot on one end of the bracelet. Repeat on the other end.

DESIGN NOTE:
Make a matching pair of earrings with just two single flowers: Work steps 1–4 of "Daisies," but in step 4, pick up a soldered jump ring at the end of the last petal, and sew back through the B and D. Open the loop of an earring finding (Basics), and attach it to the soldered jump ring.

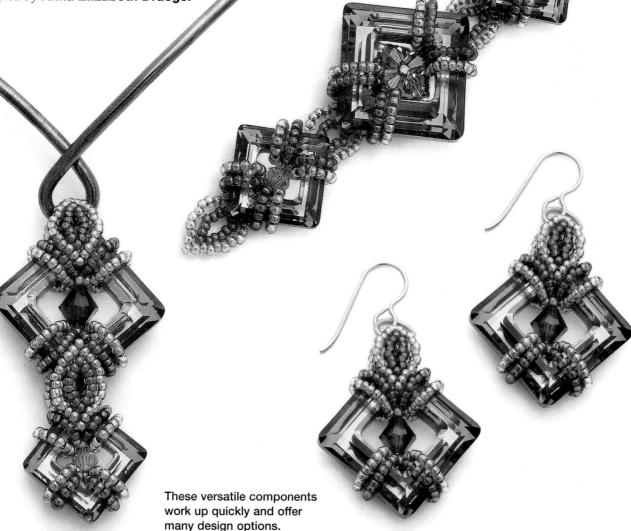

Point of connection

Bicone crystals play peek-a-boo, letting square crystal components take center stage

designed by **Anna Elizabeth Draeger**

These versatile components work up quickly and offer many design options.

materials

three linked components 3½ in. (8.9 cm)

- **20 mm** large crystal square (Swarovski, Bermuda blue)
- **2 14 mm** small crystal squares (Swarovski, Bermuda blue)
- **6 4 mm** bicone crystals (Swarovski, light tanzanite)
- **1 g 11º** seed beads (Miyuki 378, light olive-lined crystal luster)
- **2–3 g 15º** seed beads
  color A (Miyuki 1884, violet gold luster)
  color B (Toho 457, gold lustered green tea)
- Fireline 6 lb. test
- beading needles, #1

DESIGN NOTE:

For the large component in the pieces on p. 115, I used a 6 mm bicone in place of the four 4 mms, working as for the small component. I used Swarovski amethyst 6 mm crystals for the earrings and pendant.

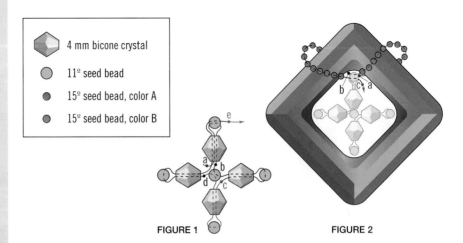

FIGURE 1   **FIGURE 2**

Layer sparkle upon sparkle by filling in the spaces of these square Swarovski Elements. Use a few components for a smashing pendant, or link several to wrap around your wrist.

stepbystep

Large component

[1] On 1½ yd. (1.4 m) of Fireline, pick up a 4 mm bicone crystal and an 11º seed bead, leaving a 12-in. (30 cm) tail. Skip the 11º, and sew back through the 4 mm **(figure 1, a–b)**.

[2] Pick up an 11º, a 4 mm, and an 11º. Skip the last 11º picked up, and sew back through the last 4 mm **(b–c)**.

[3] Pick up a 4 mm and an 11º, skip the last 11º, sew back through the last 4 mm, and then sew through the center 11º **(c–d)**.

[4] Pick up a 4 mm and an 11º, skip the last 11º, sew back through the last 4 mm, and then sew through the first 4 mm and 11º picked up in step 1 **(d–e)**.

[5] Pick up 19 color A 15º seed beads, wrap the beads around one side of one corner of a large crystal square, and sew back through the 11º your thread exited at the start of this step **(figure 2, a–b)**. Repeat to add a loop of beads around the other side of the same corner **(b–c)**. Retrace the thread path through both loops, exiting the 11º.

[6] Repeat step 5 on the same corner, but use color B 15º seed beads, and position the loops to sit under the loops of As.

[7] Working on the back side of the component, pick up six As, and sew through the 11º at the end of the next 4 mm. Repeat to exit the 11º opposite the one your thread exited at the start of this step **(figure 3)**, and then repeat steps 5 and 6 on the opposite corner of

the large crystal square **(figure 4, a–b)**. Pick up six As, and sew through the 11º at the end of the next 4 mm **(b–c)**. Pick up six As, and sew through all four sets of six As, skipping the end 11ºs. This will make a tight frame around the center bicone embellishment. Sew through the 11º connecting the first set of loops, and then continue through the first four As of one of the loops on the back of the component **(c–d)**.

[8] Using the tail, sew through the beadwork to exit the corresponding As on the opposite end of the crystal square, so the working thread exits a loop of As on one end of the square and the tail exits a loop of As on the other end. Don't end the working thread or tail; these threads are used to connect bails or links to the components later.

Small component

[1] On 1 yd. (.9 m) of Fireline, pick up an 11º, a 4 mm, and an 11º, leaving a 12-in. (30 cm) tail. Skip the last 11º, and sew back through the 4 mm and the first 11º so the working thread and tail are exiting opposite ends of the same bead **(figure 5)**.

[2] Pick up 13 As, wrap the beads around one side of one corner of a small crystal square, and sew back through the 11º your thread exited at the start of this step. Repeat to add a loop to the other side of the same corner **(figure 6)**. Retrace the thread path through the first two loops. Repeat this step using Bs to add a second set of loops to sit under the loops of As on this corner.

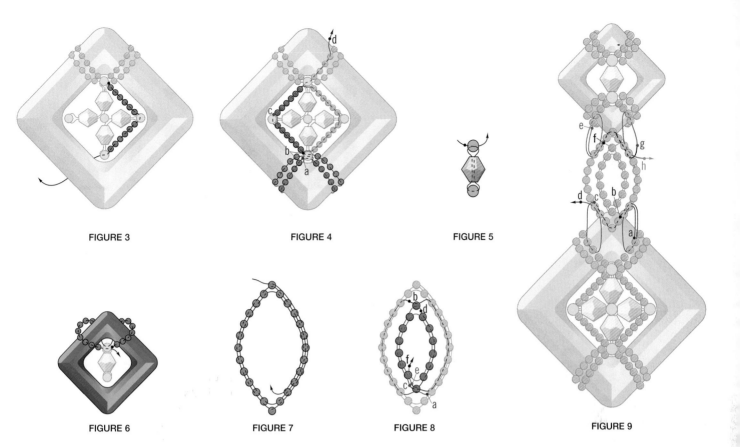

FIGURE 3

FIGURE 4

FIGURE 5

FIGURE 6

FIGURE 7

FIGURE 8

FIGURE 9

[3] Sew through the 4 mm and the next 11º on the opposite end of the small crystal square. Repeat step 2 to add two more sets of loops.

[4] Sew through the first four As of one of the loops on this end of the small crystal square on the back of the component. Using the tail, sew through the beadwork to exit the corresponding As on the opposite end of the small crystal square, so the working thread exits a loop of As on one end of the square and the tail exits a loop of As on the other end. Don't end the working thread or tail; these threads are used to connect bails or links to the components later.

Bails or links

[1] On 1 yd. (.9 m) of Fireline, pick up 24 Bs, leaving a 6-in. (15 cm) tail. Sew through the first 12 Bs, skip the next B in the ring, and sew through the following 11 Bs. Skip the next B, and sew through the following 10 Bs (figure 7).

[2] Pick up an A, skip three Bs in the outer round, and sew through the next nine Bs (figure 8, a–b). Pick up an A, skip three beads in the outer round, sew through the following nine Bs, and continue through the first A picked up at the start of this step (b–c).

[3] Pick up six As, and sew through the A at the opposite end (c–d). Repeat (d–e). Retrace the thread path, skipping the two end As (e–f). End the working thread and tail (Basics).

Assembly

• Attach a bail: Position one end of the bail at the top of a large or small component on the back surface. Align two As from one of the loops on this end of the component to two Bs along one edge of the bail. Using one of the threads from the component, sew through these corresponding beads (figure 9, a–b). Sew through the next five Bs, exiting the corresponding Bs on the other edge of the bail (b–c). Sew through the corresponding beads (c–d). Retrace the thread path of the join, and end the thread.

• Connect two components: Work as for attaching a bail on one end of the link, and then align the remaining end of the link to the loops on one end of the next component. Use one of the threads from the next component to sew through the corresponding Bs on this edge of the link (e–f). Sew through the next five Bs to exit the corresponding beads on the other edge

of the link (f–g). Sew through the corresponding beads (g–h). Retrace the thread path of the join. End the thread.

Design ideas

• Bracelet: Connect small and large components in an alternating pattern until you reach the desired length, ending with a bail at both ends. Attach a clasp to the end bails with jump rings.

• Earrings: Attach a bail at the top of a large or small component, or connect a few components with links, ending with a bail at the top. Attach earring findings to the bails with jump rings.

• Pendant: Connect a large component and a small crystal component with a link, ending with a bail at the top. Attach it to a chain or necklace cord with a jump ring.

• Attach a bail to both the front and back surfaces of a large or small component to create additional design details. Stitch the top Bs together to create a closed shape. Connect two components with a link on both the front and back surfaces to make the join more secure. This makes the connection stiffer than if only connecting the links to the back, so this technique works best with earrings or pendants.

BEADWEAVING

Spellbinding

Use modified right-angle weave to create sparkling pearl nests

designed by **Grace Nehls**

Embellish bezeled pearls with bicone crystals, add fire-polished bead connectors, filigree bead caps, and larger round crystals, then finish off with lengths of chain for the look of old-world splendor.

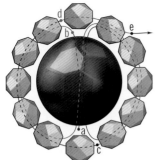

FIGURE 1

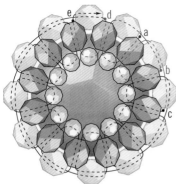

FIGURE 2

FIGURE 3

stepbystep

Bezeled pearls

[1] On 1½ yd. (1.4 m) of Fireline, pick up a 9 mm pearl and five 3 mm fire-polished beads, leaving a 5-in. (13 cm) tail. Sew through the pearl again (**figure 1, a–b**). Pick up five 3 mms, and sew through the pearl and the first five 3 mms again (**b–c**).
[2] Pick up a 3 mm, and sew through the next five 3 mms (**c–d**). Pick up a 3 mm, and sew through the next 3 mm (**d–e**) to create a ring of 12 3 mms around the center pearl.
[3] Embellish the front of the pearl: Pick up a 3 mm, a 2 mm round crystal, and a 3 mm, and sew through the 3 mm your thread exited at the start of this step and the next 3 mm in the original ring (**figure 2, a–b**).
[4] Pick up a 3 mm and a 2 mm, and sew through the first 3 mm added in the previous stitch, the 3 mm your thread exited at the start of this stitch, and the following 3 mm in the original ring (**b–c**). Repeat this step nine more times (**c–d**), and snug up the beads.
[5] Sew through the adjacent 3 mm added in the first stitch, pick up a 2 mm, and sew through the 3 mm added in the previous stitch (**d–e**).

[6] Embellish the back of the pearl: With the thread exiting a 3 mm in the original ring, pick up a 15º seed bead, an 11º seed bead, and a 15º, and sew through the 3 mm your thread exited at the start of this step and the next 3 mm in the original ring (**figure 3, a–b**).
[7] Pick up a 15º and an 11º, and sew through the first 15º added in the previous stitch, the 3 mm your thread exited at the start of this step, and the next 3 mm in the original ring. Repeat this step nine times (**b–c**).

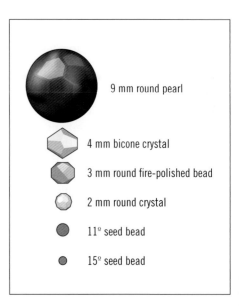

9 mm round pearl

4 mm bicone crystal

3 mm round fire-polished bead

2 mm round crystal

11º seed bead

15º seed bead

spangles

For a budget-friendly option, substitute fire-polished beads for the pearls, and use seed beads for the 2 mm round crystals.

DESIGN NOTE:
Make your own fancy bead caps by using flatnose pliers to bend each petal of a filigree bead cap at a 45-degree angle.

materials

copper necklace 18½ in. (47 cm)

- **11** x 5.5 mm briolette drop (Swarovski, aqua satin)
- **4** 9 mm faceted round freshwater pearls (copper)
- **4** 8 mm round crystals in each of **2** colors: A (Swarovski, Indian sapphire), B (Swarovski, crystal golden shadow)
- **56** 4 mm bicone crystals (Swarovski, sand opal AB 2X)
- **42** 4 mm round fire-polished beads (bronze)
- **96** 3 mm round fire-polished beads (copper luster)
- **48** 2 mm round crystals (Swarovski, crystal golden shadow)
- **2 g** 11º seed beads (Miyuki 457, dark metallic gold)
- **3 g** 15º seed beads (Miyuki 457, dark metallic gold)
- **15 mm** lobster claw clasp with decorative ring (antique brass)
- **8** 9 mm blossom bead caps (antique brass)
- **8** 9 mm foliage bead caps (natural brass)
- **8½ in.** (21.6 cm) 7 x 4 mm square curb chain (natural brass)
- **8½ in.** (21.6 cm) 5 mm round double-link chain (natural brass)
- **4** 9.5 mm etched jump rings (natural brass; Bead Haven Las Vegas, 702-233-2450)
- Fireline 8 lb. test
- beading needles, #12
- **2** pairs of pliers
- wire cutters

purple necklace colors:

- 10 mm Czech glass pearls (plum)
- 8 mm round crystals: color A (Swarovski, garnet AB), color B (Swarovski, black diamond)
- 4 mm bicone crystals (Swarovski, sapphire helio)
- 4 mm round fire-polished beads (silver)
- 3 mm round fire-polished beads (garnet AB)
- 11º seed beads (Toho 88, metallic cosmos)
- 11º cylinder beads (Toho 1955-007, hexagon silver-lined clear)
- 15º seed beads (Toho 89, metallic moss)
- 25 x 19 mm toggle clasp (silver)
- 10 mm filigree bead caps (antique silver)
- 10 mm foliage bead caps (silver)
- 10 x 10 mm steampunk chain (antique silver)
- 6 x 3 mm oval etched-link chain (antique silver)
- 9.5 mm jump rings (gray)

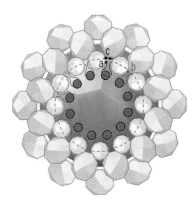

FIGURE 4

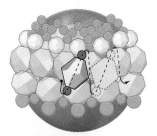

FIGURE 5

[8] Sew through the 15º in the first stitch. Pick up an 11º, and sew through the 15º added in the previous stitch (c–d), the 3 mm your thread exited at the start of this step, and the 15º and 11º in the first stitch (d–e).

[9] Sew through all the 11ºs, and gently snug up the beads around the pearl. Retrace the thread path to reinforce.

[10] Sew through the beadwork to exit a 2 mm on the front of the pearl. Pick up a 15º, and sew through the next 2 mm (figure 4, a–b). Repeat around the ring (b–c).

[11] Create a picot embellishment: With the thread exiting a 2 mm, pick up three 15ºs, sew through the 2 mm your thread exited at the start of this step and the next 15º and 2 mm in the ring. Repeat this step 11 times, then sew through an adjacent 3 mm.

[12] Pick up a 15º, a 4 mm bicone crystal, and a 15º, and sew through the next 3 mm in the bezel so the 4 mm sits diagonally between the two 3 mms (figure 5). Repeat this step 11 times, and end the threads.

[13] Make a total of four bezeled pearls to make the copper necklace on p. 119 or three bezeled pearls to make the purple necklace.

Necklace base

[1] Thread a needle on each end of 1½ yd. (1.4 m) of Fireline. Pick up eight 11ºs, and center them on the thread. With each needle, pick up a 4 mm fire-polished bead and an 11º. With one needle, pick up an 11º, and cross the other needle through it.

[2] Over both needles, pick up a blossom bead cap from outside to inside, a color A 8 mm round crystal, and a foliage bead cap from inside to outside.

[3] With one needle, pick up an 11º, and cross the other needle through it.

[4] With each needle, pick up an 11º and a 4 mm fire-polished bead. With one needle, pick up a 4 mm bicone crystal, and cross the other needle through it.

[5] With each needle, pick up a 4 mm fire-polished bead and an 11º. With one needle, pick up an 11º, and cross the other needle through it.

[6] Over both needles, pick up a foliage bead cap from outside to inside, a color B 8 mm round crystal, and a blossom bead cap from inside to outside.

[7] Repeat steps 3 and 4.

[8] With each needle, pick up a 4 mm fire-polished bead and an 11º, and cross both needles through a 3 mm in the original ring of a bezeled pearl.

[9] With each needle, sew through the next six 3 mms in the bezel, exiting the opposite 3 mm in the ring.

[10] With each needle, pick up an 11º and a 4 mm fire-polished bead. With one needle, pick up a 4 mm bicone crystal, and cross the other needle through it.

[11] With each needle, pick up a 4 mm fire-polished bead and an 11º. With one needle, pick up an 11º, and cross the other needle through it.

[12] Repeat steps 2–4 and 8–9 to connect the second bezeled pearl.

[13] Work the second half of the necklace base as a mirror image of the first. The necklace base will have three bezeled pearls. End the threads.

Bezeled pearl dangle

[1] Thread a needle on each end of 18 in. (46 cm) of Fireline, and center an 11 x 5.5 mm briolette.

[2] With each needle, pick up two 11°s. With one needle, pick up an 11°, and cross the other needle through it.

[3] Over both needles, pick up a blossom bead cap from outside to inside, a B, and a foliage bead cap from inside to outside. With one needle, pick up an 11°, and cross the other needle through it.

[4] With each needle, pick up an 11°, a 4 mm fire-polished bead, and an 11°, and cross both needles through a 3 mm in the original ring of the remaining bezeled pearl. With each needle, sew through the next six 3 mms in the bezel, exiting the opposite 3 mm in the ring.

[5] With each needle, pick up an 11°, a 4 mm fire-polished bead, and an 11°, and cross both needles through an 11°.

[6] Over both needles, pick up a foliage bead cap from outside to inside, a B, and a blossom bead cap from inside to outside. With one needle, pick up an 11°, and cross the other needle through it.

[7] With each needle, pick up an 11°, a 4 mm fire-polished bead, and an 11°. Cross both needles through the center 3 mm at the bottom of the middle bezeled pearl in the base. End the threads.

Chain

[1] Cut two 4-in. (10 cm) pieces of curb chain and two 4-in. (10 cm) pieces of double-link chain.

[2] Open a 9.5 mm etched jump ring (Basics), and attach the beaded loop on one end of the necklace base and an end link of a curb chain and a double-link chain, making sure the double-link chain is to the outside.

[3] Open a 9.5 mm jump ring, and attach half of the clasp and the remaining end links of the chains.

[4] Repeat steps 2 and 3 on the other end of the necklace base.

Exploring
the angles

It can be a challenge to figure out what to do with beads in unusual shapes. This bracelet combines three bead shapes with fun results.

Angled beads nestle together to make spiky flower shapes

designed by **Cheryl Erickson**

Combine two-hole Tila beads with elongated magatamas and drop beads to make this fun geometric-yet-organic design. This bracelet goes together quickly so you can wear it right away.

Before beginning this project, familiarize yourself with the elongated magatamas. The hole through each magatama is on an angle. On one side, the hole is near the center of the bead **(photo a, left)**. In this project, we'll refer to this side as the high side. On the other side, the hole is closer to the end of the bead

(photo a, right). In this project, we'll refer to this as the low side. If you wish, separate the magatamas into two piles; turn all the magatamas in one pile so the high side is facing up, and turn all the magatamas in the other pile so the low side is facing up.

stepbystep

[1] On 2 yd. (1.8 m) of Fireline, attach a stop bead (Basics), leaving an 8-in. (20 cm) tail.

[2] Pick up a repeating pattern of a 5 mm Tila bead, a high-side magatama, and a low-side magatama (figure 1) until you reach the desired length. Allow for about 10 percent shrinkage, and make sure you use an even number of Tilas.

[3] Pick up a Tila, and then sew through the other hole of the same Tila. Sew through both holes again (figure 2) to lock the thread in place.

[4] Pick up a high-side magatama, a low-side magatama, a Tila, a high-side magatama, and a low-side magatama. Skip five beads on the previous strand,

and sew through the remaining hole of the next Tila (figure 3). Repeat this step to the end of the strand.

[5] Remove the stop bead, and, making sure both sides are snug, tie the working thread and tail with a square knot (Basics). Sew through the first hole of the first Tila, the next two magatamas, and the following Tila (figure 4, a–b).

[6] Pick up a 3.4 mm drop bead, and sew through the opposite Tila, going through the same hole you sewed through before (b–c). Pick up a drop, sew through the opposite Tila and the first drop added in this step (c–d), and pull tight. This will cause the Tilas adjacent to the drops to angle upward like wings. Sew through the next six beads on this side of the bracelet (d–e). Repeat this step to the end of the band.

[7] Pick up a drop bead, half of the clasp, and a drop bead, and sew through the other hole of the end Tila (photo b). Retrace the thread path through the clasp connection several times, and end the thread (Basics). Repeat this step with the tail at the other end of the bracelet.

a

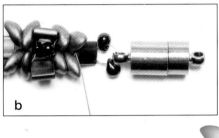

b

materials

purple bracelet 7½ in. (19.1 cm)
- 28 5 mm Tila beads (Miyuki 455, multi iris matte)
- 72 elongated magatamas (Miyuki 1884, blue crystal with violet luster)
- 22 3.4 mm drop beads (Miyuki 181, galvanized silver)
- clasp
- Fireline 6 lb. test
- beading needles, #10

green bracelet colors:
- 5 mm Tila beads (Miyuki 458, metallic green gold)
- elongated magatamas (Miyuki 459, metallic olive)
- 3.4 mm drop beads (Miyuki 27, apricot-lined chartreuse)

bronze/black/pink bracelet colors:
- 5 mm Tila beads (Miyuki 401, opaque black)
- elongated magatamas (Miyuki 457, metallic dark bronze)
- 3.4 mm drop beads (Miyuki 3, pink-lined smoky amethyst)

matte green/purple bracelet colors (shown in how-to photos):
- 5 mm Tila beads (Miyuki 401FR, matte black AB)
- elongated magatamas (Miyuki 2008, matte metallic patina iris)
- 3.4 mm drop beads (Miyuki 454, purple iris)

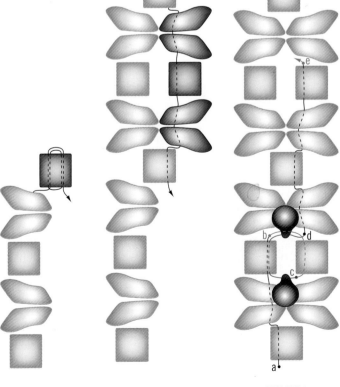

FIGURE 1   FIGURE 2   FIGURE 3   FIGURE 4

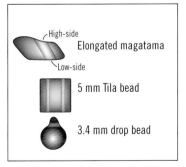

High-side — Elongated magatama

Low-side

5 mm Tila bead

3.4 mm drop bead

BEADWEAVING
Gift wrapped
glam

Wrap crystal clusters with ribbons of
seed beads and top them off with a
crystal bow, creating a glittering gift

designed by **Samantha Mitchell**

Make matching earrings:
Work one cluster, and
add embellishments to
the front and back of
each. Or, try 6 mm pearls
instead of 6 mm crystals
for a classic look.

stepbystep

[1] On 3 yd. (2.7 m) of Fireline, pick up a repeating pattern of a 10º cylinder bead and a 6 mm bicone crystal four times, leaving a 24-in. (61 cm) tail. Sew through all the beads again to form a ring, exiting the first cylinder picked up.

[2] Pick up three 15º seed beads, two 3 mm bicone crystals, and three 15ºs, and sew through the next cylinder in the ring (**figure 1, a–b**). Pick up three 15ºs, and sew back through the last 3 mm picked up in the previous stitch (**b–c**).

[3] Pick up a 3 mm and three 15ºs, and sew through the next cylinder in the ring (**c–d**). Pick up three 15ºs, and sew back through the last 3 mm picked up in the previous stitch (**d–e**). Repeat this step (**e–f**).

[4] Sew through the first 3 mm picked up in step 2, pick up three 15ºs, and sew through the next cylinder in the ring (**f–g**). Sew through the next four beads in the outer ring (**g–h**).

[5] Pick up a repeating pattern of a 15º and a cylinder three times. Pick up a 15º, and sew through the cylinder your thread exited at the start of this step. Sew through the next four beads (**figure 2, a–b**).

[6] Pick up a repeating pattern of a 6 mm and a cylinder three times. Pick up a 6 mm, and sew through the cylinder your thread exited at the start of this step (**b–c**).

[7] Repeat steps 2–6 eight times, and then repeat steps 2–5 once. End the working thread (Basics).

[8] Using the tail, repeat step 5 on the starting end of the bracelet, but sew through all the beads picked up in the step to exit at **figure 3, point a**.

[9] Sew through the next three 15ºs and 3 mm (**a–b**). Pick up a cylinder, and sew through the opposite 3 mm, the next three 15ºs, and the following cylinder (**b–c**). Sew through the next four beads in the connecting ring (**c–d**). Repeat this step nine times, and then sew through the next four beads in the end ring. Retrace the thread path through the beads added in this step, but sew through the other 15ºs in the clusters. End the tail.

[10] Open a jump ring (Basics), and attach half of the clasp to an end ring of beads. Repeat on the other end.

- 6 mm bicone crystal
- 3 mm bicone crystal
- 10º cylinder bead
- 15º seed bead

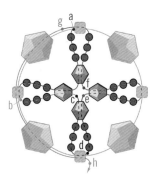

FIGURE 1

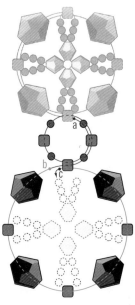

FIGURE 2

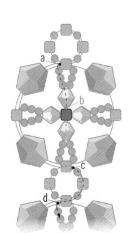

FIGURE 3

materials

red bracelet 7½ in. (19.1 cm)
- 40 6 mm bicone crystals (Swarovski, garnet)
- 40 3 mm bicone crystals (Swarovski, garnet satin)
- 1 g 10º cylinder beads (Miyuki 0089, olive-lined amber AB)
- 1–2 g 15º seed beads (Miyuki 401, opaque black)
- clasp
- 2 4–6 mm jump rings
- Fireline 6 lb. test
- beading needles, #12
- 2 pairs of pliers

black bracelet colors:
- 6 mm bicone crystals (Swarovski, jet)
- 3 mm bicone crystals (Swarovski, Siam AB 2X)
- 10º hex-cut cylinder beads (Miyuki 464, nickel plated)
- 15º seed beads (Miyuki 401F, matte black)

green bracelet colors:
- 6 mm bicone crystals (Swarovski, chrysolite and tourmaline)
- 3 mm bicone crystals (Swarovski, khaki)
- 11º seed beads (Miyuki 464A, deep silver)
- 15º seed beads (Miyuki 464, nickel plated)

DESIGN NOTE:
Make a two-tone bracelet by alternating crystal colors as you work the clusters.

Show off your shapes!

Four favorite bead shapes
work harmoniously in this
elegant bracelet

designed by **Helena Tang-Lim**

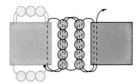

FIGURE 1

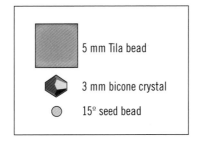

FIGURE 2

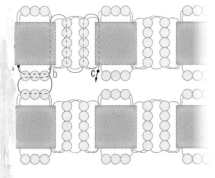

FIGURE 3

□ 5 mm Tila bead

⬡ 3 mm bicone crystal

○ 15º seed bead

materials
bronze bracelet 7 in. (18 cm)
- **3** 8 mm margarita crystals (Swarovski, heliotrope)
- **66** 3 mm bicone crystals (Swarovski, Siam AB 2X)
- **10 g** 5 mm Tila beads (Miyuki 2006, matte metallic dark bronze)
- **7 g** 15º Japanese seed beads (Toho 557, galvanized gold)
- Fireline 4 lb. test conditioned with Thread Heaven or microcrystalline wax
- beading needles, #12 or #13

hematite bracelet colors:
- 8 mm margarita crystals (Swarovski, crystal satin)
- 3 mm bicone crystals (Swarovski, crystal comet argent light)
- 5 mm Tila beads (Miyuki 464, hematite/gunmetal)
- 15º Japanese seed beads (Miyuki 951, bright silver)

's no surprise that Tila beads lend themselves well to a grid, and a framework of metallic round seed beads is another natural choice. But who would have imagined that 3 mm bicone crystals would nestle so nicely into this structure? Another sweet surprise: A trio of margarita crystals serves as the closure for this glamorous bracelet.

stepbystep

Tila bead strips

[1] On 2 yd. (1.8 m) of conditioned Fireline (Basics), pick up a 5 mm Tila bead, leaving a 6-in. (15 cm) tail.
[2] Pick up three 15º seed beads, and sew through the other hole of the Tila bead. Pick up three 15ºs, and sew through the first hole of the Tila bead, the three 15ºs picked up at the start of this step, and the second hole of the Tila bead (figure 1).
[3] Pick up five 15ºs, sew through the second hole of the Tila bead, and continue through the five 15ºs just picked up. Pick up five 15ºs, sew through the previous five 15ºs, and continue through the five new 15ºs. Pick up a Tila bead, sew through the previous five 15ºs, and continue through the first hole of the new Tila bead (figure 2).

[4] Repeat steps 2 and 3 to the desired bracelet length, ending with step 2. End the working thread and tail (Basics).
[5] Make three more Tila bead strips.

Connecting the strips

[1] Add (Basics) 1 yd. (.9 m) of conditioned Fireline to a Tila bead strip, exiting the outermost hole of an end Tila bead (figure 3, point a).
[2] Sew through the adjacent three 15ºs, the corresponding three 15ºs on another Tila bead strip, and the three 15ºs from the first strip again (a–b). Sew through all six 15ºs again to reinforce.
[3] Sew through the second hole of the end Tila bead in the first strip, zigzag through the two stacks of five 15ºs, and continue through the first hole of the next Tila bead (b–c).
[4] Repeat steps 2 and 3 to connect the first two Tila bead strips. End the thread.
[5] Work as in steps 1–4 to attach the third and fourth strips to the first two.

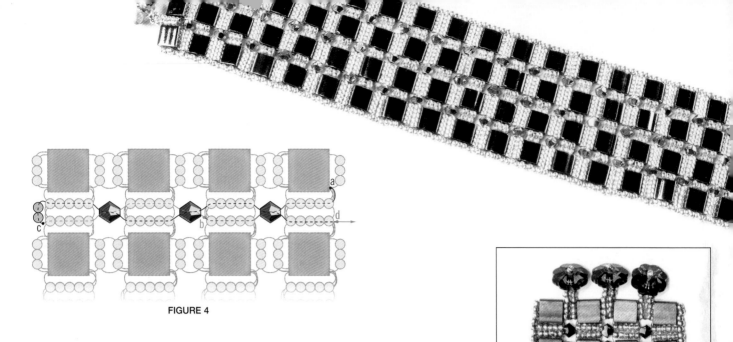

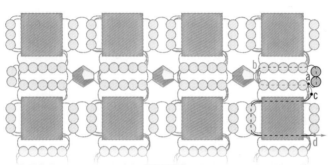

FIGURE 4

FIGURE 5

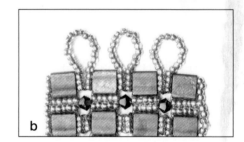

a

b

Embellishments

[1] Turn the beadwork so that one end of the base is at the top of your work surface. Add 2 yd. (1.8 m) of conditioned Fireline to the base, exiting the bottom hole of a corner Tila bead with your thread pointing away from the beadwork (**figure 4, point a**).
[2] Sew through the top set of five 15ºs below the corner Tila bead, pick up a 3 mm bicone crystal, and continue through the bottom set of five 15ºs below the next Tila bead (**a–b**). Pick up a 3 mm, sew through the top set of five 15ºs below the following Tila bead, pick up a 3 mm, and sew through the bottom set of five 15ºs below the last Tila bead in the row (**b–c**).
[3] Pick up two 15ºs, and sew through the top set of 15ºs below the last Tila bead in the row. To reinforce the crystals, sew back through the crystals and the sets of 15ºs you did not sew through in the previous step (**c–d**).
[4] Pick up two 15ºs, sew through the top set of five 15ºs below the corner Tila bead (**figure 5, a–b**), and continue

through the bottom set of 15ºs below the same Tila bead (**b–c**). Sew through the top hole of the next Tila bead along the edge, the adjacent three 15ºs, and the bottom hole of the Tila bead (**c–d**).
[5] Repeat steps 2–4 for the length of the bracelet, ending with your thread exiting the bottom hole of a corner Tila bead. Sew through the adjacent three 15ºs along this edge of the bracelet.
[6] Pick up a 15º, and sew through the next two 15ºs along the edge. Pick up a 15º, and sew through the next three 15ºs along the edge. Repeat these two stitches along this edge, and then sew through the beadwork to add this embellishment on the other edge. End the thread.

Clasp

[1] If necessary, turn the beadwork so that one end of the base is again at the top of your work surface. Add 18 in. (46 cm) of conditioned Fireline to the base, exiting the bottom hole of a corner

Tila bead with your thread pointing toward the opposite edge of the base.
[2] Sew through the adjacent three 15ºs, and a pick up four 15ºs, an 8 mm margarita crystal, and a 15º. Skip the last 15º, and sew back through the margarita and one 15º. Pick up three 15ºs, and sew through the next three 15ºs in the base. Retrace the thread path through the connection a few times, and sew through the beadwork to exit the bottom hole of the next Tila bead.
[3] Repeat step 2 twice to add the remaining margaritas, and end the thread (**photo a**).
[4] Repeat step 1 on the other end of the base.
[5] Sew through the adjacent three 15ºs, pick up 18–20 15ºs, and sew through the next three 15ºs in the base. Retrace the thread path of the connection a few times, and sew through the beadwork to exit the bottom hole of the next Tila bead.
[6] Repeat step 5 twice, and end the thread (**photo b**).

Cubes and circles

designed by **Julia Gerlach**

Fashion an everyday bracelet with a simple pattern of shapes

Sew-through bead frames are available in a variety of sizes, styles, and materials. Adjust your bead choices to suit the frames you use.

materials

bracelet 7½ in. (19.1 cm)
- **8** 10 mm sew-through bead frames (ohiobeads.com)
- **8** 6 mm round crystals (Swarovski, crystal celadon)
- **18** 4 mm crystal cubes (Swarovski, crystal vitrail medium)
- **1 g** 11º seed beads (Toho 995, gold-lined rainbow aqua)
- clasp
- Power Pro or Fireline (crystal), 8 lb. test
- beading needles, #10

stepbystep

[1] On 1 yd. (.9 m) of Power Pro or Fireline, attach a stop bead (Basics), leaving a 6-in. (15 cm) tail.

[2] Pick up two 11º seed beads, a 4 mm crystal cube, two 11ºs, one hole of a 10 mm bead frame, a 6 mm round crystal, an 11º, and the other hole of the same bead frame. Repeat this sequence seven times, and then pick up two 11ºs, a cube, and two 11ºs.

[3] Pick up three 11ºs, half of the clasp, and three 11ºs. Skip the last six 11ºs and the clasp, and sew back through the previous 11º.

[4] Pick up an 11º, a cube, and an 11º. Skip the next 11º, cube, and 11º in the initial strand, and sew through the following 11º, bead frame hole, 11º, 6 mm, bead frame hole, and 11º **(photo)**.

[5] Repeat step 4 until you've sewn through the 11º after the last bead frame.

Repeat step 4 once more, but sew through only the 11º at the end of the strand.

[6] Repeat step 3 to attach the other clasp half at this end of the bracelet.

[7] Retrace the thread path through the entire bracelet, and end the working thread (Basics). Remove the stop bead, and end the tail.

Wreathed rivolis

Sandwich a crystal stone between two filigree rings, and link a series of rivolis for a bracelet that's a little metal, a little magic

designed by **Cary Bruner**

To add interest, change up the colors of your rivolis and 3 mm bicone crystals, and alternate the finishes of the filigrees.

stepbystep

Each filigree ring has 12 petals with three holes per petal. The hole at the tip of the petal will be called hole 1, the hole at the base of the petal on the left will be called hole 2, and the hole at the base of the petal on the right will be called hole 3 (photo a).

Rivoli components

[1] On 1½ yd. (1.4 m) of Fireline, sew through hole 2 of a filigree ring from back to front, and then sew through hole 3 from front to back, leaving a 6-in. (15 cm) tail. Tie the working thread and tail with a square knot (Basics).
[2] Place the filigree face down on your work surface; this is the bottom filigree. Place a 14 mm rivoli face up on the

bottom filigree. Place a new filigree face up on the rivoli; this is the top filigree. Sew up through hole 3 in a corresponding petal on the top filigree.
[3] Pick up three 3 mm bicone crystals, sew down through hole 1 of the next petal on both filigrees (photo b), and sew up through hole 3 of the same petal on both filigrees (photo c). Repeat this stitch around the filigrees, but in the last repeat, don't sew up through hole 3. Your thread should be exiting hole 1 on the bottom filigree.
[4] Pick up five 15º seed beads, and sew through hole 1 of the next petal on the bottom filigree from the inside surface of the filigree to the outer surface (photo d). Repeat this stitch around the bottom filigree, and sew through the first five 15ºs picked up in this step.

[5] Pick up a 15º, and sew through the next five 15ºs. Repeat this stitch around the bottom filigree, and sew down through hole 1 of any petal on the bottom filigree.
[6] Pick up six 11º seed beads, and sew down through hole 1 of the next petal on both filigrees (photo e). Repeat this stitch around the filigrees. End the tail (Basics) but not the working thread.
[7] Make a total of five rivoli components.

Bracelet

[1] Lay out the rivoli components in the desired order, with the working thread from each component pointing toward the next component.
[2] Using the working thread from an end component, sew through the

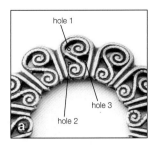

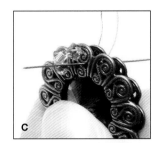

hole 1
hole 3
hole 2

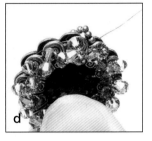

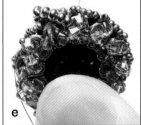

materials

bracelet 7 in. (18 cm)

- **10** 22 mm filigree rings (Bead Haven Las Vegas, 702-233-2450)
- **5** 14 mm rivolis
- **8** 4 mm bicone crystals
- **180** 3 mm bicone crystals
- 8–10 g 11º seed beads
- 5 g 15º seed beads
- 2-strand slide clasp
- Fireline 6 lb. test
- beading needles, #12

beadwork to exit the bottom three 11ºs in a loop of 11ºs (**photo f**).

[3] Pick up an 11º, a 4 mm bicone crystal, and an 11º. Sew through the top three 11ºs in a loop of 11ºs on the next component (**photo g**). Sew down through hole 1 of both filigrees in this component and the bottom three 11ºs in the same loop. Sew back through the 11º, 4 mm, and 11º picked up in this step, and sew through the top three 11ºs in the loop on the first component. Retrace the thread path of the connection.

[4] Sew through the beadwork to exit the bottom three 11ºs in an adjacent loop of 11ºs. Repeat step 3, sewing through the corresponding loop on the second component. Leave this working thread for step 9.

[5] Using the working thread from the new component, sew through the beadwork to exit the bottom three 11ºs in a loop of 11ºs opposite one of the loops in the previous connection.

[6] Repeat steps 2–5 to connect all five components, but in step 4, end the working thread. Make sure to complete step 5 on the last component.

[7] With a thread exiting an end component, pick up an 11º, and sew

through one loop of half of the clasp. Sew back through the 11º just added and the top three 11ºs in the loop. Retrace the thread path.

[8] Sew through the beadwork to exit the bottom three 11ºs in the adjacent loop, and repeat step 7 to attach the other loop of the clasp. End the working thread.

[9] Using the remaining thread from the first component, repeat steps 5, 7, and 8.

individual rivoli component colors:

component #1

- 22 mm filigree rings (copper)
- 14 mm rivoli (Swarovski, crystal copper)
- 3 mm bicone crystals (Swarovski, silver shade)
- 11º seed beads (brass)
- 15º seed beads (copper)

component #2

- 22 mm filigree rings (silver)
- 14 mm rivoli (Swarovski, silver shade)
- 3 mm bicone crystals (Swarovski, crystal copper)
- 11º seed beads (brass)
- 15º seed beads (silver)

component #3

- 22 mm filigree rings (gold)
- 14 mm rivoli (Swarovski, jet)
- 3 mm bicone crystals (Swarovski; silver shade, black diamond, crystal copper, and golden shadow)
- 11º seed beads (brass)
- 15º seed beads (gold)

component #4

- 22 mm filigree rings (copper)
- 14 mm rivoli (Swarovski, golden shadow)
- 3 mm bicone crystals (Swarovski, black diamond)
- 11º seed beads (brass)
- 15º seed beads (copper)

component #5

- 22 mm filigree rings (silver)
- 14 mm rivoli (Swarovski, black diamond)
- 3 mm bicone crystals (Swarovski, golden shadow)
- 11º seed beads (brass)
- 15º seed beads (silver)

BEADWEAVING
Bugle core

So often relegated to decorative fringe, bugle beads form the foundation of these elegant earrings

designed by **Barbara Klann**

Transform bugle beads into a square frame that forms the base of these earrings. That plain square then becomes a diamond with cube bead corners and crystal elements.

stepbystep

Bugle squares

[1] On 24 in. (61 cm) of Fireline, pick up four 6 mm bugle beads, and tie them into a ring with a square knot (Basics), leaving a 6-in. (15 cm) tail. Sew through the first bugle again.

[2] Pick up a 1.5 mm cube bead, and sew through the next bugle (**figure 1, a–b**). Repeat this stitch three times to complete the round, and step up through the first cube (**b–c**).

[3] Pick up a bugle, and sew through the next cube (**figure 2, a–b**). Repeat this stitch to complete the round, and step

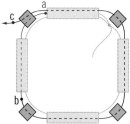

FIGURE 1

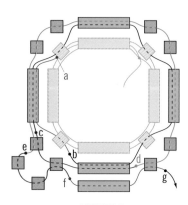

FIGURE 2

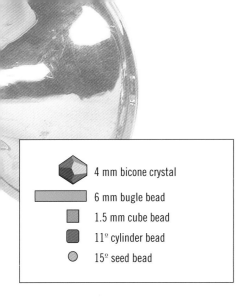

materials

orange earrings 2 in. (5 cm)

- **2** 9 x 6 mm faceted teardrops (Swarovski, topaz AB)
- **12** 4 mm bicone crystals (Swarovski, fire opal)
- **32** 6 mm bugle beads (Miyuki 72003, melon)
- **1 g** 1.5 mm cube beads (Toho 952, rainbow light topaz/sea foam lined)
- **1 g** 11º cylinder beads (Miyuki 0883, matte opaque dark cream AB)
- **1 g** 15º seed beads (Czech three-cut, silver-lined gold)
- **2** 4 mm jump rings
- pair of earring findings
- Fireline 6 lb. test
- beading needles, #12
- **2** pairs of pliers

blue earring colors:

- 9 x 6 mm faceted teardrops (Swarovski, crystal AB)
- 4 mm bicone crystals (Swarovski, jet AB 2X)
- 6 mm bugle beads (Miyuki 413FR, opaque turquoise blue)
- 1.5 mm cube beads (Toho 712, gold)
- 11º cylinder beads (Miyuki 0918, color-lined dark turquoise blue)
- 15º seed beads (Miyuki 25, capri blue)

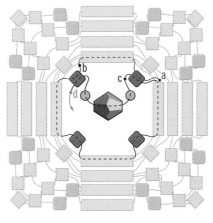

FIGURE 3

up through the first bugle added in this round (b–c).

[4] Pick up two cubes, and sew through the next bugle added in the previous round (c–d). Repeat this stitch to complete the round, and step up through the first cube added in this round (d–e).

[5] Pick up two cubes, and sew through the next cube added in the previous round (e–f). Pick up a bugle, and sew through the next cube (f–g). Repeat these two stitches to complete the round, and step up through the first cube added in this step.

[6] Pick up two cubes, and sew through the next cube added in the previous round. Pick up an 11º cylinder bead, and sew through the next bugle. Pick up a cylinder, and sew through the next cube added in the previous round. Repeat these three stitches to complete the round, and step up through the first cube added in this round.

[7] Pick up a cube, and sew through the next cube added in the previous round. Pick up a cylinder, and sew through the next cylinder. Pick up a bugle, and sew through the next cylinder. Pick up a cylinder, and sew through the next cube. Repeat these four stitches to complete the round.

Center embellishment

[1] Sew through the beadwork to exit a bugle in the center of the square. Pick up a cylinder, and sew through the next bugle (figure 3, a–b). Repeat this stitch to complete the round, and step up through the first cylinder added (b–c).

[2] Pick up a 15º seed bead, a 4 mm bicone crystal, and a 15º, and sew through the next cylinder in the center ring (c–d). Repeat this stitch to complete the round, retrace the thread path, and step up through a 4 mm. Sew through all the 4 mms several times, and snug up the beads.

Dangle

[1] Sew through the beadwork to exit a corner cube in the outer edge of the square. Pick up a cube, a 4 mm, a cube, 15º, a 9 x 6 mm faceted teardrop, and a 15º. Skip the last 15º, and sew back through the drop. Pick up a 15º, a cube, a 4 mm, and a cube, and sew through the cube your thread exited at the start of this step. End the working thread and tail (Basics).

[2] Make a second earring.

Assembly

Open a 4 mm jump ring (Basics), slide it through the corner cube on the outer edge of the square opposite the dangle, and attach an earring finding. Repeat for the other earring.

DESIGN NOTE:

For a 7¼-in. (18.4 cm) bracelet: Stitch five "Bugle squares" with "Center embellishments." Do not end the threads. Using the working thread on one square, make a dangle, but instead of adding the drop, sew through the corresponding cube bead at the corner of another square to join. Join all the squares in this manner. On the end square, add 9 in. (23 cm) of Fireline (Basics), and exit the corner opposite the join. Work as if to add the "Dangle," but add another cube instead of the drop and 15º. Open a 4 mm jump ring, and attach the end cube to half of the clasp. Repeat on the remaining end.

Queen of the tile

A regal but wearable chain offers a subtle nod to Macedonian majesty

designed by **Amy Kohn**

Gold and silver beads
and rings frame colorful
Tilas that almost look
like gemstone tiles.

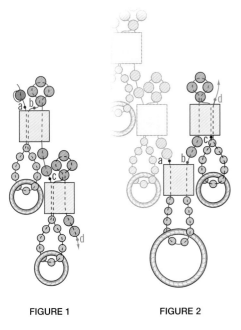

FIGURE 1

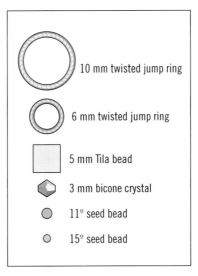

FIGURE 2

10 mm twisted jump ring

6 mm twisted jump ring

5 mm Tila bead

3 mm bicone crystal

11º seed bead

15º seed bead

materials

gold/white necklace 19½ in. (49.5 cm)
- **41** 5 mm Tila beads (Miyuki 471, white pearl AB)
- **39** 3 mm bicone crystals (Preciosa, crystal diamond gold aurum half coated)
- **8–10 g** 11º seed beads (metallic gold)
- **5–6 g** 15º seed beads (metallic gold)
- clasp (gold)
- **13** 10 mm twisted jump rings (gold; Fire Mountain Gems and Beads, firemountaingems.com)
- **52** 6 mm twisted jump rings (gold; Fire Mountain Gems and Beads)
- Fireline 6 lb. test
- beading needles, #10
- **2** pairs of pliers

silver/blue necklace colors:
- 5 mm Tila beads (Miyuki 451, hematite)
- 3 mm bicone crystals (Preciosa, Montana AB)
- 11º seed beads (metallic silver)
- 15º seed beads (metallic silver)
- clasp (silver)
- 10 mm twisted jump rings (silver; Fire Mountain Gems and Beads, firemountaingems.com)
- 6 mm twisted jump rings (silver; Fire Mountain Gems and Beads)

This necklace brings together an unlikely pair — the round, twisted jump ring and the smooth, square Tila bead. Choose 11º and 15º seed beads in a metallic hue to match your jump rings, lending the look of fine jewelry fit for an Egyptian queen. Long lines of Tila beads with glinting bicone crystals create a river of color that culminates in a delicate delta front and center.

stepbystep

Tila bead chain

[1] On 2 yd. (1.8 m) of Fireline, attach a stop bead (Basics), leaving an 8-in. (20 cm) tail.

[2] Pick up a 5 mm Tila bead, 10 15º seed beads, and a 6 mm twisted jump ring. Sew back through the first 15º just picked up and the same hole of the Tila bead, forming a loop of beads around the jump ring **(figure 1, a–b)**.

[3] Pick up four 11º seed beads, sew back through the first 11º just picked up, and sew through the second hole of the Tila bead. Keep your tension tight, and position the loop of 11ºs directly above the second hole of the Tila bead. Pick up two 11ºs **(b–c)**.

[4] Repeat steps 2 and 3 **(c–d)** until you have a total of 20 Tila beads, creating the first half of the chain.

[5] To work the center of the chain: Pick up a Tila bead, 10 15ºs, and a 10 mm twisted jump ring, and sew through the second hole of the Tila bead **(figure 2, a–b)**.

[6] Pick up two 11ºs, a Tila bead, and four 11ºs. Sew back through the first of the four 11ºs just picked up, and then sew through the second hole of the Tila bead **(b–c)**. Keep your tension tight, and position the loop of 11ºs directly above the first hole of the Tila bead.

[7] Pick up 10 15ºs and a 6 mm twisted jump ring, and sew back through the first 15º just picked up and the same hole of the Tila bead **(c–d)**.

[8] Repeat steps 6 and 7 until you have a total of 20 Tila beads in the second half of the chain, not counting the Tila bead at the center of the chain. End and add thread (Basics) as needed.

DESIGN NOTE:

Make sure all the jump rings in "Tila bead chain" are completely closed (Basics) before incorporating them into your beadwork.

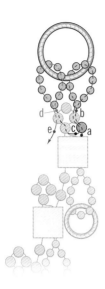

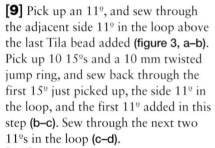

FIGURE 3

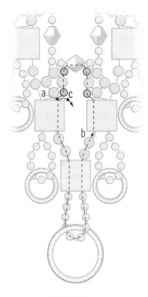

FIGURE 4

[9] Pick up an 11º, and sew through the adjacent side 11º in the loop above the last Tila bead added (figure 3, a–b). Pick up 10 15ºs and a 10 mm twisted jump ring, and sew back through the first 15º just picked up, the side 11º in the loop, and the first 11º added in this step (b–c). Sew through the next two 11ºs in the loop (c–d).

[10] Pick up 10 15ºs, sew through the 10 mm twisted jump ring added in step 9, and sew back through the first 15º just picked up and the side 11º your thread exited at the start of this step (d–e). Do not end the working thread.

[11] On the starting end of the chain, remove the stop bead, and repeat steps 9 and 10. End the tail.

Crystal embellishment

Before adding the embellishment, lay the Tila bead chain flat on your work surface, arranging it so all the twisted jump rings sit along the outer edge. Work the embellishment with medium tension; pulling too tight will make the sides bunch up instead of lying flat, so adjust your tension as necessary.

[1] With the working thread, pick up two 15ºs, a 3 mm bicone crystal, and two 15ºs, and sew through the top 11º in the loop of 11ºs above the next Tila bead (photo). Repeat this step until you exit the top 11º above the Tila bead just before the center Tila in the chain.

[2] Pick up a 15º, a 3 mm, and a 15º, and sew through the top 11º in the loop

of 11ºs above the corresponding Tila bead in the other half of the chain.

[3] Pick up two 15ºs, a 3 mm, and two 15ºs, and sew through the top 11º in the loop of 11ºs above the next Tila bead. Repeat this step to the end of the chain, and end the thread.

[4] Add 10 in. (25 cm) of thread to the chain, exiting the inner hole of a Tila bead above the center Tila bead (figure 4, point a).

[5] Pick up a 15º, and sew through the adjacent side 11º in the loop of 11ºs above the Tila bead. Pick up a 15º, and sew through the center 3 mm. Pick up a 15º, and sew through the adjacent side 11º in the loop of 11ºs above the corresponding Tila bead on the other side of the chain. Pick up a 15º, and sew through the adjacent hole of the Tila bead (a–b). Continue through the next two 11ºs, the center Tila bead, the 10 15ºs below it, the other hole of the center Tila bead, the following two 11ºs, and the next Tila bead (b–c). Retrace the thread path of this step, and end the thread.

Neck straps

On one end of the Tila bead chain, open a 6 mm twisted jump ring (Basics), and attach the end 10 mm twisted jump ring to a new 10 mm jump ring. Repeat to attach a total of five new 10 mm twisted jump rings. Use a 6 mm twisted jump ring to attach the end 10 mm to half of the clasp. Repeat this step on the other end of the chain.

DESIGN NOTE:
If you prefer not to wear metal findings, replace the twisted jump rings in this design with 5 mm fringe drops.

Circle meets square

Pearls are the perfect fit for these beaded cubes

designed by **Kathleen Burke**

materials

blue/gray bracelet with nine beaded beads
8½–9 in. (21.6–23 cm)

- 16 8 mm crystal pearls (Crystazzi, light gray)
- 36 6 mm crystal pearls (Crystazzi, light gray)
- 80 4 mm bicone crystals (Swarovski, heliotrope)
- 54 3 mm fire-polished beads (Czech, silver)
- 2 3–4 mm round metal beads (silver)
- 2 g 11º cylinder beads (Miyuki DB0146, silver-lined smoky amethyst)
- 5 g 15º seed beads (Miyuki 452, metallic dark blue iris)
- toggle clasp
- 2 crimp beads
- 2 crimp covers (optional)
- Fireline 6 lb. test
- beading needles, #10
- flexible beading wire, .014–.019
- crimping pliers
- wire cutters
- drinking straw, 6 mm diameter
- Bead Stopper or tape

rainbow bracelet colors:

- 8 mm crystal pearls (Crystazzi, white)
- 6 mm crystal pearls (Crystazzi, white)
- 4 mm bicone crystals (Swarovski; fire opal, light sapphire, amethyst, lime, light Siam, blue zircon, light amethyst, capri blue, rose, and light topaz)
- 3 mm fire-polished beads (Czech, in colors to match the 4 mm bicones)
- 3–4 mm round metal beads (gold)
- 8º seed beads, in place of the 4 mm bicones between pearls (gold)
- 11º cylinder beads (silver)
- 15º seed beads (gold)

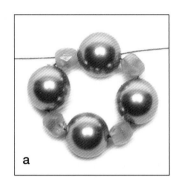
a

b

c

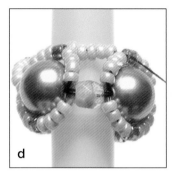
d

Square off a set of beaded beads with equally angular bicone crystals, and then soften the lines with round crystal pearls. These unique shapes require consideration: As you string your bracelet, check that it's long enough to fit around your wrist, and form it into a circle before crimping to ensure there's enough space between beads for a proper fit.

stepbystep

Beaded bead

Work the following steps with tight tension.

[1] On 2 yd. (1.8 m) of Fireline, pick up a pattern of a 3 mm fire-polished bead and a 6 mm pearl four times, leaving a 6-in. (15 cm) tail. Sew through all the beads again to form a ring, and continue through the first 3 mm and pearl (photo a). Place the ring of beads on a 6 mm drinking straw.

[2] Pick up four 15º seed beads, an 11º cylinder bead, and four 15ºs. Sew through the pearl your thread exited at the start of this step to form a loop around the top of the pearl (photo b). Retrace the thread path through the loop and the pearl, and continue through the next 3 mm and pearl. Repeat this step to form a loop around the top of each pearl.

[3] Work as in step 2 to add a loop around the bottom of each pearl (photo c).

Sew through the first four 15ºs and cylinder of a loop around the top of a pearl.

[4] Pick up five 15ºs, and sew through the cylinder above the next pearl (photo d). Repeat this step around the top of the pearls, and then sew through all the 15ºs and cylinders from this step to reinforce the ring.

[5] Sew through the bead-work to exit the first four 15ºs and cylinder of a loop around the bottom of a pearl. Work as in step 4 around the

DESIGN NOTE:
Even if you don't normally work tubular beadwork around a form, you'll want to use one for these beaded beads. Without it, the opening at the top and bottom of the bead won't be circular. I found a drinking straw works better than a dowel or other solid form; the straw is sturdy enough to support the bead, but its hollow core allows it to be compressed slightly as you work with tight tension.

pair of earrings

- **4** 8 mm crystal pearls (Swarovski, white)
- **8** 6 mm crystal pearls (Swarovski, bright gold)
- **20** 4 mm bicone crystals (Swarovski, light rose)
- **12** 3 mm fire-polished beads (Czech, light rose)
- **16** 11º cylinder beads (Miyuki DB0913, sparkle salmon-lined topaz)
- **2 g** 15º seed beads (Miyuki 429, opaque salmon)
- **2** 2–3-in. (7.6 cm) head pins (gold)
- pair of earring findings (gold)
- Fireline 6 lb. test
- beading needles, #10
- chainnose pliers
- roundnose pliers
- wire cutters
- drinking straw, 6 mm diameter

DESIGN NOTE:

In steps 2 and 3 of "Beaded bead," don't try to speed the process by working two loops around each 6 mm pearl before moving on to the next pearl. The extra thread path created by working step 2 and then step 3 strengthens the inner core of the beaded bead.

To make an earring or a dangle for a clasp: On a 2–3-in. (5–7.6 cm) head pin, string a 4 mm bicone crystal, an 8 mm pearl, a beaded bead, two 3 mm fire-polished beads (to sit inside the beaded bead), an 8 mm pearl, and a 4 mm bicone. Make a plain or wrapped loop (Basics) to attach to an earring finding or clasp.

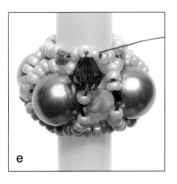

e

f

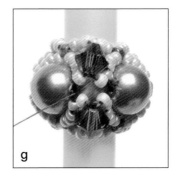

g

bottom of the pearls, and then sew through the beadwork to exit a 3 mm.

[6] Pick up a 15º, a 4 mm bicone crystal, and a 15º. Sew through the center 15º in the set of five 15ºs above the 3 mm **(photo e)**. Pick up a 15º, sew back through the bicone, pick up a 15º, and sew through the 3 mm in the same direction your thread exited it at the start of this step **(photo f)**. Retrace the thread path through the crystal embellishment, exiting the same 3 mm. Repeat this step, but sew through the center 15º in the set of five 15ºs below the 3 mm **(photo g)**. Sew through the next pearl and 3 mm.

[7] Repeat step 6 around the beaded bead. End the

working thread and tail (Basics).

Bracelet

[1] Make nine beaded beads, or as many as desired, keeping in mind that their square shape means that the inside diameter of your bracelet will be smaller than the overall length of the piece. My bracelets have nine beaded beads and measure 8½–9 in. (21.6–23 cm) with an inside diameter of 6½–7 in. (16.5–18 cm) when clasped.

[2] Cut 12 in. (30 cm) of beading wire. Center the following beads: an 8 mm pearl, a beaded bead, two 3 mms (to sit inside the beaded bead), an 8 mm, a beaded bead, two 3 mms, an 8 mm, a beaded

beads, two 3 mms, and an 8 mm. On each end of the wire, string the following pattern three times: a 4 mm bicone, an 8 mm, a beaded bead, two 3 mms, and an 8 mm. Temporarily secure one end of the wire with a Bead Stopper or tape.

[3] On the other end, string a 4 mm, a 3–4 mm round bead, a crimp bead, and half of the clasp. Go back through the crimp bead, the round bead, and the 4 mm. Crimp the crimp bead (Basics), and trim the excess wire. Form the strand into a circle, remove the Bead Stopper or tape, and repeat this step on the other end. Close a crimp cover over each crimp if desired.

Filigree fanfare

designed by **Nealay Patel**

Rows of beaded fans run through a framework of filigree beads

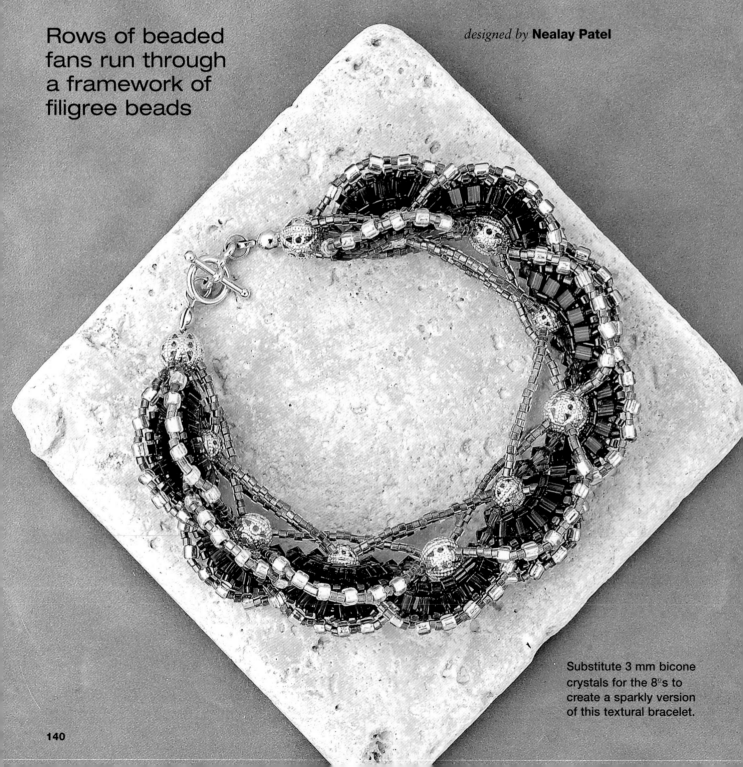

Substitute 3 mm bicone crystals for the 8⁰'s to create a sparkly version of this textural bracelet.

This project brings together the best of both worlds — stringing and stitching! Slide stitched fans onto beading wire, and weave through filigree beads to construct this intricate bracelet.

stepbystep

Beaded fans

[1] On 18 in. (46 cm) of Fireline, attach a stop bead (Basics), leaving a 6-in. (15 cm) tail. Pick up a 3 mm cube bead, a color A 11º cylinder bead, and an 8º seed bead. Skip the 8º, and sew back through the A and the cube bead **(figure 1, a–b)**.

[2] Pick up an 11º triangle bead, a cube, and a color C 11º cylinder bead, and sew back through the previous cube, the triangle, and the cube just added **(b–c)**. Pick up an A and an 8º, skip the 8º, and sew back through the A and the cube added in this step **(c–d)**.

[3] Repeat step 2 until you have a total of six cubes **(d–e)**. Sew back through all the triangles, and snug up the beads to create a fan. End the threads (Basics).

[4] Make a total of 23 fans.

Foundation strand

Filigree beads are essential to this bracelet. The strategically placed holes provide entry and exit points for the multiple pieces of beading wire that create the undulating design. Except for the first and last 8 mm filigree beads in the bracelet, the wires go through holes surrounding the center hole, cross through the bead diagonally, and exit a corresponding hole on the opposite side of the bead.

[1] Cut a 12-in. (30 cm) piece of beading wire, and temporarily secure the end of the strand with a Bead Stopper or piece of tape, leaving a 3-in. (7.6 cm) tail. String an 8 mm filigree bead, three 4 mm bicone crystals, a 6 mm filigree bead, and three 4 mms. Repeat this pattern four more times.

[2] String an 8 mm, and temporarily secure this end of the wire.

Stringing the fans

[1] Cut eight 12-in. (30 cm) pieces of beading wire. Temporarily secure one end of each strand, leaving a 3-in. (7.6 cm) tail.

[2] With each strand, go through the center hole of the first 8 mm filigree bead of the "Foundation strand," and exit one of the holes surrounding the center hole on the opposite side of the 8 mm, with each strand exiting a different hole **(figure 2)**.

Strand 1

Select one wire to be strand 1. You will use **figure 2** to determine the strand numbers of the other wires based on their placement in relation to strand 1.

materials

purple bracelet 7 in. (18 cm)
- **6** 8 mm round filigree beads (silver; Michaels, michaels.com)
- **5** 6 mm round filigree beads (silver; Michaels, michaels.com)
- **30** 4 mm bicone crystals (Swarovski, tanzanite)
- **10 g** 3 mm cube beads (Miyuki 157, transparent amethyst)
- **8 g** 8º seed beads (Miyuki 1024, silver-lined light amethyst AB)
- **6–8 g** 11º triangle beads (Toho 477D, higher royal metallic purple)
- **4–6 g** 11º cylinder beads in each of **3** colors: A (DB695, silver-lined frost violet), B (DB923, sparkling amethyst-lined crystal), C (DB105, metallic royal purple)
- clasp
- 2 clamshell bead tips
- **2** 2 mm crimp beads
- Fireline 6 lb. test
- beading needles, #11
- flexible beading wire, .012 (silver)
- Bead Stoppers or tape
- E6000 adhesive or two-part epoxy
- chainnose pliers
- crimping pliers
- roundnose pliers
- wire cutters

blue bracelet (p. 74) colors:
- 4 mm bicone crystals (Swarovski, tanzanite)
- 3 mm cube beads (Miyuki, sparkling pewter-lined crystal)
- 8º seed beads (Miyuki 452, metallic dark blue iris topaz)
- 11º triangle beads (Toho T82, metallic nebula)
- 11º cylinder beads in each of 3 colors: A (DB0006, gunmetal iris), B (DB128, transparent luster rainbow amethyst purple gold), C (DB0086, color-lined gunmetal rainbow)

8 mm round filigree bead

6 mm round filigree bead

4 mm bicone crystal

3 mm cube bead

8º seed bead

11º triangle bead

11º cylinder bead, color A

11º cylinder bead, color B

11º cylinder bead, color C

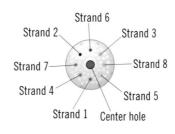

FIGURE 1

Strand 6
Strand 2
Strand 3
Strand 7
Strand 8
Strand 4
Strand 5
Strand 1   Center hole

FIGURE 2

141

[1] On strand 1, string 21 color B 11º cylinder beads. Skip the next 6 mm in the foundation strand, go through the hole below the center hole of the next 8 mm **(figure 3, a–b)**, cross through the 8 mm diagonally, and exit a hole above the center hole on the opposite side of the 8 mm **(b–c)**.

[2] String six Bs and the first 8º of a beaded fan **(c–d)**. String two Bs and the next 8º of the fan **(d–e)**. Continue adding two Bs between the 8ºs in the fan, and exit the last 8º in the fan **(e–f)**.

[3] String six Bs, skip the next 6 mm in the foundation strand, go through the hole above the center hole of the following 8 mm, cross through the 8 mm diagonally, and exit a hole below the center hole on the opposite side of the 8 mm.

[4] Repeat steps 1–3, and then repeat step 1, but exit the center hole in the last 8 mm in the foundation. Temporarily secure this end of the strand.

Strands 2 and 3

Work the following steps for strand 2 and then for strand 3.

[1] String 10 Bs, and go through a hole on the next 6 mm that corresponds to the hole the wire is exiting on the 8 mm in the foundation strand. Cross through the 6 mm diagonally, and exit the corresponding bottom hole on the opposite side of the 6 mm.

[2] String 21 Bs, skip the next 8 mm in the foundation strand, go through a hole below the center hole of the following 6 mm, cross through the 6 mm diagonally, and exit the corresponding top hole on the opposite side of the 6 mm.

[3] String eight Bs and the first 8º of a fan. String two Bs and the next 8º of the fan. Continue adding two Bs between the 8ºs in the fan, and exit the last 8º in the fan. String eight Bs, skip the next 8 mm in the foundation strand, go through a hole above the center hole of the following 6 mm, cross through the 6 mm diagonally, and exit the corresponding bottom hole on the opposite side of the 6 mm.

[4] Repeat steps 2 and 3, using corresponding holes in the next two 6 mms.

[5] String 10 Bs, go through the corresponding hole surrounding the center hole of the last 8 mm, cross through the 8 mm, and exit the center hole on the opposite side of the 8 mm. Temporarily secure this end of the strand.

Strands 4 and 5

Repeat the steps from "Strands 2 and 3" in the following order: step 1, step 3, step 2, step 3, step 2, and step 5.

Strand 6

[1] String four Bs and the first 8º of a fan. String two Bs and the next 8º of the fan. Continue adding two Bs between the 8ºs in the fan, and exit the last 8º in the fan. String six Bs, skip the next 6 mm in the foundation strand, go through the corresponding hole above the center hole of the following 8 mm, cross through the 8 mm diagonally, and exit the corresponding hole below the center hole on the opposite side.

[2] String 21 Bs, skip the next 6 mm in the foundation strand, go through the corresponding hole below the center hole of the following 8 mm, cross through the 8 mm diagonally, and exit the corresponding hole above the center hole on the opposite side of the 8 mm.

[3] String six Bs and the first 8º of a fan. String two Bs and the next 8º of the fan. Continue adding two Bs between the 8ºs in the fan, and exit the last 8º in the fan. String six Bs, skip the next 6 mm in the foundation strand, go through a hole above the center hole of the following 8 mm, cross through the 8 mm diagonally, and exit a hole below the center hole on the opposite side of the 8 mm.

[4] Repeat step 2.

[5] String six Bs and the first 8º of a fan. String two Bs and the next 8º of the fan. Continue adding two Bs between the 8ºs in the fan, and exit the last 8º in the fan. String four Bs, skip the next 6 mm in the foundation strand, go through the corresponding hole surrounding the center hole in the following 8 mm, cross through the 8 mm, and exit the center hole on the opposite side of the last 8 mm. Temporarily secure this end of the strand.

Strands 7 and 8

[1] String four Bs and the first 8º of a fan. String two Bs and the next 8º of the fan. Continue adding two Bs between the 8ºs in the fan, and exit the last 8º in the fan.

[2] String six Bs, skip the next 6 mm in the foundation strand, go through the corresponding side hole surrounding the center hole in the following 8 mm, cross through the 8 mm diagonally,

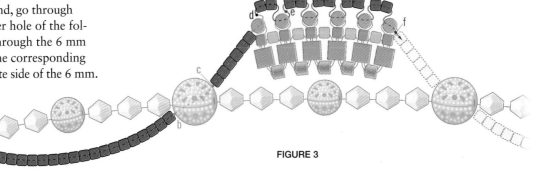

FIGURE 3

and exit the corresponding side hole surrounding the center hole on the opposite side of the 8 mm.

[3] String six Bs and the first 8º of a fan. String two Bs and the next 8º of the fan. Continue adding two Bs between the 8ºs in the fan, and exit the last 8º in the fan. String six Bs, skip the next 6 mm in the foundation strand, go through the corresponding side hole surrounding the center hole in the following 8 mm, cross through the 8 mm diagonally, and exit the corresponding side hole surrounding the center hole on the opposite side of the bead. Repeat this step three times, but at the end of the last repeat, pick up four Bs, go through the corresponding side hole surrounding the center hole in the last 8 mm, cross through the 8 mm, and exit the center hole of the last 8 mm. Temporarily secure this end of the strand.

Assembly

[1] On one end of the bracelet, remove the Bead Stoppers or tape from all nine strands. Over all nine strands, string a clamshell bead tip and a crimp bead, and snug up the beads so the crimp bead is inside the open clamshell. Crimp the crimp bead (Basics), and trim the wires flush with the crimp.

[2] Apply a dab of E6000 adhesive or two-part epoxy over the crimp. Using chainnose pliers, close the clamshell over the crimp.

[3] Using roundnose pliers, open the loop of the clamshell, and attach half of the clasp. Close the loop.

[4] Repeat steps 1–3 on the remaining end of the bracelet.

When it reigns...

Jewel-tone beads and metallic accents lend the look of royalty, minus the silver spoon

designed by **Isabella Lam**

Picots of silver or gold seed beads create the structure for perfectly planned rows of fire-polished beads. You'll feel like a queen wearing colors that imitate your favorite gem (but your loyal subjects will never know you paid a lot less than you would for the real thing!).

stepbystep

[1] On 2 yd. (1.8 m) of Fireline, attach a stop bead (Basics), leaving a 10-in. (25 cm) tail. Pick up a repeating pattern of an 11º seed bead and a 3 mm fire-polished bead until the strand reaches the desired length, ending with an 11º and an even number of 3 mms. Skip the last 11º, and sew back through the next 3 mm and 11º **(figure 1, a–b)**.

[2] Pick up three 11ºs, and sew through the 11º your thread exited at the start of this step to form a picot. Continue through the next 3 mm and 11º **(b–c)**. Repeat this step across the strand, but for the last repeat, sew through the first two 11ºs in the end picot instead of the next 3 mm and 11º **(c–d)**.

[3] Pick up three 11ºs, and sew through the 11º your thread exited at the start of this step to form a picot **(figure 2, a–b)**. Pick up a 3 mm, sew through the center 11º of the next picot, pick up a 3 mm, and sew through the center 11º of the following picot **(b–c)**. Repeat this step across the strand, ending and adding thread (Basics) as needed, to embellish every other 11º with a picot, ending with a picot **(c–d)**. Sew through the first two 11ºs in the end picot **(d–e)**.

[4] Pick up a 4 mm fire-polished bead and four 11ºs. Sew through the first 11º picked up in this step to form a

materials

red necklace 16–18 in. (41–46 cm)
- **166–170** 4 mm round fire-polished beads (Czech, ruby silver lined)
- **210–216** 3 mm round fire-polished beads (Czech, silver)
- 10 g 11º seed beads (Toho 712, 24K gold plated)
- clasp
- **2** 6 mm jump rings
- Fireline 6 lb. test
- beading needles, #10 or #12
- **2** pairs of pliers

purple necklace colors:
- 4 mm round fire-polished beads (Czech, tanzanite silver lined)
- 3 mm round fire-polished beads (Czech, gold matte metallic)
- 11º seed beads (Toho 711, nickel-plated silver)

⬡	4 mm round fire-polished bead
⬡	3 mm round fire-polished bead
○	11º seed bead

DESIGN NOTE:
Got a lot of bicone crystals on hand? Swap them in for the fire-polished beads to achieve a super-sparkly variation.

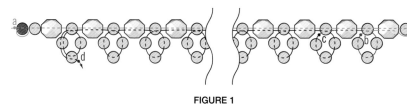

FIGURE 1

FIGURE 2

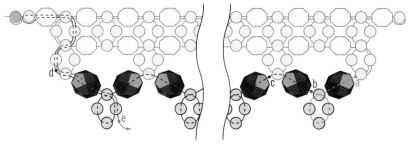

FIGURE 3

picot **(figure 3, a–b)**. Pick up a 4 mm, and sew through the center 11º in the next picot **(b–c)**. Repeat this step across the strand **(c–d)**. Sew through the beadwork as shown to exit a side 11º in the last picot created in this step **(d–e)**.

[5] Pick up a 4 mm, an 11º, a 3 mm, and three 11ºs. Skip the three 11ºs, and sew back through the 3 mm and the single 11º **(figure 4, a–b)**. Pick up a 4 mm, and sew through the top three 11ºs in the next picot **(b–c)**. Repeat this step across the strand **(c–d)**, and then sew through the beadwork to exit the 11º on one end of the row of beads picked up in step 1.

[6] Pick up seven 11ºs, and sew through the end 11º again in the same direction to form a ring. Retrace the thread path through the ring a few times, and end the thread. Open a jump ring (Basics), and attach half of the clasp to the ring of beads.

[7] Remove the stop bead, and repeat step 6 on the other end of the necklace.

Metallic accents, like these nickel-plated seed beads and matte gold fire-polished beads, carry the look of fine jewelry throughout the piece.

FIGURE 4

Choose silver-lined ruby or tanzanite fire-polished beads for gem-inspired jewelry.

We've got Christmas covered

Wrap up your holiday gift list with traditional ornament covers

designed by
LindaMay Patterson

These ornaments are sure to dazzle with their striking colors and dramatic fringe.

materials

blue/white ornament cover
2½ x 4 in. (6.4 x 10 cm)

- **2½-in. (6.4 cm)** diameter glass ball ornament
- **21** 8 mm bicone crystals (crystal AB)
- **21** 6 mm bicone crystals (crystal AB)
- **21** 5 x 7 mm rondelle crystals (crystal AB)
- **63** 4 mm pearls (cream)
- **21** 3 mm round crystals (crystal AB)
- **15–20 g** 11º seed beads (pearlized white)
- nylon beading thread, size D
- beading needles, #10 or #12

fuchsia/white ornament cover colors:

- 8 mm fire-polished glass beads (red AB)
- 6 mm fire-polished glass beads (red AB)
- 5 x 7 mm rondelle crystals (crystal AB)
- 4 mm fire-polished glass beads (red AB)
- 4 mm round crystals (crystal AB)
- 3 mm round crystals (crystal AB)
- 11º seed beads (fuchsia AB)

A netted band supplies ample space through which a neutral or colorful glass ornament can peek. Suspend the bands from a beaded collar, and then embellish it with lots of sparkling fringe.

step by step

Netted band
Round 1

[1] On a comfortable length of thread, attach a stop bead (Basics), leaving a 6-in. (15 cm) tail. Pick up two 11º seed beads, skip the last 11º, and sew back through the first 11º **(figure 1, a–b)**.
[2] Pick up seven 11ºs. Skip the last 11º, and sew back through the next 11º **(b–c)**.
[3] Pick up three 11ºs. Skip three 11ºs, and sew through the next 11º **(c–d)**.
[4] Pick up three 11ºs. Skip the last 11º, and sew back through the next 11º **(d–e)**.
[5] Repeat steps 3 and 4 until you have 42 11º points along both edges of the band, ending and adding thread (Basics) as needed.
[6] Form the band into a ring: Pick up an 11º, and sew through the center 11º in the corresponding stitch from the start of the band **(figure 2, a–b)**. Pick up an 11º, and sew through the center 11º in the corresponding stitch from the end of the band **(b–c)**. Pick up an 11º, skip the stop bead, and sew through the first two 11ºs picked up in step 1, following the established thread path **(c–d)**. End the working thread.
[7] Remove the stop bead, and use the tail to retrace the thread path of the join. End the tail.

Round 2

Round 2 is joined to the bottom points of round 1. There are two versions of this ornament: one with crystals in this round and one without crystals. Steps 1–7 below are written for the version without crystals. To make the crystal version, see the Design Note, p. 149.
[1] On a comfortable length of thread, attach a stop bead, leaving a 6-in. (15 cm) tail. Pick up an 11º, sew through a point 11º along the bottom edge of round 1, and sew back through the 11º picked up in this step **(figure 3, a–b)**.
[2] Repeat steps 2 **(b–c)** and 3 **(c–d)** of "Round 1."
[3] Pick up two 11ºs, sew through the next point 11º along the bottom edge of round 1, and then sew back through the last 11º picked up in this step **(d–e)**.
[4] Pick up three 11ºs. Skip three 11ºs, and sew through the next 11º.
[5] Pick up three 11ºs. Skip the last 11º, and sew back through the next 11º.
[6] Repeat these steps in the following order: 4, 3, 4, and 5. Continue repeating these steps until you have sewn through all the point 11ºs along the bottom edge of round 1, ending and adding thread as needed.
[7] Complete the round by joining the ends as in steps 6 and 7 of "Round 1."

FIGURE 1

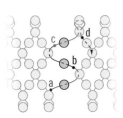

FIGURE 2

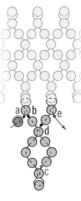

FIGURE 3

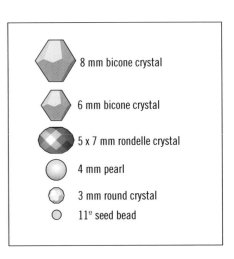

8 mm bicone crystal

6 mm bicone crystal

5 x 7 mm rondelle crystal

4 mm pearl

3 mm round crystal

11º seed bead

Collar and assembly

[1] On 2 yd. (1.8 m) of thread, attach a stop bead, leaving a 6-in. (15 cm) tail. Pick up 42 11ºs, and sew through all the beads again to form a ring. Sew through the first 11º picked up once more.

[2] Pick up an 11º, sew through the 11º your thread exited at the start of this step, and continue through the 11º just picked up **(figure 4, a–b)**.

[3] Pick up three 11ºs, and sew through the 11º your thread exited at the start of this step to form a picot **(b–c)**. Sew through the 11º your thread exited in the ring **(c–d)**, and retrace the thread path through all the beads added in this step, exiting the same 11º in the ring. Sew through the next two 11ºs in the ring **(d–e)**.

[4] Repeat steps 2 and 3 until you have a total of 21 picots. Sew through the next picot, exiting the center 11º picked up in step 3 **(figure 5, point a)**. Place the collar around the neck of the 2½-in. (6.4 cm) glass ball ornament.

[5] Place the netted band around the circumference of the ornament. Using the working thread from the collar, pick up 18 11ºs, and sew through a point 11º along the top edge of the band **(a–b)**.

[6] Pick up 18 11ºs, and sew through the center 11º at the end of the next picot in the collar **(b–c)**. Sew back through 15 of the 18 11ºs just picked up **(c–d)**. Pick up three 11ºs, skip a point 11º along the top edge of the band, and sew through the next point 11º along the edge **(d–e)**. Repeat this step 19 more times.

[7] Pick up three 11ºs, and sew through the first 15 11ºs picked up in step 5, the first point 11º, and back through the 18 11ºs picked up in step 5. End the working thread and tail.

Fringe

[1] On 3 yd. (2.7 m) of thread, center a stop bead, and sew through a point 11º along the bottom edge of the netted band, directly across from one of the 11ºs connecting the top of the band to the collar **(figure 6, point a)**.

[2] Pick up four 11ºs, a 4 mm pearl, two 11ºs, a 3 mm round crystal, two 11ºs, a 6 mm bicone crystal, two 11ºs, a 4 mm, two 11ºs, a 5 x 7 mm rondelle crystal, two 11ºs, a 4 mm, two 11ºs, an 8 mm bicone crystal, and an 11º. Skip the last 11º picked up, and sew back through the previous 19 beads, exiting after the first pearl picked up in this step **(a–b)**. Pick up four 11ºs, skip a point 11º along the bottom edge of the netted band, and sew through the next point 11º **(b–c)**.

[3] Repeat step 2 20 times, ending the thread when it runs out. Remove the stop bead, and switch to the remaining thread. End any remaining threads.

FIGURE 4

FIGURE 5

FIGURE 6

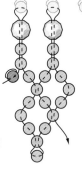

DESIGN NOTE:

To add 3 mm round or bicone crystals while joining rounds 1 and 2, as in the fuchsia/white ornament cover, make the following changes:

- In step 1 of "Round 2," pick up two 11ºs and a 3 mm crystal instead of one 11º before sewing through the point 11º. Sew back through the 3 mm and both 11ºs picked up.
- In step 3 of "Round 2," pick up three 11ºs and a 3 mm instead of two 11ºs before sewing through the next point 11º. Sew back through the 3 mm and two 11ºs.
- Before adding the fringe, work one more round of netting by picking up nine 11ºs between every other point 11º along the bottom edge of the netted band. Exit a center 11º in one of the nine-bead netted stitches. Work as in "Fringe" to add fringe to the center 11º in each nine-bead netted stitch in the last round. Use more accent beads if desired, alternating with more 11ºs to create longer fringe.

Count your chickens

Lighten up with an airy bracelet and a whimsical parade of poultry

designed by **Michele Trondsen**

Use as many or as few bead colors as you wish. The bracelet in primary colors (above) uses 12, and the bracelet in warm tones (below) uses eight.

We've been told, "Don't count your chickens before they're hatched," and often it puts a damper on our hopes and dreams. When you need a reason to smile, go for this feather-light netted bracelet, and count your chickens all you want.

stepbystep

Chicken pattern

[1] On comfortable length of thread or Fireline, attach a stop bead (Basics), leaving a 20-in. (51 cm) tail. Pick up 35 color A 11° seed beads. This is row 1 (pattern, a–b).
[2] Work a turn stitch: Pick up four As, skip the last two As in row 1, and sew back through the next A in row 1 (b–c).
[3] Row 2: Pick up three As, skip the next three As in row 1, and sew back

through the following A in row 1 (c–d). Repeat this stitch until you sew through the first A in row 1 (d–e).
[4] Work a turn stitch: Pick up two As, a color B 11° seed bead, and an A, and sew back through the middle A in the last stitch of row 2 (e–f).
[5] Row 3: Pick up an A, a B, and an A. Sew back through the middle A in the next stitch of row 2 (f–g). Repeat this stitch until you sew through the third A in the turn stitch between rows 1 and 2 (g–h).

[6] Continue working in netting, following the **pattern** to determine which color 11°s to pick up. Remember that each turn stitch adds four beads, and each row will have eight stitches of three beads each. Always sew through the middle bead in the next stitch of the previous row when working a new row. End and add thread (Basics) as needed while you stitch, but do not end the working thread or tail when you complete the pattern.

Toggle bar

[1] Remove the stop bead from the 20-in. (51 cm) tail, and sew through the beadwork to exit the center A in the center stitch of row 1.
[2] Pick up four As, an 8° seed bead, enough As to equal about half the

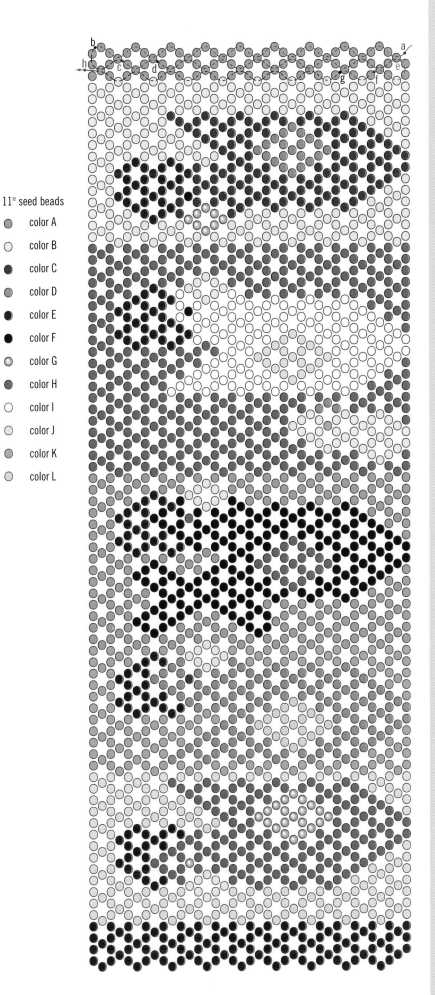

materials

primary color bracelet
7½–8 in. (19.1–20 cm)
- 13–15 mm oval bead (green)
- **3** 8º seed beads (red)
- 11º seed beads
  3 g color A (green)
  3 g color B (yellow)
  1 g color C (brown)
  2 g color D (orange)
  3 g color E (red)
  1 g color F (black)
  1 g color G (gold)
  3 g color H (blue)
  1 g color I (white)
  2 g color J (beige)
  1 g color K (teal)
  1 g color L (pink)
- nylon beading thread or
  Fireline 6 lb. test
- beading needles, #10

pastel bracelet colors:
- 13–15 mm oval bead (iridescent white)
- 8º seed beads (Miyuki 2, silver-lined
  light gold)
- 11º seed beads
  color A (Miyuki 596, opaque tea rose
  luster)
  color B (Miyuki 304, garnet gold luster)
  color C (Miyuki 2021, matte opaque
  cream)
  color D (Miyuki 642, dyed salmon
  silver-lined alabaster)
  color E (F457B, dark bronze matte)
  color F (Miyuki 1936, semi-matte
  daffodil-lined crystal)
  color G (F403B, opaque matte dark
  peach)
  color H (Miyuki 2036, matte opaque
  tea rose)

11º seed beads

- ◐ color A
- ○ color B
- ◕ color C
- ◑ color D
- ● color E
- ● color F
- ◔ color G
- ◕ color H
- ○ color I
- ○ color J
- ◐ color K
- ○ color L

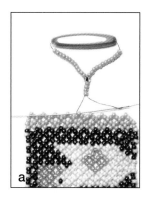

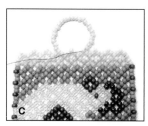

length of the 15–20 mm oval bead, the oval bead, and the same number of As picked up after the 8º. Sew back through the 8º and the first four As picked up in this step, and then continue through the A your thread exited at the start of this step, sewing in the same direction as before (photo a).

[3] Sew through the first two rows of beadwork, following the existing thread path, to exit the center A again. Retrace the thread path of the toggle bar. Repeat this step several times to reinforce the toggle connection.

[4] Sew through the beadwork to exit the oval bead in the toggle. Pick up an 8º and an A, and sew back through the 8º and the oval bead. Pick up an 8º and an A on this side of the oval, and sew back through the 8º and the

oval (photo b). Retrace the thread path a few times, and end the thread.

Toggle ring

[1] With the tail on the other end of the bracelet, sew through the beadwork to exit the center color E 11º seed bead in the fourth end stitch from either edge, with your thread pointing toward the nearest edge. Pick up enough Es to accommodate the toggle bar, and sew through the center E two stitches over with your thread pointing toward the first center E your thread exited in this step (photo c).

[2] Sew through the end rows of beadwork to retrace the thread path of the toggle ring several times. Work in peyote stitch (Basics) around the loop if desired. End the thread.

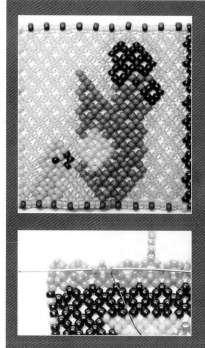

DESIGN NOTES:
- Place a sheet of paper over the pattern, covering the rows you have not yet completed. When you complete a row, slide the paper down to reveal the next.
- To give your beadwork a more finished edge, pick up an 11º between the pairs of 11ºs along both edges of the band (left, top).
- To create scallops on the ends of the bands, sew through the 11ºs on either side of the center 11º in each end stitch (left, bottom). If necessary, use your needle to pull up on the center 11º, causing it to stick out.

Bakelite delights

Combine bead embroidery with chunky vintage findings

designed by **Suzanne Branca**

These square components are just one example of the Bakelite available for including in jewelry designs.

materials

clear-crystal earrings
4 in. (10 cm)

- **2** 1¼-in. (3.2 cm) square Bakelite components (agrainofsand.com)
- **2** 16 x 12 mm vintage sew-on crystal mirrored ovals (agrainofsand.com)
- **4** 3 mm rose montees (red)
- **3–4 g** 11º seed beads (Toho, silver-lined black)
- **2 g** 15º Charlottes, color A (gunmetal)
- **3 g** 15º seed beads, color B (Toho 25D, silver-lined ruby)
- pair of oval lever-back earring findings
- Fireline 4–6 lb. test
- beading needles, #12
- 2 pairs of pliers
- E6000 adhesive
- fabric dye (optional)
- Lacy's Stiff Stuff beading foundation
- Ultrasuede

black-crystal earring colors:

- 35 mm stone rings, in place of Bakelite components (black)
- 14 x 9 mm sew-on crystals, in place of 16 x 12 mm vintage sew-on mirrored ovals (Swarovski, jet)
- 11º seed beads (Toho 711, nickel-plated silver)
- 15º seed beads, in place of Charlottes, color A (Toho 329, African sunset gold-luster)
- 3 g 15º seed beads, color B (Toho 25D, silver-lined ruby)

Lightweight Bakelite is a perfect material to use for earring designs. You get a heavy-duty fashion statement without the weight while preserving a bit of the past.

stepbystep

Embroidered dangles

If desired, dye the beading foundation according to the dye manufacturer's instructions to match your dominant color palette.

[1] Cut a piece of beading foundation about ¾ in. (1.9 cm) larger than the sew-on crystal.

[2] Put a dab of E6000 adhesive on the back of the crystal, and center it on the beading foundation. Let the glue dry.

[3] On 1 yd. (.9 m) of Fireline, tie a knot at the very end of the thread, and sew up through the foundation from back to front, exiting a hole of the crystal. Pick up an 11º seed bead, and sew back through the crystal and the foundation **(photo a)**. Retrace the thread path to secure the crystal, and then repeat for the other hole of the crystal. Sew up through the foundation to exit next to the edge of the crystal.

[4] Pick up two 11ºs, and lay them next to the edge of the crystal. Sew down through the foundation after the second 11º, sew up through the foundation between the two 11ºs, and sew through the second 11º again. Repeat this step **(photo b)** to surround the sew-on crystal. Sew through all the 11ºs to snug them up to one another and the crystal, and then sew up through the foundation at one end of the crystal.

[5] Pick up an 11º, a 3 mm rose montee, and an 11º, and lay them next to the round of seed beads. Sew down through the foundation after the last 11º **(photo c)**, and retrace the thread path. Sew through the foundation and the other hole of the rose montee to secure it **(photo d)**. Sew up through the foundation next to one of the 11ºs added in this step.

[6] Pick up two color A 15º Charlottes, and work as in step 4 **(photo e)** to surround the 11ºs and rose montee added in step 5.

[7] Repeat steps 5 and 6 on the opposite end of the crystal **(photo f)**.

[8] Trim the foundation next to the outer edge of beadwork, making sure not to cut the thread. Trace the resulting shape on a piece of Ultrasuede, and cut out the shape.

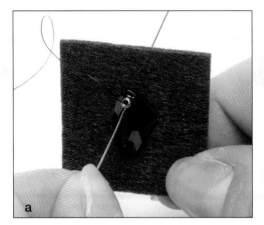

a

b

c

d

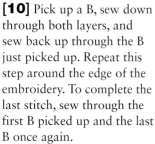

e

f

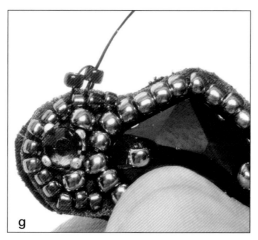

g

h

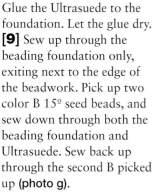

Glue the Ultrasuede to the foundation. Let the glue dry.

[9] Sew up through the beading foundation only, exiting next to the edge of the beadwork. Pick up two color B 15° seed beads, and sew down through both the beading foundation and Ultrasuede. Sew back up through the second B picked up (photo g).

[10] Pick up a B, sew down through both layers, and sew back up through the B just picked up. Repeat this step around the edge of the embroidery. To complete the last stitch, sew through the first B picked up and the last B once again.

[11] Exit one of the edge Bs on one side of the crystal. Pick up a B, an 11°, and a B. Skip a B along the edge, and sew through the next two edge Bs (photo h). Repeat this step three times, and then sew

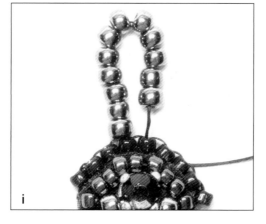

i

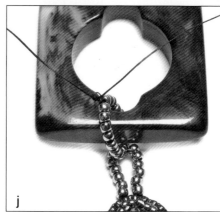

j

through to the other side of the crystal and repeat these stitches as a mirror image. Sew through the beadwork to exit an edge B at the top of the crystal.

[12] Pick up 12 11°s, and sew through the next edge B to form a loop (photo i). Retrace the thread path, and end the thread (Basics).

[13] Make a second embroidered dangle.

Assembly

[1] On 12 in. (30 cm) of Fireline, center 18 11°s. Sew through a Bakelite component and the loop of 11°s from an embroidered dangle. Tie the beads into a ring with a square knot (Basics and photo j).

[2] Sew through the ring of 11°s again, exiting next to the tail. Tie another knot, sew through the next few beads, and end the threads.

[3] On 12 in. (30 cm) of Fireline, center 18 11°s, and tie them into a ring with a square knot. Work as in step 2 to secure the ring.

[4] Repeat step 1, but sew through the ring made in step 3 and the top of the Bakelite component before tying the knot.

[5] Open the loop (Basics) of an earring finding, and attach the top ring of 11°s.

[6] Make the second earring.

Soutastic soutache!

Learn to make sinuous shapes with beads and soutache braid, a common element in the French art of passementerie

designed by **Amee McNamara** *with* **Jane Danley Cruz**

Soutache, also known as "Russian braid," is a narrow braid woven into a herringbone pattern around two strands of piping that lie side by side inside the braid. It is identified by a single groove running along the center of the braid. In soutache bead embroidery, layers of braid are stacked to create a three-dimensional form. The addition of beads provides visual interest and a framework of support for the curves and shapes of a design.

Soutache bead embroidery does not have a particular stitch or pattern associated

with it, so the technique more closely resembles sculpture or wirework. Stitching is used to secure layers of braid together around the beads that give the piece shape, and to attach a backing so frayed ends and stitches are hidden.

Basics
Positioning the soutache
Lay cut lengths of braid on your work surface. Note the center groove and the direction of threads running into the groove to make a V. Position each braid so the Vs are all pointing the same direction **(photo a)**. Create a

stack by laying one braid on top of the other with the Vs going in the same direction, and hold the stack gently on the sides between your thumb and finger **(photo b)**.

Stitch in the ditch
With the exception of ending the soutache, all stitching will be done through the center groove or "the ditch"

(photo c). This will align the layers in a stack. When you sew through the center groove, your needle will slide through easily. If you stitch through the braid at any other point, you will feel a slight resistance.

Tension
Keep your tension soft but not loose. Do not pull your stitches

The term "passementerie" refers to a wide range of trims, braids, and tassels used as decoration on haute couture fashion, draperies, and furnishings.

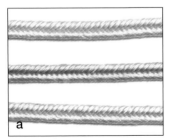
a

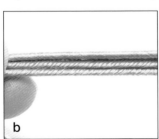
b

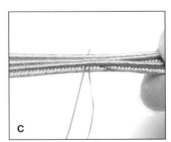
c

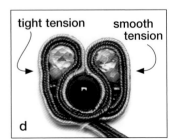
tight tension   smooth tension
d

tight as this will create bumps or waves in your work. You want to maintain a light, consistent tension to result in soft, smooth curves (photo d).

Curves

There are two things to remember when making a curve: Sew long stitches on the outside of the curve (photo e) and short stitches on the inside (photo f). Long stitches are ¼–⅜ in. (6 mm–1 cm) in length, and short stitches are about ¹⁄₁₆ in. (2 mm) in length.

Spacing

Do not crowd the beads when you add them side by side. They should barely touch each other (photo g), so be prepared to make adjustments in your work. If the beads are too close together, they will create an uneven and wavy surface.

Joining

Joining is where either two portions of the same stack or separate stacks meet, typically at the base of a bead or focal piece. To join, carefully separate the stack of braids, and pinch together both sides of the inner layer close to the bead (photo h). With the needle exiting the bead, sew through the inner layer of braid on one side of the bead (photo i), sew back through the same braid, and then sew through the inner layer on the other side of the bead (photo j). Retrace the thread path through the join, and then sew through the other layers in the stack on the first side (photo k). Sew back through the first stack, and continue through the next stack (photo l). Sew back through all layers in the other direction.

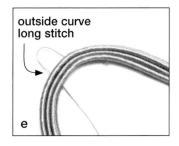

outside curve long stitch

e

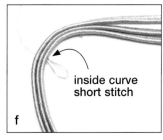

inside curve short stitch

f

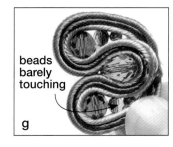

beads barely touching

g

materials
pair of earrings 1 in. (2.5 cm)

- 1 ft. (30 cm) ⅛-in. (3 mm) soutache in each of **3** colors (ice blue, chartreuse, Dijon)
- **2** 6 mm hex-cut gemstone beads (turquoise)
- **4** 4 mm fire-polished beads (pearl coating)
- **2** 8º seed beads (Toho 1207, marbled opaque turquoise blue)
- **4** 11º seed beads, color A (Toho 421, gold-lustered transparent pink)
- 1 g 11º seed beads, color B (Czech, yellow-lined green)
- **4** 15º seed beads (Toho 123, opaque luster light beige)
- **2** 6 mm soldered jump rings
- pair of earring findings
- nylon beading thread, size B
- beading needles, #11
- glue, such as E6000 adhesive
- Ultrasuede
- 2 pairs of chainnose pliers

DESIGN NOTE:
Soutache can be found in fabric, craft, and home decorating stores as well as online.

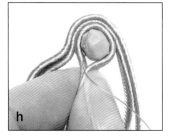
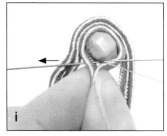
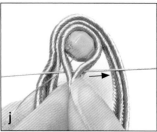
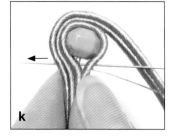
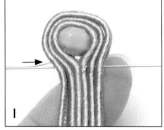
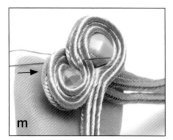

Ending a stack
Push the loose ends of the stack to the back of your work, and sew up from the back through all the layers **(photo m)**. The thread will be exiting the side of one braid. Sew down through all the layers as close as possible to the point where the thread exited, sewing through the same braid at some point other than the center groove. Repeat this last stitch several times to secure the end of the stack, and trim the ends ¼ in. (6 mm) from the last stitch **(photo n)**, being careful not to trim too closely, as the braids will fray. You can whip stitch the frayed ends together on the back of the piece to keep them contained.

Finishing techniques
Backing
The back and edges of soutache bead embroidery are finished in much the same manner as any other bead embroidery. Apply a thin coat of glue to the back of your work, making sure the glue extends to the outer edge but isn't so thick it oozes out when pressed onto the backing. Place the shape on the wrong side of a piece of Ultrasuede, and let dry completely. Trim the Ultrasuede close to the soutache piece, but not too close—make sure you cannot see the outer edge of the soutache from the back of the piece.

Beaded edging
Tie an overhand knot (Basics) at the end of a comfortable length of thread. Beginning at an inside curve, sew through a stack to the outside edge of the soutache piece. The knot should be buried in one of the small crevices on the front of the work.

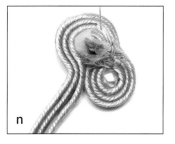

n

o

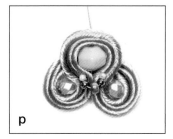

p

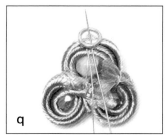

q

r

edge beads

Pick up two edge beads, sew down through the soutache and Ultrasuede, and sew back up through the Ultrasuede, the soutache, and the last edge bead just picked up. For subsequent stitches, pick up an edge bead, sew down through the soutache and Ultrasuede, and then sew back up through the Ultrasuede, the soutache, and the edge bead just picked up.

stepbystep

Earrings, p. 156
Earring front

[1] Tie a square knot (Basics) at one end of 1 yd. (.9 m) of thread, leaving a 6-in. (15 cm) tail.
[2] Cut a 6-in. (15 cm) piece of soutache braid in each of three colors. Create a stack as in "Positioning the soutache."
[3] Locate the center of the stack, and sew through all

three layers from bottom to top as in "Stitch in the ditch."
[4] Working from right to left, sew down through the stack of braids ¼ in. (6 mm) to the left. Sew up ¹⁄₁₆ in. (2 mm) to the left of the previous stitch, and then sew down ¼ in. (6 mm) to the left of that stitch.
[5] Pick up a 6 mm bead, wrap the stack around the 6 mm, and sew from the inside to the outside of the stack near the knot.
[6] Working from left to right, sew down through the stack ¼ in. (6 mm) to the right. Sew up ¹⁄₁₆ in. (2 mm) to the right of the previous stitch, and then sew down ¼ in. (6 mm) to the right of that stitch.
[7] Wrap the stack around the bead on the right-hand side, and sew back up through the 6 mm and the stack. Sew back down through the stack and the 6 mm close to where your thread just exited.
[8] Work as in "Joining" to secure the stack beneath the 6 mm.
[9] Carefully separate the braids into two stacks of three braids each. With your

thread exiting the outer layer braid, pick up a 4 mm fire-polished bead, wrap the corresponding three-layer stack around one side of the 4 mm, and sew through the stack where it meets the other end of the bead **(photo o)**. Note that the braid that was the outer layer around the 6 mm is now the inner layer going around the 4 mm. Make a few stitches in the stack as in "Curves," wrapping the stack around the other side of the 4 mm.
[10] End the stack as in "Ending a stack."
[11] Bring the thread across the back of the piece to exit the stack on the opposite side of the join in step 8, and repeat steps 9 and 10 to make a mirror image on the other side of the 6 mm.

Bridge beads and jump rings
[1] Bridges are used to add decoration and to cover joins where thread might otherwise show. Sew from back to front, exiting near the join made in step 8 of "Earring front." Pick up a 15º seed bead, a color A 11º seed bead, an 8º seed bead, an A, and a 15º, and sew back down through the stack on the other side of the join **(photo p)**. Sew back up through the first

stack your thread exited at the start of this step, sew through the 8º, and sew down through the second stack. This helps the bridge curve around the 6 mm and keeps the bridge resting on the soutache.
[2] Working on the back of the earring, bring the thread to the top of the 6 mm, and sew through the edge of the middle braid at the top of the earring. Pick up a 6 mm soldered jump ring, and sew back through the braid on the back of the earring **(photo q)**. Make sure the jump ring extends slightly past the edge of the earring, and secure it to the back with several small stitches. End the thread by tying a knot at the back of the work.

Assembly
[1] Work as in "Backing."
[2] Refer to "Beaded edging" to add color B 11º seed beads around the perimeter of the earring **(photo r)**, and end the thread in the edging beads (Basics).
[3] Open the loop of an earring finding (Basics), and attach the jump ring.
[4] Make and assemble a second earring.

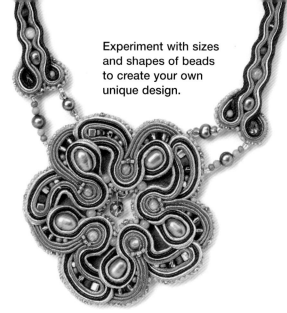

Experiment with sizes and shapes of beads to create your own unique design.

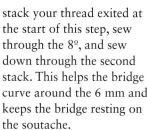

Multiple-
Technique
Projects

Hot dots
cuff

Get your bling on by stacking
two kinds of sequins to make
sparkling dots of color

designed by **Sherry Serafini**

Bezel and embellish a donut bead for a stunning focal on a suede-wrapped cuff. Then layer sequins to complete this fabulously fast bead-embroidered piece.

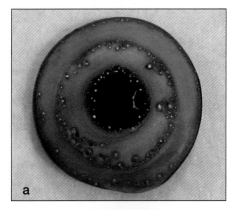

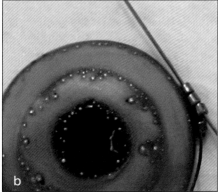

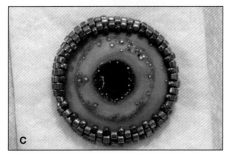

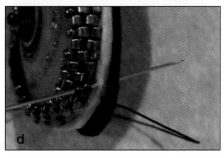

materials

cuff ½ in. (1.3 cm) wide

- ½-in. (1.3 cm) metal cuff blank (designersfindings.net)
- 20–22 mm donut bead (Angi Graham, hicoartist@gmail.com)
- **35–40** 5 mm metal or plastic sequins (gailcrosmanmoore.com)
- **35–40** 4 mm crystal sequins (Swarovski, glacier blue 2X; beyondbeadery.com)
- **10–15** 4 mm bicone crystals (Swarovski, jet AB 2X)
- **6–8** 8º seed beads (matte metallic blue/purple)
- 11º cylinder beads
  1 g color A (purple)
  1 g color B (black)
- 5 g 15º seed beads (metallic purple)
- nylon beading thread, size B or D
- beading needles, #13
- beading foundation, such as Lacy's Stiff Stuff
- Ultrasuede
- cloth tape measure
- E6000 adhesive
- white tacky adhesive
- rubber band

DESIGN NOTE:
Experiment with a different size donut bead and/or metal cuff depending on the statement you wish to make.

stepbystep

Donut component

[1] Using E6000 adhesive, glue the 20–22 mm donut bead to the center of a 3 x 3-in. (7.6 x 7.6 cm) square of beading foundation, making sure no glue shows through the center of the donut. Let the glue dry completely **(photo a)**.

[2] Tie an overhand knot (Basics) at the end of 1 yd. (.9 m) of thread, and sew through the beading foundation from back to front, exiting next to the donut.

[3] Work in beaded backstitch (Basics and **photo b**) around the donut using color A 11º cylinder beads to create the base round of the bezel. End with an even number of beads.

[4] Exiting an A in the base round, work two rounds of tubular peyote stitch (Basics) using As, and step up through the first A added in each round. If needed to accommodate the height of your donut, work an additional round with As.

[5] Work a round with 15º seed beads **(photo c)**, pulling the thread to snug the beadwork around the donut. Sew through the beadwork to exit an A in the base round of the bezel.

[6] Sew down through the foundation and back up through the center hole in the donut. Pick up a 5 mm sequin, a 4 mm crystal sequin, and a 15º. Skip the 15º, and sew back through the sequins, the donut, and the foundation. Retrace the thread path to secure, and end the thread by tying a knot on the back of the foundation.

[7] Trim the beading foundation close to the beadwork, making sure you don't cut any of the threads.

[8] Cut a piece of Ultrasuede to the size of the beading foundation. Using E6000 adhesive, glue the Ultrasuede to the foundation, and let it dry.

[9] Tie an overhand knot at the end of 2 ft. (61 cm) of thread. Sew between the foundation and Ultrasuede at the edge of the donut, and exit the front of the foundation, hiding the knot between the two layers.

[10] Make a simple beaded edge: Pick up two 15ºs, sew down through the foundation and Ultrasuede **(photo d)**, and sew back up through the foundation, the Ultrasuede, and the last 15º just picked up. For subsequent stitches, pick up one 15º, sew down through the foundation and Ultrasuede, and sew back up through the foundation, Ultrasuede, and 15º just picked up (photo e). Repeat this stitch about ¾ of the way around the donut component. Work six to eight stitches with 8º seed beads, and then complete the round using color B 11º cylinder beads. After adding the last B, sew down through the first 15º picked up in the first stitch, the foundation, and the Ultrasuede, and then sew back up through the Ultrasuede, foundation, and first 15º.

[11] To add fringe: Pick up a 15º, a 4 mm bicone crystal, and a 15º. Skip the last 15º, and sew back through the 4 mm bicone. Pick up a 15º, and sew down through the 15º adjacent to the one your thread exited at the start of this step. Sew up through the next 15º, and repeat this step for the remaining 15ºs and the first 8º along the edge.

[12] With the thread exiting an edge 8º, pick up a 5 mm sequin, a 4 mm crystal sequin, and a 15º. Skip the 15º, and sew back through the sequins and the adjacent edge 8º. Sew up through the next edge 8º, and repeat this stitch for the remaining edge 8ºs (photo f), leaving the Bs unembellished. End the thread in the beadwork (Basics).

Cuff

[1] With a cloth tape measure, measure the length and width of the inner and outer surfaces of the metal cuff blank. The outer surface will be larger than the inside. On a piece of paper, draw the measurements, allowing an extra ⅛ in. (3 mm) on all sides, and cut out the shapes. Trace them onto Ultrasuede, and cut them out.

[2] Using white tacky adhesive, glue the inner piece of Ultrasuede to the inside of the metal cuff (photo g), making sure

e

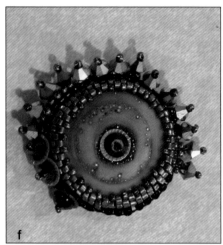

f

g

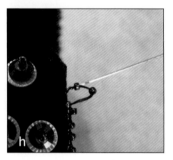

h

the glue does not seep past the edges, and let dry.

[3] Temporarily center the donut component on the outer piece of Ultrasuede. Make small marks around the donut component to denote this position for attaching it later.

[4] Tie an overhand knot at the end of 1½ yd. (1.4 m) of doubled thread; sew through the Ultrasuede from back to front on either side of the position marks for the donut component. Pick up a 5 mm sequin, a 4 mm crystal sequin, and a 15º. Skip the 15º, and sew back through the sequins and the Ultrasuede. Randomly repeat this stitch across the top piece of Ultrasuede, adding fringe as desired and leaving at least a ⅛-in. (3 mm) margin around the edges. Make sure you do not add any fringe within the area where the donut component will be attached. End the thread by tying a knot on the back of the Ultrasuede.

[5] Using white tacky adhesive, glue the outer piece of Ultrasuede to the metal cuff, and let dry.

[6] Tie an overhand knot at the end of 1 yd. (.9 m) of thread. Sew between the layers of Ultrasuede at the edge of the cuff. Exit the front of the outer Ultrasuede, hiding the knot between layers.

[7] Using 15ºs, work a picot edging: Pick up three 15ºs, sew down through both layers of Ultrasuede, and sew back up through both layers and the last 15º just picked up. For subsequent stitches, pick up two 15ºs, sew down through both layers of Ultrasuede, and sew back up through both layers and the second 15º just picked up (photo h). Repeat this stitch around the perimeter of the metal cuff. For the last stitch, pick up one 15º, sew down through the first 15º picked up in the first stitch and both layers of Ultrasuede, and then sew back up through both layers and the first 15º.

[8] Squeeze a small amount of E6000 adhesive in the center of the top of the cuff where you marked the placement of the donut component. Press the donut component in place, and hold it in position with a rubber band until thoroughly dried.

[9] Tie an overhand knot at the end of 12 in. (30 cm) of thread, and sew through the top layer of Ultrasuede close enough to the donut component to hide the knot. With small stitches, sew the Ultrasuede on the top surface of the cuff to the Ultrasuede on the back surface of the donut component. End the thread in the beadwork.

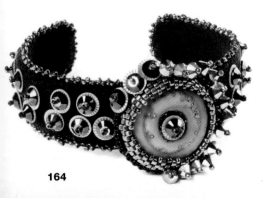

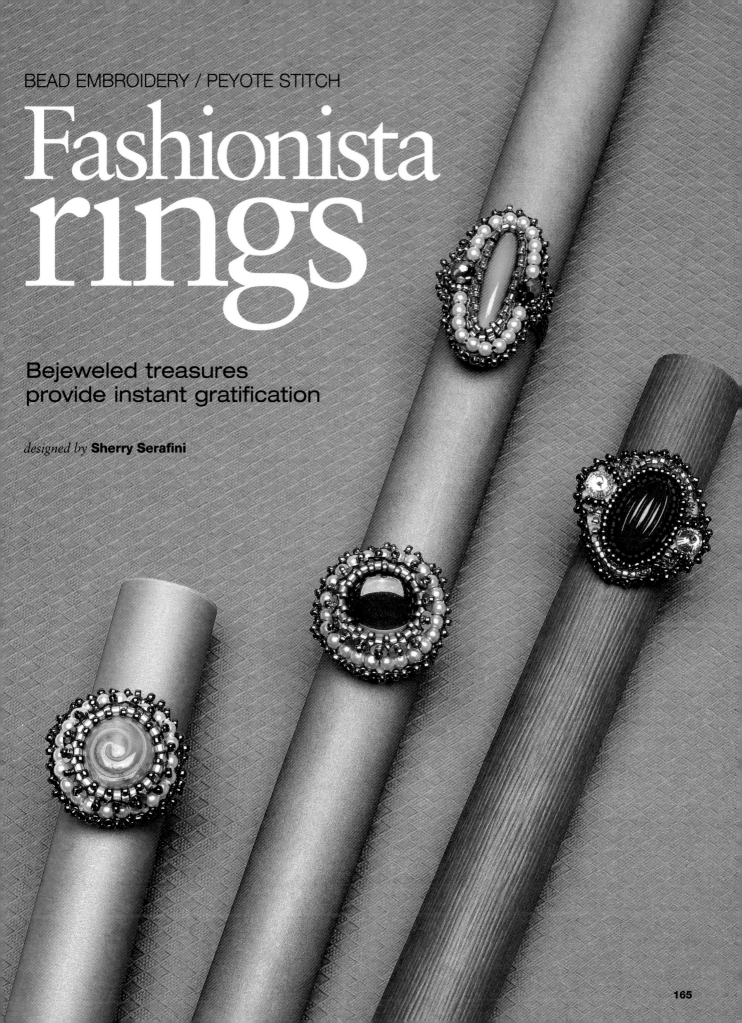

BEAD EMBROIDERY / PEYOTE STITCH

Fashionista rings

Bejeweled treasures
provide instant gratification

designed by **Sherry Serafini**

materials

ring

- **1–3** 5–10 mm glass, crystal, or gemstone cabochons
- **20–40** assorted accent beads: pearls, crystal pearls, fire-polished beads, gemstones, or other beads
- **16–24** 3 mm sequins (optional)
- **2–3 g** 15º and 11º seed beads
- **2–3 g** 11º cylinder beads
- ring finding with 10 mm platform (ringsandthings.com)
- Fireline 6 lb. test, or nylon beading thread, size D, conditioned with wax or Thread Heaven
- beading needles, #12
- beading foundation
- E6000 adhesive
- Ultrasuede

DESIGN NOTE:

Look for costume jewelry at antique stores or estate sales. Broken or discarded pieces may provide inexpensive and unusual components. Take them apart to incorporate the undamaged pieces into your new designs. You can also salvage findings from jewelry that is on clearance at your local mall or department store.

This is a perfect project for getting started with basic bead embroidery. Try your hand at beaded backstitch, peyote bezels, picot stitch, embellishments, and edging techniques.

step by step

Ring top
Focal elements

[1] Lay out the desired cabochons and/or accent beads on a piece of beading foundation cut slightly larger than the desired size of your ring top. To determine the spacing of the focal elements and beads, temporarily string a few seed beads and cylinder beads on short lengths of Fireline or thread, and place the strands between the focal elements **(photo a)**. Trace the final position of the focal elements if desired. Glue the focal elements in place, and allow the glue to dry.
[2] Cut out the desired ring top shape, leaving about ¼ in. (6 mm) of extra beading foundation on the edges.

Bezels

[1] Tie an overhand knot (Basics) at one end of 2 yd. (1.8 m) of Fireline or conditioned thread (Basics), and sew through the beading foundation from back to front next to the main cabochon.
[2] Work in beaded backstitch (Basics) around the cabochon using 11º cylinder beads to create the base round, ending with an even number of beads. If your cab has a low profile, you can skip to step 6. For a taller cab, continue on to step 3 to build up a peyote bezel.
[3] With your thread exiting a cylinder, work a round of tubular peyote stitch (Basics) using cylinders, and step up through the first cylinder added in this round. If needed, work an additional round with cylinders.
[4] Work one to two rounds with 15º seed beads to snug the beadwork to the cab.
[5] If desired, add an embellishment round using sequins: Sew through the bezel to exit the second-to-last round of cylinders. Pick up a sequin and a 15º. Skip the 15º, and sew back through the sequin and the next cylinder in the same round of the bezel **(photo b)**. Repeat to complete the round.
[6] Stitch accent beads in place as desired **(photo c)**.
[7] Using 15º or 11º seed beads or cylinders, work a round of beaded backstitch close to the bezel base and around the accent beads.

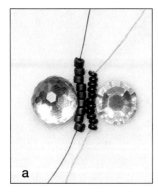

a

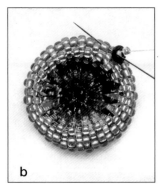

b

c

Surface embellishments

[1] Continue working in beaded backstitch to create the rest of your design using seed beads, pearls, fire-polished beads, gemstones, or other accent beads.

[2] When you are satisfied with the design, end the thread (Basics). Trim the beading foundation close to the beadwork, making sure you don't cut any of the threads.

Assembly

[1] Cut a piece of Ultrasuede to the size of the beading foundation. Glue the Ultrasuede to the foundation, and let it dry.

[2] Tie an overhand knot at the end of 1½ yd. (1.4 m) of Fireline or conditioned thread. Sew between the foundation and Ultrasuede at the edge of the ring top component, and exit the front of the foundation, hiding the knot between the two layers.

[3] Make a picot along the edge: Pick up three 15ºs, sew down through the foundation and Ultrasuede, and sew back up through the foundation, Ultrasuede, and the last 15º just picked up. For subsequent stitches, pick up two 15ºs, sew down through the foundation and Ultrasuede, and sew back up through the foundation, Ultrasuede, and the second 15º just picked up. For the last stitch, pick up one 15º, sew down through the first 15º picked up in the first stitch, the foundation, and the Ultrasuede, and sew back up through the first 15º in the first stitch. End the thread.

[4] Glue a ring finding to the center of the Ultrasuede, and let it dry.

Low-profile focal pieces speed the stitching because you can omit the peyote bezel.

This fun and easy project allows you to create beautiful rings using only a handful of materials. It's ideal for those left-over beads that end up in your stash!

DIAGONAL PEYOTE STITCH / HERRINGBONE / FRINGE

Neptune's garden

Create an underwater
vision of botanical bliss
for your wrist

designed by **Carole Horn**

Diagonal peyote stitch provides an interesting base for this bracelet. Make an arrangement of fanciful flora, and as you attach these embellishments to the base, you'll also create clever camouflage for the clasp.

step by step

Base

[1] On a comfortable length of thread or Fireline, attach a stop bead (Basics), leaving a 12-in. (30 cm) tail. Pick up 26 8º seed beads and a color A 11º seed bead. Skip the last two beads picked up, and sew back through the next 8º **(figure 1, a–b)**.

[2] Work 12 flat even-count peyote stitches (Basics) using 8ºs **(b–c)**, then work an increase turn: Pick up an 8º, an A, and an 8º. Skip the last two beads picked up, and sew back through the next 8º **(c–d)**.

[3] Work 12 peyote stitches with 8ºs **(figure 2, a–b)**, then work a decrease turn: Pick up an A, and sew back through the last 8º added **(b–c)**.

[4] Repeat steps 2 and 3 until the base is 1 in. (2.5 cm) longer than your desired length, ending and adding thread (Basics) as needed. Leave 18 in. (46 cm) of thread on this end of the base.

[5] Remove the stop bead, and using the tail, pick up an A, sew through the first up-bead of the end row, and continue diagonally through the next four 8ºs **(figure 3, a–b)**. Sew through the adjacent 8º and the following 8º **(b–c)**. Pick up a button or glass drop, skip an 8º in the base, and sew through the next two 8ºs **(c–d)**. Sew through the adjacent 8º, and retrace the thread path to secure the button. Sew through the beadwork to evenly space and attach the other two buttons, then end the tail.

[6] On the other end of the base, fold the last few rows of peyote toward the top

materials

matte green bracelet 7½ in. (19.1 cm)

- **3** 10 mm buttons with shanks (artbeads.com)
- **11–20** 6 mm bugle beads (SB0728, matte opaque blue AB)
- **6–10** 2.8 mm drop beads (Toho 518EE, hot pink Ceylon)
- 43 g 8º seed beads (Toho 0987, matte light olive)
- 11º seed beads
  5 g color A (Toho 37F, silver-lined frost olive)
  9 g color B (SB2544, sage-lined crystal clear)
  18 g color C (SB1672, matte transparent light spring green)
  10 g color D (SB2036, salmon-lined transparent light aqua)
  4 g color E (SB1906, opaque turquoise)
- 1 g 15º seed beads (Toho 37F, silver-lined frost olive)
- nylon beading thread, size D, or Fireline 6 lb. test
- beading needles, #12

shiny green bracelet colors:

- ½-in. (1.3 cm) glass drops (pastel purple, unicornebeads.com)
- 6 mm bugle beads (SB0728, matte opaque blue AB)
- 2.8 mm drop beads (Toho M162F, opaque rainbow frosted khaki)
- 8º seed beads (Toho 996, bronze-lined peridot rainbow)
- 11º seed beads: A (Miyuki 574, dyed lilac silver-lined alabaster); B (Toho 258F, frosted transparent chartreuse AB); C and E (SB356B, opaque grape AB*); D (Miyuki 1477, dyed opaque bright purple)
- 15º seed beads (Toho 397, sapphire color-lined fuchsia)

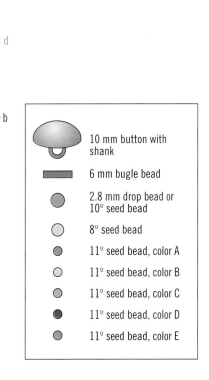

10 mm button with shank	
6 mm bugle bead	
2.8 mm drop bead or 10º seed bead	
8º seed bead	
11º seed bead, color A	
11º seed bead, color B	
11º seed bead, color C	
11º seed bead, color D	
11º seed bead, color E	

FIGURE 1   FIGURE 2   FIGURE 3

DESIGN NOTE:
To make a fun ring, create a band as in steps 1–6 of "Base" using 11º and 15º seed beads instead of 8ºs and 11ºs. Stitch the band long enough to fit around your finger, and zip up (Basics) the ends. Make a flower with petals, spikes, or both, and attach it to the band.

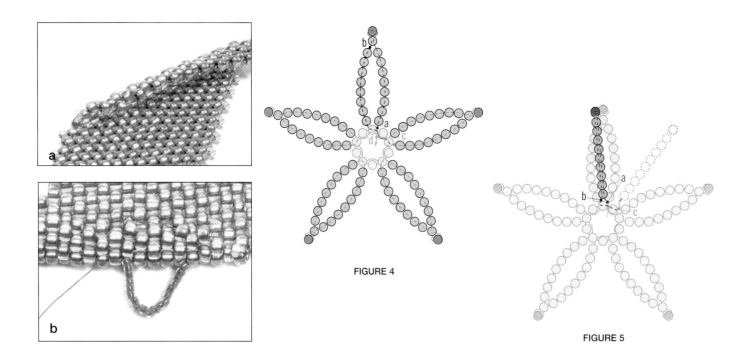

FIGURE 4

FIGURE 5

surface, and zip up (Basics) the end row
and the row of 8ºs it overlaps (photo a).
Retrace the thread path, then sew
through the beadwork to exit an 8º
along the folded end of the base that
corresponds with a button on the other
end of the base.

[7] Pick up enough 15º seed beads
(approximately 19) to make a loop
around the button. Skip four or five 8ºs,
and sew through the next five 8ºs in the
same row as the 8º your thread exited
at the start of this step (photo b). Repeat
twice to make loops for the other two
buttons. End the working thread.

Flora embellishments

Work the following embellishments
using 2 yd. (1.8 m) of thread or Fireline
each, and leaving a 12-in. (30 cm) tail.
After completing each embellishment,
end the working thread but not the tail.
The tails will be used to attach the
embellishments to the base.

Flowers with petals

[1] Pick up 10 color B 11º seed beads.
Tie the beads into a ring with a square
knot (Basics), and exit the next B in the
ring. The beads in the ring will shift to
create the first two rounds as round 3
is added in step 2.

[2] Work four rounds of tubular peyote
stitch (Basics) using Bs, stepping up

For lively flowers, use
a seed bead mix, a
gradation of dark to
light, or different colors
per round when adding
the petals and spikes.

after each round. You should have a
total of six rounds with five Bs in each
round. Exit a B in round 6 (figure 4,
point a).

[3] Make a petal: Pick up nine Bs and
an A. Skip the A, and sew back through
the last B picked up (a–b). Pick up eight
Bs, and sew through the B your thread
exited at the start of this step and the
next B in round 6 (b–c). This will pull
the beads in the end round close together
as you add the petals. Repeat this step
to complete a round of five petals (c–d).

[4] Sew through the adjacent B in
round 5. Work as in step 3, but after
completing the first petal, sew through
an adjacent B in round 4. Continue
adding petals to rounds 5 and 4 to
complete the round. Repeat for rounds
3 and 2, leaving the five Bs of round 1
unembellished.

Flowers with spikes

[1] Work as in steps 1–3 of "Flowers
with petals" using color C and color D
11º seed beads.

[2] To make spikes: Pick up nine Cs
and a D. Skip the D, and sew back
through the last nine Cs (figure 5, a–b).
Sew through the C your thread exited
at the start of this step and the next C
in the previous round (b–c). Repeat to
make a spike on each bead of each
round, leaving the five Cs of round 1
unembelllished.

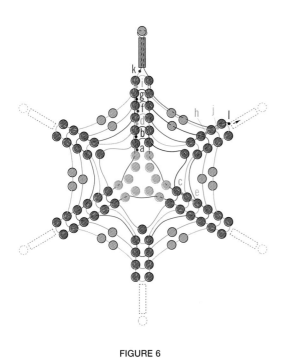

FIGURE 6

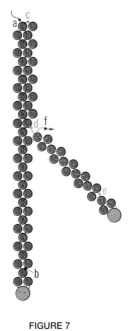

FIGURE 7

[3] Make a third flower as in steps 1 and 2 using Cs and As.

Herringbone flower

[1] Pick up four Ds. Working in ladder stitch (Basics), make a ladder two Ds high and six stitches long. Form the ladder into a ring (Basics).

[2] Work a round of tubular herringbone stitch (Basics) off the top round of the ladder using Ds. Step up through the first D of the first stitch in this round (figure 6, a–b).

[3] Work an increase round: Pick up two Ds, and sew down through the next D in the previous round. Pick up a D, and sew up through the next D in the previous round (b–c). Repeat this step to complete the round, and step up through the first D added in this round (c–d).

[4] Work an increase round: Pick up two Ds, and sew down through the next D in the previous round. Pick up two Ds, and sew up through the next D in the previous round (d–e). Repeat this step to complete the round, and step up through the first D added in this round (e–f).

[5] Work a round of six tubular herringbone stitches using Ds, working off of the original herringbone stitches and the increase Ds added in step 4 (f–g).

[6] Work an increase round: Pick up two Ds, and sew down through the next D in the previous round. Pick up a color E 11º seed bead, and sew up through

the next D in the previous round (g–h). Repeat this step to complete the round, and step up through the first D added in this round (h–i).

[7] Work an increase round: Pick up two Ds, and sew down through the next D in the previous round. Pick up two Es, and sew up through the next D in the previous round (i–j). Repeat this step to complete the round, and step up through the first D added in this round (j–k).

[8] Pick up a 6 mm bugle bead and an E. Skip the E, and sew back through the bugle bead, the top two Ds in the next stack, the following two Es, and the top two Ds of the next stack (k–l). Repeat to complete the round.

Branched coral

[1] Pick up 30 Ds, a 2.8 mm drop bead or 10º seed bead, and a D. Skip the last three beads, and sew back through the next D (figure 7, a–b). Work 14 peyote stitches using Ds (b–c).

[2] Work six peyote stitches using Ds (c–d). Pick up 12 Ds, a drop bead or 10º, and a D. Skip the last three beads, and sew back through the next D (d–e). Work five stitches using Ds (e–f).

[3] Sew through the beadwork to exit the opposite edge of the first strip of beads, and add a branch as in step 2.

[4] Add more branches as desired, varying the number of Ds to change

the length, but always start by picking up an even number of Ds.

Assembly

Arrange the embellishments on the base as desired. Use the remaining tail from each embellishment to attach it to the base. After each one is secure, end the tail.

[1] To attach a flower: Sew through the 8ºs in the base and the unembellished round of 11ºs in the flower (photo c). Retrace the thread path. Repeat for the remaining flowers, sewing through the first ladder round to attach the herringbone flower.

[2] To attach the branch coral: Lay the coral on the base, and tack the edges of the coral to the base.

[3] To add bugle fringe to fill in any gaps or add a burst of color: Add 1 yd. (.9 m) of thread or Fireline to the base, exiting an 8º where fringe is desired. Pick up six 11ºs of any color, a 6 mm bugle, and a different color 11º. Skip the last 11º, and sew back through the rest of the beads, the 8º your thread exited at the start of this fringe, and an adjacent 8º in the base. Repeat to add more fringe as desired.

Elementary engineering

Multiple components work in concert to showcase an art-glass bead focal

designed by **Jimmie Boatright**

Structure natural and organic-looking elements with beads in a variety of shapes and sizes for a necklace with chemistry.

stepbystep

Peyote rings
Side one

[1] On 1 yd. (.9 m) of Fireline, center 48 15º seed beads. Tie the beads into a ring with a square knot (Basics), and sew through the first bead again. These beads will shift to form the first two rounds in the next step.

[2] With one end of the thread, work two rounds of tubular peyote stitch (Basics) using 15ºs, stepping up at the end of each round.

[3] Work a round of peyote stitch with 11º cylinder beads, stepping up at the end of the round.

[4] Work a round of peyote stitch as follows: Work two stitches with cylinders, then work a stitch with an 11º seed bead. Repeat these three stitches to complete the round, and step up.

[5] Work a round of peyote stitch as follows: Work one stitch with a cylinder and two stitches with 11ºs. Repeat these three stitches to complete the round, and step up.

[6] Work a round of peyote stitch as follows: Work one stitch with an 11º, one stitch with a color A 8º seed bead, and one stitch with an 11º. Repeat these three stitches to complete the round. Tie a couple of half-hitch knots (Basics), but do not trim the thread.

Side two

[1] With the other thread, exit a 15º in round 1, and work two rounds of peyote stitch with 15ºs, stepping up at the end of each round.

[2] Repeat steps 3–5 of "Side one," making sure to match the pattern.

[3] Zip up (Basics) the edges of the ring. End the threads (Basics).

[4] Make a second peyote ring.

Bezeled coins

[1] On 1 yd. (.9 m) of Fireline, sew through the center hole of a mosaic shell coin bead, leaving a 12-in. (30 cm) tail. Pick up an even number of cylinder beads to fit around half of the coin. For a 17 mm coin, I used 22 cylinders.

[2] Sew through the coin, and pick up the same

Incorporate a wide variety
of shapes, sizes, and
styles of beads for this
stash-busting necklace.

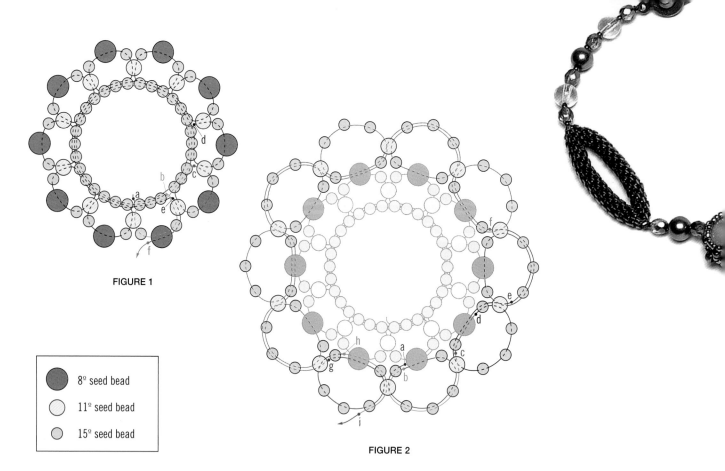

FIGURE 1

⬤	8º seed bead
◯	11º seed bead
◎	15º seed bead

FIGURE 2

number of cylinders picked up in step 1. Sew through the coin again.

[3] Sew through all the cylinders around the coin to form a ring.

[4] Work one round of peyote stitch with cylinders, then work two rounds of peyote stitch with 15ºs.

[5] Sew through the beadwork to exit a cylinder in the first round of cylinders. Work two rounds of peyote stitch with cylinders toward the other side of the coin, then work two rounds of peyote stitch with 15ºs.

[6] Sew through the beadwork to exit the center round along the edge of the coin, pick up an 11º, and sew through the next cylinder in the round. Repeat to complete the round. End the working thread and tail.

[7] Make a second bezeled coin.

Caged beads

[1] On 1 yd. (.9 m) of Fireline, pick up 30 15ºs, leaving a 6-in. (15 cm) tail. Sew through all the beads again to form a ring, and sew through the next three 15ºs **(figure 1, a–b)**.

[2] Pick up an 11º seed bead, a 15º, a color B 8º seed bead, a 15º, and an 11º, and sew through the 15º the tail

is exiting and the next five beads in the original ring **(b–c)**.

[3] Pick up an 11º, a 15º, a B, and a 15º, and sew through the adjacent 11º in the previous stitch and the next six 15ºs in the original ring **(c–d)**. Repeat this step to complete the round **(d–e)**.

[4] Sew through the first 11º, 15º, and 8º added in the first stitch of this round **(e–f)**.

[5] Pick up a 15º, an 11º, three 15ºs, an 11º, and a 15º, and sew through the B your thread exited at the start of this step **(figure 2, a–b)**. Continue through the first six beads just added **(b–c)**.

[6] Pick up a 15º, and sew through the next B **(c–d)**. Pick up a 15º, an 11º, and three 15ºs, and sew through the 11º in the previous stitch, and the next 15º, B, 15º, and 11º in this stitch **(d–e)**.

[7] Pick up three 15ºs, an 11º, and a 15º, and sew back through the next B. Pick up a 15º, and sew through the adjacent 11º in the previous stitch and the three 15ºs and 11º just added **(e–f)**.

[8] Repeat steps 6 and 7 three times **(f–g)**. For the last stitch, pick up a 15º, and sew through the next B. Pick up a 15º, and sew through the adjacent 11º in the first stitch. Pick up three 15ºs,

and sew through the 11º added in the previous stitch and the first 15º added in this stitch **(g–h)**. Sew through the next four beads to exit the outer edge **(h–i)**.

[9] Insert a 12 mm bead into the cage, and sew through all the 15ºs along the outer edge several times to snug up the cage, holding the 12 mm in place. Locate the hole in the 12 mm, and sew through it to secure the bead to the cage. End the working thread and tail.

[10] Make a second caged bead.

Assembly

The necklace is assembled using doubled thread to connect the components. The fringe is made using single thread.

[1] Add (Basics) 1 yd. (.9 m) of doubled Fireline to a caged bead, exiting a B along the edge of the cage. Starting and ending with an 11º, pick up 1½ in. (3.8 cm) of 3–8 mm beads alternating with 11ºs. Pick up seven 15ºs and half of the clasp. Skip the 15ºs, and sew back through the beads just strung and an edge B in the bead cage. Sew through the beadwork to exit a B opposite the one your thread exited at the start of this step.

[2] Starting and ending with an 11º, pick up 1 in. (2.5 cm) of 3–8 mm beads

174

Jimmie incorporated stitched oval links instead of the 15 x 30 mm flat oval gemstones for a lighter weight alternative.

materials

amazonite necklace 21 in. (53 cm)

- art-glass bead (Joanne Morash, blueirisdesigns.com)
- **4** 15 x 30 mm flat oval gemstone beads (amazonite)
- **2** 15–18 mm mosaic shell coin beads
- **2** 12 mm round beads (green agate)
- **80–90** 3–8 mm assorted beads: round glass beads, fire-polished beads, gemstone beads, coin beads
- 8º seed beads
  1 g color A (Miyuki 8-389A, fuchsia-lined cranberry AB),
  1 g color B (Miyuki 8-2035, matte metallic khaki iris)
- 4–6 g 11º seed beads (Miyuki 0577, dyed butter cream silver-lined alabaster)
- 6–8 g 11º cylinder beads (DB0380, matte metallic khaki iris)
- 6–8 g 15º seed beads (Toho 15R71, nickel-plated silver)
- S-hook clasp with **2** 6 mm soldered jump rings
- Fireline 6 lb. test
- beading needles, #12

bronze necklace colors:

- 20 mm and 12 mm art-glass bead (Rodney Andrew, randrewglass.com)
- 3–8 mm assorted beads in neutral and metallic tones
- 8º seed beads (Miyuki 342, berry-lined light topaz AB)
- 11º seed beads (Miyuki 2006, bronze)
- 11º cylinder beads
  color A used in rings (DB802, dyed shell silk satin)
  color B used in bezeled coins and pointed oval links (DB26, metallic steel iris)
- 15º seed beads (Toho 15R7119, nickel-plated silver)

alternating with cylinders. Sew through an edge 11º in a bezeled coin and back through the beads just strung. Pick up an 11º, and sew through the B in the bead cage. Retrace the thread path through the connection a few times, and end the thread.

[3] Add 12–18 in. (30–40 cm) of doubled Fireline to the bezeled coin, exiting an 11º opposite the previous connection. Starting and ending with a 15º, pick up about 2½ in. (6.4 cm) of 3–8 mm beads and a 15 x 30 mm oval gemstone alternating with 11ºs or 15ºs. Sew through an A in a peyote ring, and sew back through the beads just strung. Pick up a 15º, and sew through the 11º in the bezeled coin. Retrace the thread path through the connection a few times, and end the thread.

[4] Add 12–18 in. (30–40 cm) of doubled Fireline to the peyote ring, exiting an A opposite the previous connection. Starting and ending with a 15º, pick up 2 in. (5 cm) of 3–8 mm beads and a 15 x 30 mm oval gemstone alternating with 15ºs. Starting and ending with a 15º, pick up this exact same bead grouping in reverse order. Sew through an edge 11º on the other

bezeled coin. The two 15ºs in the middle of this 4-in. (10 cm) section mark the center of the necklace. Pick up a 15º, and retrace the thread path through the connection a couple of times, leaving about 1 mm of space between the two 15ºs at the center of the necklace. This is where you will attach the focal and fringe. End the thread.

[5] Work as in steps 1–3 for the other side of the necklace, but switch the placement of the peyote ring and the bezeled coin.

Fringe

[1] On 1 yd. (.9 m) of Fireline, pick up 1½–2 in. (3.8–5 cm) of assorted beads ending with an 11º or 15º seed bead. Skip the 11º or 15º, and sew back through all the beads just added. Pick up the art-glass bead and a 6 mm bead, and loop the thread over the 1 mm space of exposed thread at the center of the necklace. Sew back through the 6 mm and art-glass bead.

[2] Using the same thread, work as in step 1 to add fringe as desired, keeping your tension loose so the fringe will drape. End the thread.

Vines AND flowers

Here's a clever design detail: Ruffles frame the button when clasped.

Combine stitches to create a feminine bracelet that epitomizes the word "pretty"

designed by **Jackie Schwietz**

Add crystals, branches, buds, flowers, and leaves to this winding vine for a nature-inspired bracelet design. Clasp it with a button to complete the romantic look.

stepbystep

Base and ruffle

[1] On a comfortable length of Fireline, attach a stop bead (Basics), leaving a 10-in. (25 cm) tail. Pick up 12 color A 11º seed beads, and work in flat even-count peyote stitch (Basics) to make a base that is 12 beads wide and long enough to fit around your wrist. End and add thread (Basics) as needed.
[2] With your thread exiting an end A along one edge of the base, pick up three color B 11º seed beads, and sew through the next two edge As **(figure 1)**. Repeat this step along the edge.
[3] If the last A on this edge of the base is an up-bead, work as in **figure 2** to add

materials

burgundy bracelet 7 in. (18 cm)
- 12–18 mm button with shank
- **14–20** assorted crystals
  4 x 6 mm rondelles (Czech, light gold)
  3 mm bicone crystals (Swarovski; light Colorado topaz, light amethyst, and gold aurum)
- 11º seed beads
  15–20 g color A (Miyuki 469, metallic dark plum)
  2–3 g color B (light bronze)
  4–6 g color C (Toho 222, dark bronze)
- 15º seed beads
  3–4 g color D (bronze iris)
  1–2 g color E (copper-lined crystal)
- Fireline 6 lb. test
- beading needles, #12

white bracelet colors:
- crystals (crystal, white opal)
- 11º seed beads
  color A (Miyuki 131FR, matte crystal AB)
  color B (Miyuki 242, sparkle pewter-lined crystal)
  color C (Miyuki 650, dyed rustic gray silver-lined alabaster)
- 15º seed beads
  color D (Miyuki 458, metallic brown iris)
  color E (Miyuki 551, gilt-lined white opal)
  color F (Toho 994, gold-lined rainbow crystal)

DESIGN NOTE:
Use as many or as few colors as desired for your color palette; the white bracelet includes one extra color 15º seed bead.

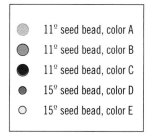

- 11º seed bead, color A
- 11º seed bead, color B
- 11º seed bead, color C
- 15º seed bead, color D
- 15º seed bead, color E

FIGURE 1

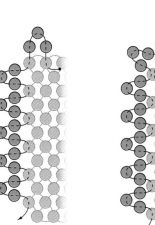

FIGURE 2

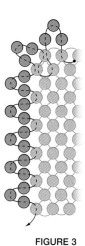

FIGURE 3

FIGURE 4

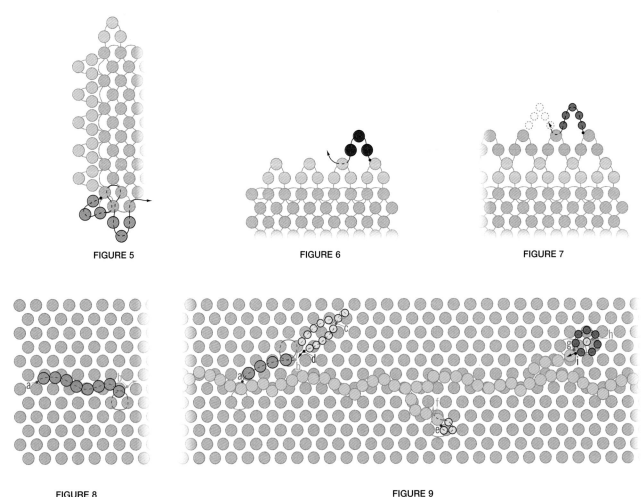

FIGURE 5

FIGURE 6

FIGURE 7

FIGURE 8

FIGURE 9

three Bs to each stitch along the end of the base. If the last A on this edge of the base is a down-bead, work as in **figure 3** to add three Bs to each stitch along the end of the base.

[4] If the last A on this end of the base is an up-bead, work as in **figure 4** for the turn. If the A at the end of the base is a down-bead, work as in **figure 5** for the turn.

[5] Add three Bs to each stitch along the remaining edge as in step 2.

[6] Add three Bs to each stitch along the remaining end as in step 2, and step up through the center B of the first stitch worked in step 2.

[7] Pick up three color C 11º seed beads, and sew through the center B of the next stitch **(figure 6)**. Repeat this

step around the edges and ends of the base, and step up through the center C of the first stitch worked in this step.

[8] Pick up five color D 15º seed beads, and sew through the center C of the next stitch **(figure 7)**. Repeat around the edges and ends of the base, and sew through the beadwork to exit a center A at one end of the base.

Embellishments

Using the working thread from "Base and ruffle," add the embellishments below as desired, ending and adding thread as needed.

Vine

[1] Pick up eight to 10 B 11ºs, lay them along the surface of the base as desired, and sew through a nearby A in the base. Sew through an adjacent A in the base, and continue through the last B added in the vine **(figure 8, a–b)**.

[2] Repeat step 1 for the length of the bracelet, curving the vine as desired.

Branches

Sew through several beads in the vine, and exit where you want to add a branch. Pick up two to five Bs, sew through the corresponding A in the base, continue through an adjacent A in the base, and sew through the last B added in the branch **(figure 9, a–b)**.

A monochromatic color palette lends itself nicely to a subtle, sophisticated style.

Leaves

Exiting an end bead in a branch, pick up seven color E 15º seed beads. Skip the last E, and sew back through the sixth E added **(b–c)**. Pick up five Es **(c–d)**, and sew through the bead your thread exited at the start of this step.

Buds

Exiting an end bead in a branch, pick up three Es, and sew back through the bead your thread exited at the start of this step **(e–f)**.

Flowers

Exiting an end bead in a branch, pick up seven Ds, and sew through the first four Ds picked up **(g–h)**. Pick up an E, sew through the last D again **(h–i)**, and sew back through the bead your thread exited at the start of this step.

Crystals

Sew through the beadwork to exit a B in a branch or an A in the base. Pick up a crystal and a 15º seed bead of any color. Skip the 15º, and sew back through the crystal and the 11º your thread exited at the start of this step.

Button-and-loop clasp

[1] Sew through the beadwork to exit a center A on the back of the base at the end of the bracelet opposite the tail. Pick up six As, the button, and six As. Sew through the A your thread exited at the start of this step. Retrace the thread path a couple of times to reinforce the join, and end the thread.

[2] Using the tail, sew through the beadwork to exit a center A on the back of the base at the other end. Pick up enough As to fit around the button, and sew through the A your thread exited at the start of this step. Retrace the thread path a couple of times to reinforce the join, and end the thread.

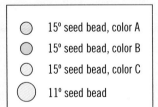

Daisy

Make a beaded daisy chain just like the real thing

This necklace is made by working a herringbone stem off a daisy head and then splitting the stem. Connect the ends of the split around the stem of another daisy to link them together.

stepbystep

Daisy
Center
[1] On 2 yd. (1.8 m) of thread, pick up four color A 15º seed beads, leaving a 24-in. (61 cm) tail. Sew through all the beads again to form a ring.

[2] Pick up an A, and sew through the next A. Repeat this stitch around the ring, and step up through the first A picked up in this round (figure 1, a–b).

[3] Work an increase round: Pick up two As, skip the next A in the original ring, and sew through the following A added in step 2 (b–c). Repeat this stitch to complete the round, and step up through the first A picked up in this round (c–d).

[4] Work an increase round: Pick up an A, and sew through the second A in the first stitch of the previous round. Pick up an A, and sew through the first A of the next stitch. Repeat these two stitches to complete the round, and step up through the first A picked up in this round (d–e).

[5] Work a round by picking up an A between all the beads added in the previous round, and step up (e–f).

◐	15º seed bead, color A
●	15º seed bead, color B
○	15º seed bead, color C
◯	11º seed bead

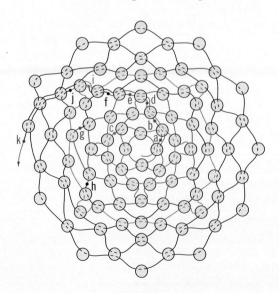

FIGURE 1

FIGURE 2

chain

PEYOTE STITCH / HERRINGBONE STITCH / FRINGE

designed by **Huib Petersen**

Connect one flower
to the next to make
a necklace as long
as you like.

[6] Work a gradual increase round by increasing every other stitch: Pick up two As, and sew through the next A in the previous round (f–g). Pick up an A, and sew through the following A in the previous round (g–h). Repeat these two stitches to complete the round, and step up through the first A added in this round (h–i).

[7] Work an increase round: Pick up an A, and sew through the second A in the first stitch of the previous round. Pick up an A, and sew through the A of the next stitch. Pick up an A, and sew through the first A of the following stitch. Repeat these three stitches to complete the round, and step up through the first A picked up in this round (i–j).

[8] Work three rounds by picking up an A between all the beads added in the previous round, and step up after each round (j–k).

[9] Work three rounds using a color B 15º seed bead between all the beads added in the previous round, and step up after each round (figure 2, a–b).

[10] Work a decrease round: Pick up a B, and sew through the next two "up-beads" (b–c). Repeat this stitch to complete the round, and step up (c–d).

[11] Work a round using Bs between all the beads added in the previous round, and step up (d–e).

[12] Work a gradual decrease round: Pick up a B, and sew through the next two up-beads (e–f). Pick up a B, and sew through the next up-bead (f–g). Repeat these two stitches to complete the round, and step up (g–h).

Stem

[1] Use the four up-bead Bs of the "Center" to work a round in tubular herringbone stitch (Basics): With your thread exiting an up-bead, pick up two Bs, and sew through the next two up-beads (figure 3, a–b). Repeat this stitch once, and step up through the first B added in this round (b–c).

[2] Work in tubular herringbone using Bs to make a rope that is 1¾ in. (4.4 cm) long.

[3] Work a split: Pick up two Bs, sew down through the next B, up through the B your thread exited at the start of this stitch, and up through the first B just picked up (figure 4, a–b). Repeat this stitch (b–c) on one side of the rope eight times.

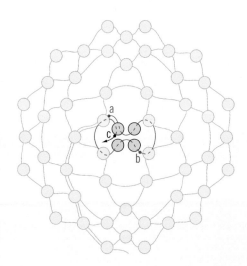

FIGURE 3

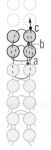

FIGURE 4

materials

necklace 15 in. (38 cm)
- 1–2 g 11º seed beads (white)
- 15º seed beads
  3–5 g color A (yellow)
  15–20 g color B (green)
  2–3 g color C (white)
- toggle bar
- nylon beading thread, size D
- beading needles, #12

DESIGN NOTES:

- Make as many daisies as desired to adjust the length of your necklace.
- For a bracelet, make the stems about 1 in. (2.5 cm) long.
- To make a pair of earrings: Work as in "Center," but sew through all the up-bead Bs in step 12, and end the thread. Work as in "Calyx and petals," but for the last calyx, pick up 13 Bs, skip the last five Bs, sew through the next B, pick up seven Bs, and sew through the next 15º. Use a jump ring (Basics) to attach an earring finding to the loop made in the last calyx.
- To make a ring: Work a daisy, but make the stem long enough to fit around your finger, and join the split after placing the head of the daisy through the split.

[4] Sew through the beadwork to exit the remaining side of the rope at the start of the split, and work as in step 3 for the other half of the split.

[5] Join the split: With your thread exiting one column of a split, sew down through the B in the adjacent column of the same split. Sew up through the corresponding B of the other split, down through the B in the next column, and up through the B in the first side of the split your thread exited at the start of this step.

[6] Continue working in tubular herringbone for four rounds.

[7] Close up the end of the tube: Pick up a B, and sew through the next two Bs (figure 5, a–b). Sew through the B just added and the following two Bs (b–c). End the working thread (Basics).

Calyx and petals

[1] Using the tail, sew through the beadwork to exit a B in the first round of Bs.

[2] Pick up nine Bs, skip the last B picked up, and sew back through the next B (figure 6, a–b). Pick up seven Bs, and sew through the next B (b–c). Repeat this step to complete the round, and step up through the adjacent A in the next round of the daisy center.

[3] Pick up two 11º seed beads and seven color C 15º seed beads, skip the last C picked up, and sew back through all the beads just added and the next A in the round (figure 7). Repeat this step to complete the round, and step up through the adjacent A in the next round.

[4] Repeat step 3, and end the tail.

Assembly

[1] Make five daisies.

[2] Make two more daisies for the clasp with the following changes:

Toggle-bar daisy:
- Make a stem 2½ in. (6.4 cm) long without a split.
- With your thread exiting an end column, pick up seven Bs and a toggle bar, and sew through the opposite column. Sew through the beadwork, retrace the thread path to reinforce the join, and end the thread.

Toggle-loop daisy:
- Work three rounds of tubular herringbone at the start of the stem.
- Work a split as in steps 3–5 of "Stem."
- Work 1½ in. (3.8 cm) of tubular herringbone, and then work a second split and end of the stem as in steps 3–7 of "Stem."

[3] String a daisy through the end of the stem of the toggle-loop daisy (photo).

[4] String a daisy stem through the last daisy strung, and repeat to string all the daisies, ending with the toggle-bar daisy.

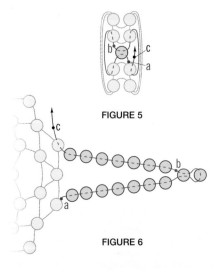

FIGURE 5

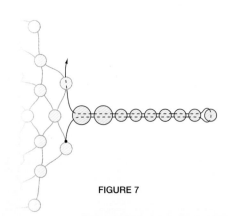

FIGURE 6

FIGURE 7

Victorian charm

Draped seed beads paired with dramatic fringe make for old-world charm

designed by **Cathy Lampole**

Herringbone rounds with peyote stitch inclusions create a scalloped base that begs to be embellished with layers of seed bead loops and graduated pearls.

stepbystep

Collar

[1] On 2 yd. (1.8 m) of Fireline, attach a stop bead (Basics), leaving a 15-in. (38 cm) tail. Pick up two 8º seed beads and an 11º seed bead, and sew back through the first 8º **(figure 1, a–b)**.

[2] Pick up an 8º, and sew back through the 11º just added **(b–c)**.

[3] Pick up an 8º, and sew back through the last 8º added **(c–d)**. Repeat this step once **(d–e)**.

[4] Pick up an 11º, and sew back through the last 8º added **(e–f)**.

[5] Pick up an 8º, and sew back through the last 11º added **(f–g)**.

[6] Repeat steps 3–5 until you have 32 beads along each edge **(g–h)**.

[7] To join the ends: Sew through the adjacent 8º on the other end **(figure 2, a–b)** and the last 8º added **(b–c)**, then sew back through the next two 8ºs **(c–d)**.

Retrace the thread path to reinforce the join, then sew through the beadwork to exit an 8º on the outer round with your thread pointing away from the ring. Don't end the working thread.

[8] Remove the stop bead from the tail, and sew through the beadwork to exit an 11º in the inner round with your thread pointing toward the center of the ring **(figure 3, point a)**.

[9] Pick up an 11º, a 4 mm pearl, and an 11º. Skip the last 11º, and sew back through the 4 mm. Pick up an 11º, and sew through the next 8º in the inner round **(a–b)**. Sew through the next 11º in the inner round **(b–c)**. Repeat this step to complete the round. End the tail.

materials

cream-colored ornament 2⅝ in. (6.7 cm)

- 2⅝-in. (6.7 cm) diameter glass ornament
- **8** 11 x 8 mm pearl drops (Swarovski, bronze)
- **24** 6 mm pearls (Swarovski, bronze)
- **24** 4 mm pearls (Swarovski, bronze)
- 12 g 8º seed beads (Toho 2125, gilt-lined buttercup)
- 10 g 11º seed beads (Toho 122, opaque lustered Navaho white)
- Fireline 6 lb. test
- beading needles, #11

pink ornament colors:

- 11 x 8 mm pearl drops (Swarovski, cream)
- 6 mm pearls (Swarovski, cream)
- 4 mm pearls (Swarovski, cream)
- 8º seed beads (Toho 38, silver-lined pink)
- 11º seed beads (Toho 907, Ceylon petunia)

DESIGN NOTE:

Keep your tension firm in steps 4–7 of "Herringbone jacket" so the peyote stitches cup.

Since the mid-19th century, glass ornaments have been used as holiday decorations.

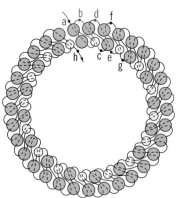

FIGURE 1

11 x 8 mm pearl drop

6 mm pearl

4 mm pearl

8º seed bead

11º seed bead

FIGURE 2

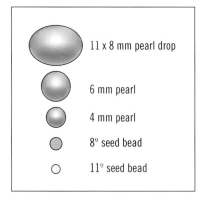

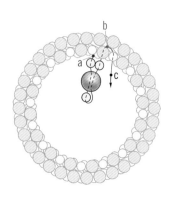

FIGURE 3

Herringbone jacket

[1] Using the working thread, work a herringbone stitch (Basics) with two 8°s (figure 4, a–b).

[2] Pick up an 8°, and sew down through the next 8° and up through the following 8° (b–c).

[3] Repeat steps 1 and 2 to complete the round, and step up through the first 8° added in step 1 (c–d). You will have eight two-bead stacks of 8°s with a single 8° between each pair of stacks.

[4] Pick up two 8°s, and sew down through the next 8° in the previous round (d–e). Pick up an 8°, and sew through the next 8° in the previous round. Pick up an 8°, and sew through the following 8° (e–f). Repeat this step to complete the round, stepping up at the end of the round. End and add thread (Basics) as needed.

[5] Alternate between herringbone and peyote stitch (Basics) as follows. Work a herringbone stitch with two 8°s (figure 5, a–b). Working in peyote, pick up an 8°, and sew through the next 8°; pick up an 11°, and sew through the next 8° (b–c); pick up an 8°, and sew up through the next 8° (c–d). Repeat this step to complete the round, and step up.

[6] Work a herringbone stitch with two 8°s (figure 6, a–b). Working in peyote, pick up an 8°, and sew through the next 8°; pick up an 11°, and sew through the next 11°; pick up an 11°, and sew through the next 8°; pick up an 8°, and sew up through the next 8° (b–c). Repeat this step to complete the round, and step up.

[7] Repeat step 6 until you have eight pairs of 8°s in each herringbone stack, but work an extra 11° stitch in each peyote section of each round. There should be six 11°s in each peyote section in the last round.

Pearl arches

Pick up two 8°s, and sew through the next 8°. Pick up an 8°, and sew through the next 8° in the previous round.

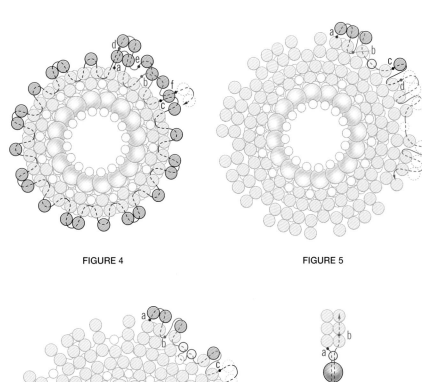

FIGURE 4

FIGURE 5

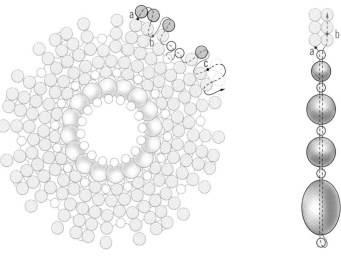

FIGURE 6

FIGURE 7

Pick up two 11°s, a 6 mm pearl, and two 11°s, and sew through the corresponding 8° on the other side of the peyote section. Pick up an 8°, and sew up through the next 8° of the following herringbone stack. Repeat this step to complete the round, and snug up the beads so the beadwork cups. If necessary, retrace the thread path through this round again. Step up through the first 8° added in this step.

Seed bead swags

[1] Pick up an 8°, 18 11°s, and an 8°. Switching the stitching direction, sew up through the next 8° in the previous herringbone stack and down through the adjacent 8°. Repeat this step to complete the round, and step up.

[2] Repeat step 1 four times, adding 22 11°s in each swag of the second round,

24 11°s in each swag of the third round, 28 11°s in each swag of the fourth round, and 34 11°s in each swag of the fifth round. End the thread.

Fringe

[1] Place the beadwork on the glass ornament. Add 1 yd. (.9 m) of Fireline to the jacket, exiting an 8° at the end of a herringbone stack (figure 7, point a).

[2] Pick up an 11°, a 4 mm pearl, an 11°, a 6 mm, an 11°, a 6 mm, an 11°, an 11 x 8 mm pearl drop (from the small end), and an 11°. Skip the last 11°, and sew back through all the beads just added and the adjacent 8° in the herringbone stack (a–b). Sew through the beadwork to exit an end 8° in the next herringbone stack.

[3] Repeat step 2 to complete the round, and end the thread.

Go for a spin

Drop beads accentuate a sculptural spiral centerpiece

designed by **Emi Yamada**

Incorporating large and small seed beads in each round of tubular herringbone causes one side of the rope to "grow" faster than the other, resulting in a spiral. Use drop beads to set off the twists and turns, then finish with a strung necklace or chain neck straps.

stepbystep

Spiral herringbone rope

[1] On a comfortable length of thread or Fireline, pick up two 8º seed beads, leaving an 8-in. (20 cm) tail. Sew through both beads again, and position them side by side. Working in ladder stitch (Basics), add one bead per stitch: an 11º seed bead, a 15º seed bead, an 11º, and an 11º. Form the ladder into a ring (Basics).

[2] With your thread exiting the first 8º in the ring, work the following rounds in tubular herringbone stitch (Basics) in a counterclockwise motion. End and add thread (Basics) as needed.
Round 2: Pick up an 8º, a 6 mm drop bead, and an 8º, and sew down through the next 8º in the ring and up through the following 11º **(figure, a–b)**. Pick up an 11º and a 15º, and sew down through the next 15º in the ring and up through the following 11º **(b–c)**. Pick up two 11ºs, and sew down through the next 11º in the ring and up through the following 8º. Step up through the first 8º added in this round **(c–d)**.

Round 3: Pick up an 8º, an 11º, and an 8º, and sew down through the next 8º in the previous round and up through the following 11º. Continue working the round in tubular herringbone stitch following the established bead pattern, and step up through the first 8º added in this round **(d–e)**.
Rounds 4–26: Alternate between rounds 2 and 3.
Round 27: Work a round following the established bead pattern, but substitute an 11º for the 15º.

[3] Repeat rounds 2–27 five times, then work rounds 2–26 again. Work a round without adding a drop bead or an 11º between the 8ºs. To stabilize the last round, work a herringbone stitch thread path through the beads without adding any new beads.

[4] With your thread exiting the first 8º in the last round, pick up three 11ºs, and sew down through the 15º across from it on the rope. Retrace the thread path to reinforce the three beads just added, and end the thread. Repeat on the other end of the rope.

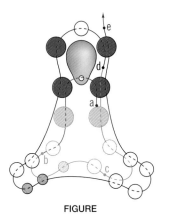

FIGURE

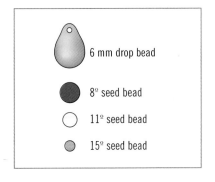

6 mm drop bead

8º seed bead

11º seed bead

15º seed bead

materials

both necklaces
- nylon beading thread or Fireline 6 lb. test
- beading needles, #10 or #12

warm-tone strung necklace, p. 186, 16½ in. (41.9 cm)
- **7** 11–12 mm faceted round glass beads (amethyst)
- **8** 7–8 mm accent beads (bronze)
- **92–96** 6 mm gemstone drop beads (amber)
- **8** 5–6 mm round glass beads (marbled red)
- **30** 6º seed beads (gold)
- 10 g 8º seed beads (gunmetal)
- 8 g 11º seed beads (rust)
- 3 g 15º seed beads (amethyst)
- toggle clasp

cool-tone chain necklace, p. 188 18 in. (46 cm)
- **7** 11–12 mm faceted round beads (medium blue)
- **92–96** 6 mm glass drop beads (sky blue with AB finish)
- **8** 5–6 mm round beads (light blue)
- **30** 6º seed beads (F463A, blue matte metallic iris)
- 10 g 8º seed beads (F463A, blue matte metallic iris)
- 7 g 11º seed beads (Miyuki 11-577, dyed butter cream silver-lined alabaster)
- 3 g 15º seed beads (Miyuki 15-1524, sparkle peony pink-lined crystal)
- toggle clasp
- 24 in. (61 cm) 22-gauge wire
- 15 in. (38 cm) chain, 6 mm links
- 4 5–6 mm jump rings
- chainnose pliers
- roundnose pliers
- wire cutters

Necklace

Follow the appropriate steps below to make a strung necklace (like the one on p. 186) or a chain necklace (right).

Strung necklace

[1] On 2 yd. (1.8 m) of thread or Fireline, attach a stop bead (Basics), leaving a 24-in. (61 cm) tail. Pick up an 8º, a 6º seed bead, an 8º, a 5–6 mm round bead, an 8º, a 6º, an 8º, and a 7–8 mm accent bead. Repeat this bead pattern three times.

[2] Sew through the three 11ºs on one end of the spiral herringbone rope.

[3] Pick up an 8º, a 6º, an 11–12 mm faceted round bead, a 6º, and an 8º. Sew through the first 11º in the column of 15ºs on the rope with your needle pointing toward the other end of the rope (photo).

[4] Repeat step 3 five times, sewing through each subsequent 11º in the column of 15ºs and repositioning the rope so it spirals around the beads in the same direction. Repeat once more, but sew through the three 11ºs on the other end of the rope.

[5] Pick up the bead pattern from step 1 to work the second side of the necklace as a mirror image of the first.

[6] Pick up six 11ºs, half of the clasp, and four 11ºs. Sew back through the first two 11ºs picked up.

[7] Sew through all the strung beads on this side of the necklace; continue through the three 11ºs at this end of the rope. Sew through a round of beads in the rope, then sew back through the three end 11ºs. Sew back through all the strung beads on this side of the necklace, and retrace the thread path through the clasp connection. Sew through a few beads on this side of the necklace, and end the working thread.

[8] Remove the stop bead, and use the tail to repeat steps 6 and 7 on the other end of the necklace.

Chain necklace

[1] Add thread or Fireline to one end of the spiral herringbone rope, and work steps 2–4 of "Strung necklace." End the thread.

[2] Cut a 3½-in. (8.9 cm) piece of chain.

[3] Determine where you would like to attach a bead connector, and cut the chain at that point. Determine where you would like to attach a second connector, and cut the chain at that point, creating three chain segments.

[4] Cut a 3-in. (7.6 cm) piece of 22-gauge wire, and make the first half of a wrapped loop (Basics) on one end. Slide an end link of one chain segment into the loop, and complete the wraps. String a 5–6 mm round bead on the wire, and make the first half of a wrapped loop. Slide an end link of another chain segment into the loop, and complete the wraps.

[5] Repeat step 4 to attach the second bead connector to the chain.

[6] Repeat steps 2–5 three times to make a total of four chains with two bead connectors each.

Stagger the placement of the bead connectors along the chains in steps 3–6 of "Chain necklace."

[7] Open a 5–6 mm jump ring (Basics), and attach the end links of two chains and the three 11ºs on one end of the rope. Use another 5–6 mm jump ring to attach the remaining end links of the chains and half of the clasp.

[8] Repeat step 7 to attach the remaining chains and half of the clasp to the other end of the rope.

DESIGN NOTES:

- Try alternating drop bead colors, or gradate the colors from one end of the rope to the other.
- For a more dramatic spiral herringbone rope, substitute dagger beads for the drop beads. The sample (right) uses 10 mm dagger beads (sea-foam with AB finish); 8º seed beads (Miyuki 8-576, dyed smoky opal silver-lined alabaster); 11º seed beads (Toho 11R278, gold-lined rainbow topaz); and 15º seed beads (Miyuki 15-595, Ceylon light beige).

Glittering globes

Dream up any color combination, from ethereal to bold, for this elegant ornament

designed by
Cathy Lampole

materials

gold ornament 2⅝ in. (6.7 cm) diameter

- 2⅝-in. (6.7 cm) diameter glass ball ornament
- **24** 6 mm fire-polished beads (crystal AB)
- **250** 4 mm fire-polished beads (crystal AB)
- **12 g** 11º seed beads (gold)
- nylon beading thread, size D
- beading needles, #12

amethyst ornament colors:

- 10 x 7 mm fire-polished teardrops (amethyst)
- 4 mm fire-polished beads (amethyst purple AB)
- 11º seed beads (amethyst AB)

blue ornament colors:

- 6 mm fire-polished beads (cobalt blue AB)
- 4 mm fire-polished beads (cobalt blue)
- 11º seed beads (silver)

Pale and glistening or bold and bright, fire-polished beads set the tone for this globe. Highlight, complement, or contrast with seed beads, and finish off with fringe.

stepbystep

Diamond band

[1] On 2 yd. (1.8 m) of thread, pick up a 4 mm fire-polished bead, an 11º seed bead, a 4 mm, and an 11º, leaving a 6-in. (15 cm) tail. Tie the beads into a ring with a square knot (Basics), and sew through the first three beads again. Work two right-angle weave stitches (Basics) using an 11º, a 4 mm, and an 11º for each stitch (**figure 1, a–b**).

[2] To make a corner, pick up an 11º, a 4 mm, an 11º, a 4 mm, and an 11º, and sew through the 4 mm your thread exited at the start of this step and the first two beads just added (**b–c**).

[3] Work three right-angle weave stitches using an 11º, a 4 mm, and an 11º for each stitch (**c–d**).

[4] Repeat steps 2–3 twice (**d–e**).

[5] Join the ends to create a diamond: Pick up an 11º, and sew through the adjacent 4 mm of the first stitch. Pick up an 11º, a 4 mm, and an 11º, and sew through the last 4 mm added in the previous stitch (**e–f**) and all the beads in this step. Tie a couple of half-hitch knots (Basics), but do not trim the working thread. End the tail (Basics).

[6] Make a total of six diamonds.

[7] Join the diamonds to make a band: With the working thread exiting a corner 4 mm of a diamond, pick up a 4 mm, sew through the corresponding 4 mm in the next diamond, pick up a 4 mm, and sew through the 4 mm your thread exited at the start of this step (**figure 2**). Retrace the thread path, and

end the working thread. Repeat this step to join the other four diamonds.

Swag

[1] Add 1½ yd. (1.4 m) of thread (Basics) to a diamond, and exit the third 4 mm from the join (**figure 3, point a**).

[2] Pick up seven 11ºs, a 4 mm, and seven 11ºs, and sew through the corresponding 4 mm on the adjacent diamond (**a–b**). Pick up three 11ºs, a 4 mm, and three 11ºs; sew through the corresponding 4 mm on the adjacent leg of the diamond (**b–c**). Pick up nine 11ºs, a 4 mm, and nine 11ºs, and sew through the corresponding 4 mm of the previous diamond (**c–d**). Pick up three 11ºs, a 4 mm, and three 11ºs, and sew through the 4 mm your thread exited at the start of this step. Sew through the beadwork to exit the 4 mm in the center of the next diamond (**d–e**). Pick up three 11ºs, and sew through the corresponding 4 mm on the next leg of the diamond (**e–f**).

[3] Pick up nine 11ºs, a 4 mm, and nine 11ºs, and sew through the corresponding 4 mm of the adjacent diamond. Pick up three 11ºs, a 4 mm, and three 11ºs, and sew through the corresponding 4 mm on the opposite leg of the diamond. Pick up seven 11ºs, a 4 mm, and seven 11ºs, and sew through the corresponding 4 mm of the previous diamond. Pick up three 11ºs, and sew through the next 4 mm, three 11ºs, and 4 mm exited at the start of this step. Sew through the beadwork to exit the 4 mm in the center of the next diamond. Pick up three 11ºs, and sew through the coresponding 4 mm on the next leg.

FIGURE 1

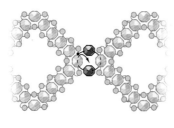

FIGURE 2

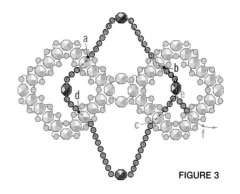

FIGURE 3

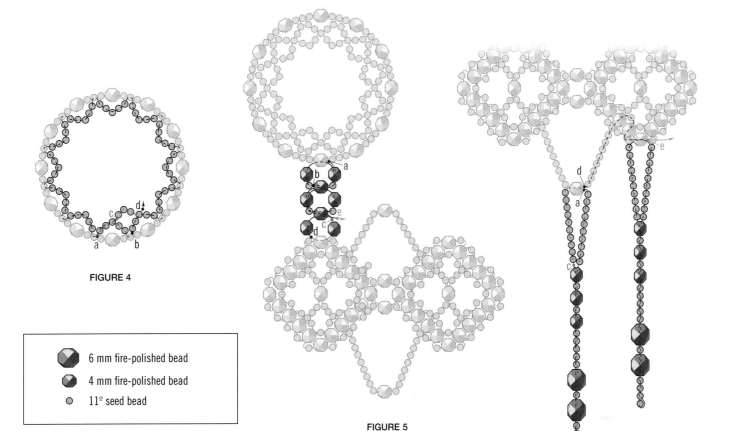

FIGURE 4

FIGURE 5

FIGURE 6

6 mm fire-polished bead

4 mm fire-polished bead

11º seed bead

[4] Continue working as in steps 2 and 3 to add swags to the remaining diamonds, sewing through the existing 4 mm in the center of each diamond as necessary.

Collar

[1] On 2 yd. (1.8 m) of thread, pick up a repeating pattern of three 11ºs and a 4 mm 12 times, leaving a 6-in. (15 cm) tail. Sew through the beads again, exiting next to the tail. Tie a square knot with the working thread and tail.

[2] With the thread exiting a center 11º (figure 4, point a), pick up five 11ºs, skip the next three beads in the ring, and sew through the next center 11º (a–b). Repeat around the ring, and step up through the first three 11ºs (b–c).

[3] Pick up three 11ºs, and sew through the center 11º in the next stitch of the previous round (c–d). Repeat around the ring. Place the collar over the neck of the ornament to check the fit. If it is too tight, loosen up on the tension so the collar slides easily over the neck of the ornament. Retrace the thread path through all the beads in this round, and snug up the beads. At this point, it may be easier to work with the collar on the glass ornament.

[4] With the thread exiting a 4 mm in the first round of the collar (figure 5, point a), work in right-angle weave: Pick up a 4 mm, an 11º, a 4 mm, an 11º, and a 4 mm, and sew through the 4 mm your thread exited at the start of this step and the first three beads just added (a–b). Repeat (b–c). Place the diamond band around the ornament with the short swags closest to the collar at the top of the ornament.

[5] Join the collar to the diamond band: Pick up a 4 mm, and sew through a top corner 4 mm of one of the diamonds in the band (c–d). Pick up a 4 mm, and sew through the 4 mm your thread exited at the start of this step (d–e). Retrace the thread path, and sew through the beadwork to exit the 4 mm in the collar at the top of this connector strip. Sew through the next eight beads in the original ring.

[6] Repeat steps 4 and 5 to connect the remaining diamonds to the collar. End the working thread and tail.

Fringe

[1] Add 2 yd. (1.8 m) of thread to a diamond, and sew through the beadwork to exit a 4 mm of a bottom swag (figure 6, point a).

[2] Pick up 10 11ºs, a 4 mm, an 11º, a 4 mm, an 11º, a 4 mm, five 11ºs, a 6 mm fire-polished bead, an 11º, a 6 mm, and four 11ºs (a–b). Skip the last 11º, and sew back through the last 16 beads just added, exiting the first 4 mm added in this step (b–c). Pick up 10 11ºs, and sew through the 4 mm your thread exited at the start of this step (c–d).

[3] Sew through the beadwork to exit the bottom corner 4 mm on the next diamond, and add fringe as in step 2 (d–e).

[4] Repeat steps 2 and 3 for a total of 12 fringes, ending and adding thread as needed.

Colors
in motion

Create bold yet flexible waves of
color with a variety of right-angle
weave techniques

designed by **Teri Dannenberg Lawson**

**Choose colors that are
close together on the
color wheel to blend
harmoniously across the
width of the bracelet.**

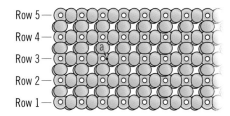

Row 5 — Row 4 — Row 3 — Row 2 — Row 1 —

a

FIGURE 1

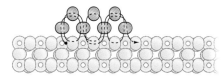

FIGURE 2

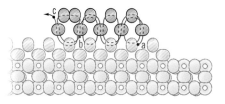

FIGURE 3

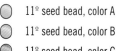

○	11º seed bead, color A
○	11º seed bead, color B
○	11º seed bead, color C
○	11º seed bead, color D
○	11º seed bead, color E
○	11º seed bead, color F

FIGURE 4

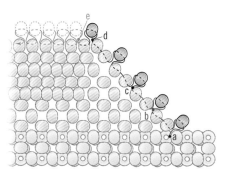

FIGURE 5

Work rows of cubic right-angle weave to provide a sturdy base for rolling ribbons of color. Attain these shapely lines by alternating rows of regular right-angle weave with increase right-angle weave.

stepbystep

Base

On a comfortable length of thread, work in cubic right-angle weave (see "Cubic Right-Angle Weave," p. 195) using color A 11º seed beads. Make the base four stitches wide and 55 stitches long, leaving a 12-in. (30 cm) tail, and ending and adding thread (Basics) as needed. The colorful waves will be added to five rows of beads on the surface of the base as shown in **figure 1**.

Waves

[1] Add a comfortable length of thread to one end of the base, and sew through the beadwork to exit the third A in the center row **(figure 1, point a)**. End and add thread as needed to work a wave. **Row 1:** Work a row of right-angle

weave (Basics) using color B 11º seed beads off the center row of As along the surface of the base **(figure 2)**, ending the row on the third stitch from the end of the base. Sew through the beadwork to exit the top B in the second-to-last stitch in this row of the wave **(figure 3, point a)**. **Row 2:** Work three stitches of right-angle weave using Bs **(figure 3, a–b)**. Work an increase stitch by picking up three Bs instead of two **(b–c)**. Continue working increase stitches across the previous row of the wave, stopping short of the last four stitches. Work three stitches of regular right-angle weave, leaving the last stitch of the previous row open to mirror the other end of the row. Sew through the beadwork to exit the second-to-last stitch in this row of the wave. **Row 3:** Work a row of right-angle weave with Bs off of the top beads in

the previous row of the wave, adding a stitch to each top bead in each increase stitch **(figure 4)**. Continue across the row, stopping short of the last stitch. Sew through the beadwork to exit the second-to-last stitch in this row of the wave. **Row 4:** Work a final row of right-angle weave with Bs off the top bead of each stitch in the previous row of the wave. **[2]** Sew through the beadwork to exit the second A in the center row of the base with your thread pointing toward the first stitch of the wave **(figure 5, point a)**. **[3]** Pick up a B, and sew through the two adjacent Bs in the first stitch of the first row of the wave **(a–b)**. Pick up a B, and sew through the next two edge Bs in the first stitch of the second row **(b–c)**. Repeat for the end stitches of the next two rows, exiting the top bead of the end stitch of the last row of the wave **(c–d)**. Pick up a B, and sew through the top B of the next stitch **(d–e)**. Repeat this stitch across the row, stopping when you reach the taper at

materials

warm-tone bracelet 7½ in. (19.1 cm)

- 11º seed beads in **6** colors:
  25–30 g color A (green)
  15–20 g in each of colors
  B (light orange), C (orange), D (yellow),
  E (red), and F (crystal AB)
- 2-strand clasp
- **4** 5–6 mm jump rings
- nylon beading thread, size D
- beading needles, #12
- **2** pairs of pliers

cool-tone bracelet colors:

- 11º seed beads
  A (matte blue AB; eclecticabeads.com)
  B (T11-3990, emerald color-lined teal;
  whimbeads.com)
  C (11-149, transparent aqua;
  eclecticabeads.com)
  D (T11-928, rainbow rosaline/opaque
  purple-lined; beadaholique.com)
  E (11-151, transparent cobalt;
  eclecticabeads.com)
  F (11-574, dyed lilac silver-lined
  alabaster; eclecticabeads.com)

DESIGN NOTE:

Time-saving tip! Stitch a single layer of peanut beads in flat right-angle weave to achieve the same thickness as the cubic right-angle weave base of 11ºs.

a

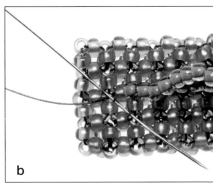

b

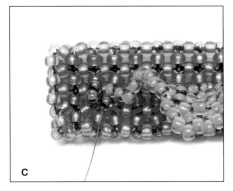

c

d

the other end. Pick up a B, and sew through the next two edge Bs. Repeat this stitch three times, then pick up a B, and sew through the next A in the center row of the base.

[4] Sew through the beadwork to exit the second A in the center row of the base, with the thread pointing toward the wave of Bs **(photo a)**.

[5] Sew diagonally under the adjacent thread bridges **(photo b)**, pick up three color C 11º seed beads, and sew under the thread bridges again and through the first C added **(photo c)**. Work as in row 1, using Cs instead of Bs, adding this first row of Cs to the adjacent base row, and working a diagonal stitch at the end of the first row of Cs. Work rows 2–4 and steps 2 and 3 using Cs to

mirror the starting end.

[6] Repeat steps 4 and 5 on the other side of the wave of Bs using color D 11º seed beads.

[7] Work the two remaining waves as in steps 1–6 using color E and F 11º seed beads, but in step 4, exit the first A in the center row of the base instead of the second A, and work two diagonal stitches at the beginning and end of each initial row of right-angle weave instead of one. End any remaining threads.

[8] Open a jump ring (Basics), and attach a center stitch at one end of the base **(photo d)** to one loop of half of the clasp. Repeat to attach the other loop of this half of the clasp. Attach the other half of the clasp to the other end of the bracelet.

The cool colors in this version of the bracelet evoke the rolling waves of surf on a warm summer day.

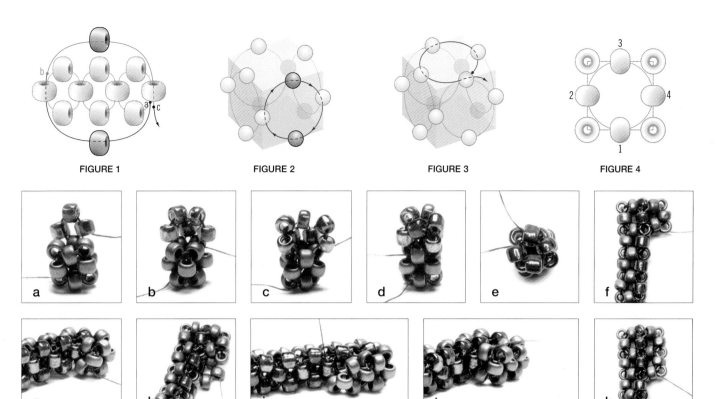

FIGURE 1 FIGURE 2 FIGURE 3 FIGURE 4

a b c d e f
g h i j k

Cubic Right-Angle Weave
Row of cubes

Each cube has six surfaces — four sides, a top, and a bottom. Each surface is made up of four beads, but since the beads are shared, 12 beads are used to make the first cube, and only eight beads are used for each cube thereafter. We used two colors in the photos above for clarity.

[1] To begin the first cube, work three right-angle weave stitches (Basics). Join the first and last stitches to form a ring: Pick up a bead, sew through the end bead in the first stitch (**figure 1, a–b**), pick up a bead, and sew through the end bead in the last stitch (**b–c**). **Figure 2** shows a three-dimensional view of the resulting cube. To make the cube more stable, sew through the four beads on the top of the cube (**figure 3**). Sew through the beadwork to the bottom of the cube, and sew through the four remaining beads.

[2] To make subsequent cubes, work off of the four top beads in the previous cube (**figure 4**): Exit one of the top beads. For the first stitch: Pick up three beads, and sew through the top bead your thread exited at the start of this step and the three beads just picked up (**photo a**). Sew through the next top bead in the previous cube. For the second stitch: Pick up two beads, and sew through the side bead in the previous stitch, the top bead your thread exited at the start of this stitch (**photo b**), and the next top bead in the previous cube. For the third stitch: Repeat the second stitch (**photo c**), and continue through the side bead from the first stitch. For the fourth stitch: Pick up a bead, and sew through the side bead in the previous stitch and the top bead in the previous cube (**photo d**).

[3] To complete the cube, sew through the beadwork to exit a top bead in the new cube. Sew through the four new top beads to stabilize them (**photo e**).

[4] Repeat steps 2 and 3 until you reach your desired length.

Subsequent rows

To make multiple rows, you'll share the beads along one edge of the first row of cubes. The shared edge beads are shown in purple in photos f–k.

[1] Work the first cube in the new row as in steps 2 and 3 of "Row of cubes," working off of the four shared edge beads of the last stitch in the previous row (**photo f**). Exit the bottom bead of the new cube (**photo g**).

[2] Pick up two beads, and sew through the bottom edge bead in the next cube of the previous row. Sew through the bead your thread exited at the start of this step and the first bead added in this stitch (**photo h**).

[3] Pick up two beads, and sew through the edge bead of the previous cube in this row, the bead your thread exited at the start of this step, the adjacent bead of the previous stitch, and the shared center edge bead of the next cube in the previous row (**photo i**).

[4] Pick up a bead, sew through the center edge bead of the previous stitch, the adjacent bottom bead, the bead your thread exited at the start of this step, and the bead just added (**photo j**).

[5] To complete the cube, sew through the four top beads of the new cube to stabilize them. Flip the beadwork over so the bead your thread is exiting is now a bottom bead (**photo k**).

[6] Work as in steps 2–5 until you reach the other end of the previous row of cubes.

glitz

Express your
unique style with
the right combination
of decorative accents

designed by **Ludmila Raitzin**

Cubic right-angle weave creates a supple
rope with both structure and texture and
provides an excellent base for embellishing.
The optional crown and swag shown in
the purple necklace allow you to add more
crystal embellishments.

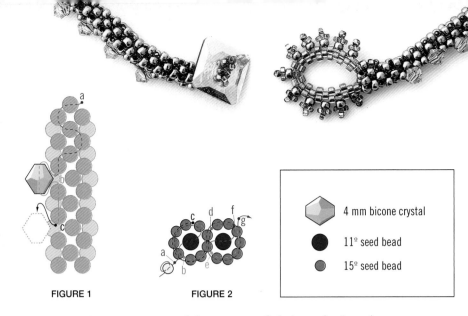

FIGURE 1   FIGURE 2

4 mm bicone crystal

● 11º seed bead

● 15º seed bead

materials

bronze necklace 26 in. (66 cm)

- 27 mm round Chinese crystal stone (vitrail AB, beadseast.com)
- 10 mm crystal button (Swarovski, crystal AB)
- **90–92** 4 mm bicone crystals (Swarovski, peridot satin)
- 30–35 g 11º seed beads (mixture of Toho 11R1706, gilded black marble, and Toho 11R1704, gilded marble lavender)
- 1 g 11º cylinder beads (DB1055, matte metallic gray dusk gold iris)
- 3 g 15º seed beads (Miyuki 457L, metallic light bronze)
- Fireline 6 lb. test
- beading needles, #12

purple necklace colors:

- 27 mm vintage pear drop pendant (Swarovski, AB)
- 10 mm crystal button (Swarovski, vitrail)
- 4 mm bicone crystals
  color A (Swarovski, tanzanite)
  color B (Swarovski, fuchsia xilion)
- 11º seed beads (Miyuki P479, galvanized purple)
- 11º cylinder beads (light purple)
- 15º seed beads (medium purple)

Capture a 27 mm crystal in a net of daisy chain, then turn up the glamour with a crystal rope and additional embellishments.

stepbystep

Crystal rope

[1] On a comfortable length of Fireline, use 11º seed beads to make a cubic right-angle weave rope (see "Cubic Right-Angle Weave," p. 195) 22½ in. (57.2 cm) long, ending and adding thread (Basics) as necessary. End the threads.

[2] Add 1½ yd. (1.4 m) of Fireline to one end of the rope, leaving a 15-in. (38 cm) tail. Select a column of stitches to face outward, and lay out the rope, making sure the rope does not twist. Sew through the beadwork to exit the outer edge 11º in the third row of right-angle weave **(figure 1, a–b)**.

[3] Pick up a 4 mm bicone crystal, and sew through the next two outer edge 11ºs **(b–c)**. Repeat for the length of the rope, stopping short of the last two outer edge 11ºs. Sew through the beadwork to exit an end 11º.

Clasp

[1] Pick up five 15º seed beads, sew through one hole of the 10 mm crystal button, and pick up three 15ºs. Skip the last three 15ºs, and sew back through the same hole of the button, the following five 15ºs, and the 11º in the rope your thread exited at the start of this step. Repeat for the other hole of the button. Retrace both thread paths to reinforce, and end the working thread.

[2] Using the tail at the remaining end of the rope, pick up an even number of 11º cylinder beads to fit around the button (about 24), and sew through the end 11º your thread exited at the start of this step.

[3] Work a round of peyote stitch (Basics) with cylinders. Sew through the end 11º, and step up through the first cylinder added in this round.

[4] Pick up an 11º and three 15ºs. Skip the 15ºs, and sew back through the 11º just added and the next cylinder in the previous round. Repeat to complete the round, and end the tail.

Daisy chain bezel

Round 1

[1] On 18 in. (46 cm) of Fireline, attach a stop bead (Basics), leaving a 6-in. (15 cm) tail. Pick up five 15ºs and an 11º, and sew back through the first 15º toward the tail **(figure 2, a–b)**. Pick up four 15ºs, and sew through the last 15º picked up before the 11º **(b–c)**. Sew through the ring of 15ºs as shown to reinforce the stitch **(c–d)**.

[2] Pick up three 15ºs and an 11º, and sew through the second-to-last 15º added in the previous stitch **(d–e)**. Pick up four 15ºs, and sew through the last 15º before the 11º **(e–f)**. Sew through the ring of 15ºs as shown to reinforce the stitch **(f–g)**.

[3] Repeat step 2 to make a daisy chain strip one stitch short of fitting around the 27 mm crystal stone (about 24 stitches for a 27 mm round crystal or 30 stitches for a 27 mm pear drop pendant).

DESIGN NOTE:

The designer used three 4 mm bicone crystals to attach the 27 mm pear-shaped crystal to the rope, which worked well with that shape. This did not work for a round crystal because it made the crystal flop over. Use the method described in "Assembly" to stabilize the round crystal in the rope.

FIGURE 3

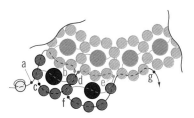

FIGURE 4

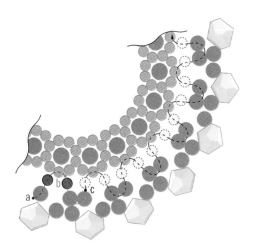

FIGURE 5

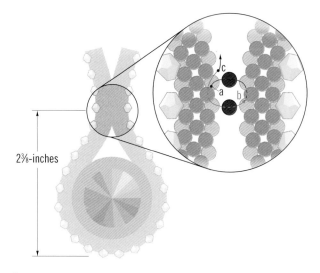

FIGURE 6

[4] Join the ends of the strip: Pick up two 15ºs, and sew through the second 15º picked up in the first stitch (**figure 3, a–b**). Pick up an 11º, and sew through the last 15º picked up in the last stitch (**b–c**). Pick up three 15ºs, and sew through the first 15º picked up in the first stitch (**c–d**). Retrace the thread path to reinforce the join, and end the working thread. Remove the stop bead, and end the tail. Note the inner edge of the daisy chain strip has two beads per stitch, while the outer edge has three.

Round 2
[1] On 18 in. (46 cm) of Fireline, attach a stop bead, leaving a 6-in. (15 cm) tail. Pick up two 15ºs, and sew through three outer edge 15ºs in a stitch of round 1 (**figure 4, a–b**).
[2] Pick up a 15º and an 11º, and sew through the first 15º picked up in step 1 (**b–c**). Pick up three 15ºs, and sew through the last 15º picked up before the 11º (**c–d**) and the next three outer edge 15ºs in the next stitch of previous round (**d–e**).
[3] Pick up a 15º and an 11º, and sew through the last 15º picked up in the

previous stitch (**e–f**). Pick up three 15ºs, and sew through the last 15º picked up before the 11º and the next three outer edge 15ºs in the next stitch of previous round (**f–g**).
[4] Repeat step 3 until you have one stitch left. To join the ends, sew through the adjacent 15º in the first stitch of round 1, pick up an 11º, and sew through the last 15º picked up in the last stitch. Pick up two 15ºs, and sew through the two 15ºs picked up in step 1.
[5] Insert the crystal stone into the bezel, sew through the inner edge 15ºs of round 1, and pull tight to snug the beads around the back of the crystal. Sew through the beadwork to exit an edge 15º in round 2. Sew through all the outer edge 15ºs, pulling tight to snug the beads around the front of the crystal. End the working thread. Remove the stop bead, and end the tail.

Assembly
[1] Fold the rope in half, and position the bezeled crystal in the loop of the rope. Center 1 yd. (.9 m) of Fireline in the center stitch of the rope, with each end of the thread exiting an 11º along

the edge opposite the 4 mm crystal embellishments.
[2] Using one end of the thread, pick up a 15º, and sew through a center shared 15º along the outer edge of the daisy chain bezel (**figure 5, a–b**). Pick up a 15º, and sew through the next two edge 11ºs in the rope (**b–c**). Continue to connect the bezeled crystal to the rope in this manner for ⅓ of the way around the bezeled crystal. End the thread.
[3] Using the remaining end of the thread, continue to connect the bezeled crystal to the rope as in step 2 around the other side of the bezeled crystal. End this thread.
[4] Measure 2⅜ in. (6 cm) from the bottom of the bezeled crystal, and add 9 in. (23 cm) of Fireline, exiting an 11º on the inner edge of one half of the rope (**figure 6, point a**). Pick up an 11º, and sew through the corresponding 11º on the other half of the rope (**a–b**). Pick up an 11º, and sew through the 11º your thread exited at the start of this step (**b–c**). Retrace the thread path several times, and end the thread.

Optional crown

[1] On 2 yd. (1.8 m) of Fireline and leaving a 6-in. (15 cm) tail, use 11ºs to make a rope of cubic right-angle weave that is 3½ in. (8.9 cm) long.

[2] To join the ends to make a ring, pick up an 11º, and sew through the corresponding 11º on the other end of the rope. Pick up an 11º, and sew through the 11º your thread exited at the start of this step and the next three 11ºs of the current stitch.

[3] Sew through the next end 11º, pick up an 11º, and sew through the corresponding 11º on the other end, the previous connector beads, and the next two beads in the new stitch. Repeat this step once, then sew through the four beads of the final stitch to complete the join.

[4] Embellish the outer edge of the ring with 4 mm crystals as in steps 2 and 3 of "Crystal rope."

[5] Fold the ring in half, and center it over the stitch that joins the two ropes above the crystal. Sew through the corresponding beads of the rope and ring to secure. End the working thread and tail.

Optional swag

[1] On 2 yd. (1.8 m) of Fireline and leaving a 6-in. (15 cm) tail, use 11ºs to make a rope of cubic right-angle weave 3 in. (7.6 cm) long.

[2] Embellish one edge of the rope with 4 mm crystals as in steps 2 and 3 of "Crystal rope."

[3] Center the swag along the bottom edge of the rope. With the thread exiting an edge 11º opposite the row of 4 mms, pick up two 15ºs, sew through the 4 mm along the bottom edge of the rope, pick up two 15ºs, and sew through the next two 11ºs in the swag. Repeat to the end of the swag, then retrace the thread path to secure. End the working thread and tail.

Ravishing rosettes

Stitched in one
continuous path, this
well-formed necklace is
a must-have

designed by **Smadar Grossman**

The rosette was a popular jewelry design in the 15th century; small gems were grouped close together to look like a single larger stone.

materials

necklace 18 in. (46 cm)

- **21** 6 mm Czech glass pearls (rose quartz)
- **118** 3 mm bicone crystals (Swarovski, garnet AB)
- 8º Japanese seed beads
  2–3 g color A (Toho 223, antique bronze)
  5–10 g color B (Miyuki 367, garnet-lined ruby AB)
- 10–15 g 11º Japanese seed beads in each of **2** colors:
  color A (Toho 223, antique bronze)
  color B (Miyuki 367, garnet-lined ruby AB)
- 12 x 6 mm lobster claw clasp
- **2** 6 mm jump rings
- Fireline 6 lb. test
- beading needles, #11
- **2** pairs of pliers

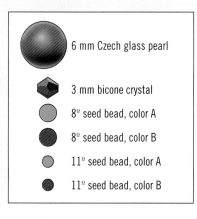

- ⬤ 6 mm Czech glass pearl
- ⬣ 3 mm bicone crystal
- ◯ 8º seed bead, color A
- ⬤ 8º seed bead, color B
- ◯ 11º seed bead, color A
- ⬤ 11º seed bead, color B

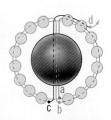

FIGURE 1

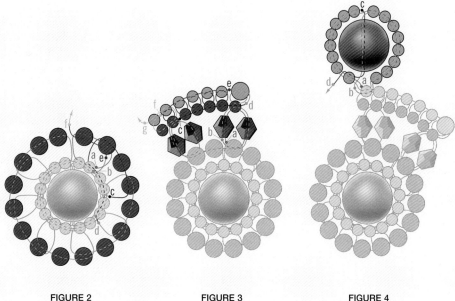

FIGURE 2   FIGURE 3   FIGURE 4

Resplendent in ruby-colored pearls and bicone crystals, this necklace naturally curves along the base of your neck.

stepbystep

First pearl rosette

[1] On 2 yd. (1.8 m) of Fireline, pick up 16 color A 11º seed beads, and tie them into a ring with a square knot (Basics), leaving a 6-in. (15 cm) tail.

[2] Pick up a 6 mm pearl, cross the ring, and sew through the first eight A 11ºs in the ring **(figure 1, a–b)**. Sew through the pearl again and the last eight A 11ºs in the ring **(b–c)**. Sew through the pearl and the next two A 11ºs in the ring **(c–d)**.

[3] Pick up two color B 8º seed beads, and sew through the two A 11ºs your thread exited at the start of this step **(figure 2, a–b)** and the following two A 11ºs in the original ring **(b–c)**.

[4] Pick up two B 8ºs, sew back through the last B 8º added in the previous step, the corresponding A 11º in the original

DESIGN NOTE:
To add an adjustable chain closure
to this necklace, attach a 3-in.
(7.6 cm) piece of 8 x 7 mm brass
chain to one of the jump rings in
step 3 of "Clasp." Embellish the
chain: On a 2-in. (5 cm) brass
head pin, string a pearl, and make
a wrapped loop (Basics). Repeat
to make two more pearl dangles.
Open a 6 mm jump ring, and attach
the end of the chain and a pearl
dangle. Repeat for the other two
pearl dangles.

ring, and the next four A 11°s (c–d).
Repeat this step six times (d–e), then
sew back through the first two B 8°s
added in this round (e–f).

[5] Pick up a 3 mm bicone crystal,
a color B 11° seed bead, and a 3 mm,
and sew through the B 8° your thread
exited at the start of this step (figure 3,
a–b). Retrace the thread path to reinforce
the stitch, then sew through the next two
B 8°s. Repeat this step, but sew through
the first 3 mm and the B 11° (b–c)
instead of the next two B 8°s.

[6] Pick up four B 11°s, and sew through
the center B 11° of the first stitch in the
previous step (c–d). Working in square
stitch (Basics), pick up a color A 8° seed
bead, and sew through the B 11° and
the A 8° again (d–e).

[7] Continue working in square stitch,
adding five A 11°s above the next five B
11°s (e–f). For the last stitch in the rosette,
pick up an A 11° and a B 11°, and sew
through the end B 11° in the previous
row and the last two A 11°s (f–g).

Subsequent pearl rosettes

[1] Pick up 16 A 11°s, and sew through
the A 11° your thread exited at the start
of this step to form a ring (figure 4, a–b).

[2] Pick up a pearl, and sew through
the last eight A 11°s just added, the
A 11° your thread exited at the start of
this step, and the next eight A 11°s in
the ring (b–c). Sew through the pearl
and the first new A 11° in the ring (c–d).

[3] Pick up a B 11°, sew through
the adjacent B 11° of the previous
rosette, the corresponding A 11°, and
the next three A 11°s in the new ring
(figure 5, a–b).

[4] Pick up two B 8°s, and sew
back through the adjacent bead,
the corresponding A 11° in the
new ring, and the next four A
11°s (b–c). Repeat this step six
times, then sew through the last A 11°
in the previous rosette (c–d).

[5] Sew through the next A 11° in the
previous rosette (d–e). Pick up a B 8°,
sew through the adjacent B 8°, and sew
back through the next four A 11°s (e–f),
the B 8° just added, and the next three
B 8°s (f–g).

[6] Pick up a 3 mm, a B 11°, and a 3 mm,
and sew through the B 8° your thread
exited at the start of this step. Retrace
the thread path to reinforce the stitch,
then sew through the next two B 8°s.
Repeat this step twice, but in the last
repeat, sew through the first 3 mm
and the B 11° again (g–h) instead of
the next two B 8°s.

[7] Pick up four B 11°s, and sew through
the previous center B 11° in the second
stitch of the previous step (h–i). Pick up
four B 11°s, and sew through the next
center B 11°. Pick up eight B 11°s, and
sew through the A 8° in the previous
rosette (i–j).

[8] Pick up two A 11°s, and sew
through the adjacent two B 11°s
and the two A 11°s just added.
Repeat this stitch five times, then
work a stitch with an A 11° and an
A 8°. Work two more stitches
using two A 11°s per stitch, then
work a stitch using one A 11° (j–k).

[9] Repeat steps 1–8 for the desired
necklace length, ending and adding
thread (Basics) as needed. In the last
repeat, stop after step 5.

FIGURE 5

Clasp

[1] Sew through the beadwork
to exit the seventh B 8° around the pearl
in the last rosette. Pick up five B 11°s,
and sew through the B 8° again to form
a loop. Retrace the thread path of the
loop several times, and end the thread.

[2] With the tail, repeat step 1.

[3] Open a jump ring (Basics), and
attach a beaded loop and the lobster
claw clasp. Attach a jump ring to
the beaded loop on the remaining
end of the necklace.

TILA tapestry

A crisscrossing pathway of beads adds a lacy look to this sturdy tiled bracelet

designed by
Connie Whittaker

A 7¼ in. (18.4 cm) bracelet has 35 Tila beads in each edging. To adjust the length, increase or decrease the number of Tila beads in each edging by three.

materials

opal-bicone bracelet (second from top)
7¾ in. (19.7 cm)

- **76** Tila beads (Miyuki 2008, matte metallic patina iris)
- **26** 4 mm bicone crystals (Swarovski, chrysolite opal)
- 3–4 g 11º seed beads in each of **2** colors: B (Miyuki 460, metallic dark raspberry), C (Miyuki 4213, Duracoat galvanized dark mauve)
- 3–4 g 15º seed beads in each of **2** colors: A (Miyuki 454, metallic iris purple), D (Toho 23B, silver-lined dark aqua)
- 3-strand slide clasp
- Fireline 6 lb. test
- beading needles, #12

fuchsia-bicone bracelet (top):
- Tila beads (Miyuki 455, metallic variegated blue iris)
- 4 mm bicone crystals (Swarovski, fuchsia)
- 11º seed beads: B (Miyuki 2011, metallic frost hematite), C (Miyuki 12, silver-lined light amethyst)
- 15º seed beads: A (Miyuki 460, metallic dark raspberry), D (Miyuki 457, metallic dark bronze)

gold-bicone bracelet (third from top):
- Tila beads (Miyuki 401, matte black AB)
- 4 mm bicone crystals (Swarovski, golden shadow)
- 11º seed beads: B (Miyuki 132, transparent amber), C (Miyuki 2016, matte metallic dark plum iris)
- 15º seed beads: A and D (Miyuki 348, purple lined light topaz luster)

dark-blue-bicone bracelet (bottom):
- Tila beads (Miyuki 2005, matte metallic dark raspberry iris)
- 4 mm bicone crystals (Swarovski, dark sapphire)
- 11º seed beads: B (Toho 81, metallic hematite), C (Toho 26, silver-lined light amethyst)
- 15º seed beads: A (F460J, matte metallic blue plum), D (Toho 222, dark copper/bronze)

Connect ladder stitch Tila bead borders with interwoven crystal and seed bead arches, experimenting with color and finishes to create a tapestry for your wrist.

step by step

Tila bead edgings

[1] On 1½ yd. (1.4 m) of Fireline, attach a stop bead (Basics), leaving a 6-in. (15 cm) tail. Sew down through the right hole of a Tila bead.

[2] Sew up through the left hole of another Tila bead (**figure 1, a–b**) and down through the right hole of the first Tila bead (**b–c**) so the beads are positioned side by side. Retrace the thread path, then sew down through the right hole of the second Tila bead (**c–d**).

[3] Repeat step 2 for the desired length of the bracelet. Remove the stop bead, and end the threads (Basics), but do not tie the half-hitch knots between the first two or last two Tila beads.

[4] Repeat steps 1–3 to create another Tila bead edging.

Connecting the edgings

[1] On 3 yd. (2.7 m) of Fireline, attach a stop bead, leaving an 18-in. (46 cm) tail. Position the Tila bead edgings across from each other.

[2] Sew through the left hole of the first Tila bead in the upper edging, pick up two color A 15º seed beads, a color B 11º seed bead, a color C 11º seed bead, an A, a 4 mm bicone crystal, an A, a C, a B, and two As, and sew down through the left hole of the corresponding Tila bead on the lower edging (**figure 2, a–b**).

[3] Pick up three Cs, and sew up through the right hole of the Tila bead and down through the left hole of the next Tila bead (**b–c**).

[4] Pick up three Cs, and sew up through the right hole of the Tila bead (**c–d**).

[5] Pick up two As, a B, a C, an A, a 4 mm, an A, a C, a B, and two As, and

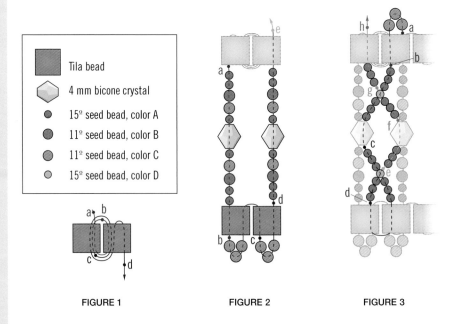

▩	Tila bead
⬡	4 mm bicone crystal
●	15º seed bead, color A
●	11º seed bead, color B
●	11º seed bead, color C
●	15º seed bead, color D

FIGURE 1

FIGURE 2

FIGURE 3

sew up through the right hole of the corresponding Tila bead in the upper edging (d–e).

[6] Pick up three Cs, and sew down through the left hole of the same Tila bead (figure 3, a–b).

[7] Pick up three As, a color D 15º seed bead, and three As, cross over the gap, and sew through the previous 4 mm (b–c). Pick up three As, a D, and three As, sew down through the left hole of the next Tila bead in the lower edging, and sew up through the right hole of the previous Tila bead (c–d).

[8] Pick up three As, and sew through the D added in the previous step (d–e). Pick up three As, and sew through the next 4 mm (e–f). Pick up three As, and sew through the first D added in the previous step (f–g). Pick up three As, and sew through the right hole of the previous Tila bead in the upper edging (g–h).

[9] Pick up three Cs, and sew down through the left hole of the same Tila bead and up through the right hole.

Zigzag up and down through the next two Tila beads (figure 4, a–b), then sew down through the left hole of the next Tila bead (b–c).

[10] Pick up two As, a B, a C, and A, a 4 mm, an A, a C, a B, and two As, and sew through the corresponding Tila on the lower edge (figure 5, a–b).

[11] Follow the bead pattern and thread path established in step 7, but sew up through the right hole of the corresponding Tila bead in the upper edging (b–c).

[12] Pick up three Cs; sew down through the left hole of the same Tila bead (c–d).

[13] Follow the bead pattern and thread path established in step 8, but sew down through the left hole of the corresponding Tila bead in the lower edging (figure 6, a–b).

[14] Pick up three Cs, and sew up through the right hole of the same Tila bead (b–c). Sew down through the left hole of the next Tila bead in the lower edging, pick up three Cs, and sew up through the right hole

of the same Tila bead (c–d).

[15] Sew down through the left hole of the next Tila bead in the lower edging, pick up three Cs, and sew up through the right hole of the same Tila bead.

[16] Repeat steps 5–15 for the length of the bracelet.

Clasp

[1] Sew through the beadwork to exit down through the right hole of the last Tila bead in the upper edging (figure 7, point a). Pick up four As, a loop of the clasp, and four As, and sew through the next 4 mm (a–b).

[2] Pick up four As, the next loop of the clasp, and four As, and sew through the 4 mm again (b–c).

[3] Pick up four As, the last loop of the clasp, and four As, and sew down through the right hole of the last Tila bead in the lower edging (c–d). Retrace the thread path, and end the thread.

[4] Repeat steps 1–3 on the remaining end of the bracelet.

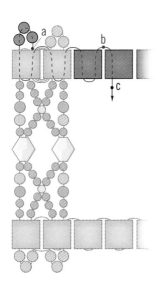

FIGURE 4

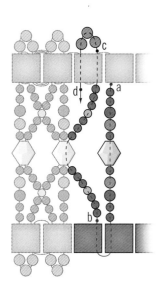

FIGURE 5

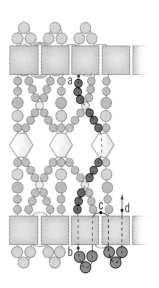

FIGURE 6

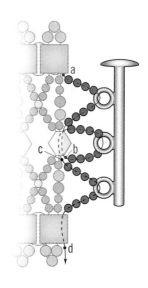

FIGURE 7

Bejeweled
garland choker

Crystal stones make pinch-me-perfect posies
to dangle from a latticework choker

Embellish a netted choker with pearls, suspend bezeled chatons from the band, and make an adjustable closure for a luxurious necklace.

stepbystep

To ensure the correct fit for this choker, measure around your neck with a flexible measuring tape, and subtract 1½ in. (3.8 cm) from that number to adjust for the tapered end and the clasp. This is the length you will need to make your netted band.

Netted band
[1] On a comfortable length of conditioned thread (Basics), attach a stop bead (Basics), leaving a 15-in. (38 cm) tail. Pick up a repeating pattern of a color B 15º seed bead and a color A 15º seed bead eight times.
[2] Pick up a B, an 11º seed bead, and a B, and sew back through the last A to make the turn (figure 1, a–b).

[3] Pick up a B, an A, and a B, skip the next three beads in the previous row, and sew through the following A (b–c). Repeat this stitch twice for a total of three netted stitches (c–d).
[4] To make the turn: Pick up a B, an A, a B, an 11º, and a B, and sew back through the last A picked up in this step (d–e).
[5] Repeat steps 3 and 4 for the desired length netted band, ending and adding thread (Basics) as necessary.
[6] To begin tapering the end, work step 3 (figure 2, a–b).
[7] Instead of making a turn as in step 4, sew back through the last two beads added in the previous step (b–c) to be in position for the next row.
[8] Work two netted stitches following the established bead pattern, and sew back through the last two beads added in this row (c–d).
[9] Work one netted stitch (d–e), and end the working thread.
[10] Remove the stop bead and the first three beads added in step 1, and use the tail to work as in steps 7–9 to taper this end of the necklace. End the thread.

Closure tab
[1] Add 18 in. (46 cm) of thread to one end of the necklace. With the thread exiting the A to one side of the end A, pick up a B, and sew through the B beside the end A (figure 3, a–b). Pick up a B, skip the end A, and sew through the next B (b–c). Pick up a B, and sew through the next A (c–d).
[2] Sew through the beadwork as shown to exit the first B added in step 1 (d–e).
[3] Work two peyote stitches using Bs (e–f).
[4] Work two peyote stitches using Bs, and then pick up a B, sew under the thread bridge between the two previous edge beads, and sew back through the B just added (f–g).
[5] Repeat steps 3 and 4 for a total of 27 rows, ending with a two-bead row.
[6] To taper the end, sew under the thread bridge between the last two edge Bs in rows 24 and 26, and sew back through the edge B in row 26 and the last B added in row 27 (figure 4, a–b). Pick up a B, and sew through the next two end beads (b–c).
[7] Stitch both parts of the 6 mm metal snap to the closure tab so they are facing up with approximately ⅜-in. (1 cm) gap between them (photo a). End the thread.

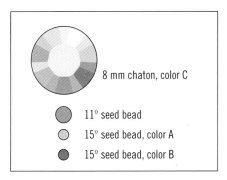

8 mm chaton, color C

11º seed bead

15º seed bead, color A

15º seed bead, color B

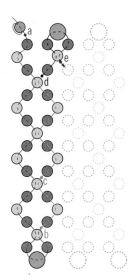

FIGURE 1

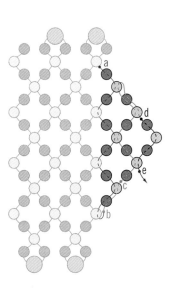

FIGURE 2

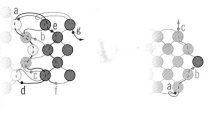

FIGURE 3   FIGURE 4

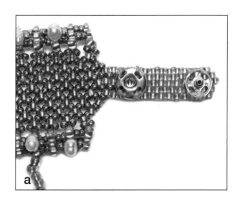

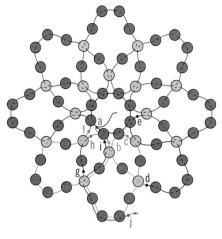

FIGURE 5

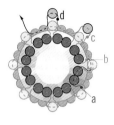

FIGURE 6

materials

silver choker 12 in. (30 cm)

- **8** 8 mm SS39 chatons, color C (Swarovski 1028, lime)
- **8** 8 mm SS39 chatons, color D (Swarovski 1028, aquamarine)
- **4** 6 mm round crystals (Swarovski, black diamond)
- **232** 2 mm potato pearls (white)
- 5 g 11º seed beads (Toho 263, rainbow crystal/light capri)
- 15º Japanese seed beads
  7 g color A (Toho 994, gold-lined rainbow crystal)
  15 g color B (Toho 176, transparent rainbow black diamond)
- 6 mm snap closure
- nylon beading thread, size B, conditioned with Thread Heaven or microcrystalline wax
- beading needles, #12
- bobbin or small piece of cardboard (optional)
- cloth measuring tape

Edge embellishment

[1] Add 2 yd. (1.8 m) of thread to the end of the band with the "Closure tab," and exit the first 11º along one edge with the needle pointing toward the other end of the band.

[2] Work the following rows:

Row 1: Pick up two Bs, and sew through the next 11º. Repeat this stitch along the edge of the band.

Row 2: Pick up an A, and sew back through the next two Bs in the previous row. Repeat this stitch to the end of the row. To make the turn at the end of the row, pick up an A, sew under the thread bridge between the end 11º and the B below it, and then sew back through the A with the needle pointing toward the other end of the band. The As in this row will sit on top of the 11ºs, and you will be in position to start the next row.

Row 3: Work as in row 1, adding two Bs between the As added in row 2.

Row 4: Repeat row 2, and work the turn in the same manner so you are in position to begin the final row.

Row 5: With the thread exiting an end A in row 4 and the needle pointing toward the opposite end of the band, pick up a B, a 2 mm pearl, and a B. Skip the next A in the previous row, and sew through the following A. Position the pearl so it sits on top of the skipped A. Repeat this stitch to the end of the row. This completes the top edge embellishment.

[3] Sew through the beadwork to exit the first 11º along the other edge of the band. Work rows 1–4 on this edge, and end the thread, but do not add the final row of pearls. You will add the pearls after adding the bezeled chaton crystals.

Bezeled chaton crystals

[1] On 24 in. (61 cm) of thread, pick up eight Bs, and tie them into a ring with a square knot (Basics), leaving a 6-in. (15 cm) tail. Sew through the first B again, and pull the thread to hide the knot **(figure 5, a–b)**.

[2] Pick up an A, a B, an A, four Bs, an A, and a B, and sew back through the first A picked up and the next B in the original ring **(b–c)**.

[3] Pick up an A and a B, and sew through the last A picked up in the previous stitch **(c–d)**.

[4] Pick up four Bs, an A, and a B, and sew through the A in the previous stitch and the next B in the original ring **(d–e)**.

[5] Repeat steps 3 and 4 five more times **(e–f)**.

[6] To join: Pick up an A and a B, and sew through the last A picked up in the previous stitch. Pick up four Bs, sew through the second A added in step 2 **(f–g)**, pick up a B, and sew through the A added at the start of this step **(g–h)** and the next B in the original ring **(h–i)**. Sew through the beadwork to exit the third B in a four-B loop **(i–j)**.

[7] Pick up an A, and sew through the two middle Bs in the next loop. Repeat this stitch to complete the round, step up through the first A added in this step, and snug up the beads to form a cup.

[8] Place a color C 8 mm chaton in the bezel face up, and hold it in place with your thumb. Pick up two Bs, and sew through the next A along the outer edge of the bezel **(figure 6, a–b)**. Repeat this stitch to complete the round, and step up through the first two Bs added in this round, the next A in the previous

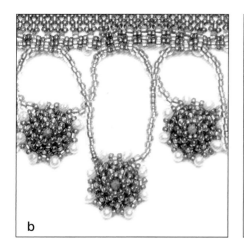

b

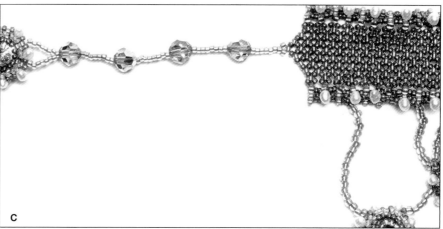

c

round, and the following two loop Bs you sewed through in step 7 (b–c).

[9] Pick up an A, and sew through the next two loop Bs (c–d). Repeat this stitch to complete the round, and step up through the first A added in this step. This round of As will sit on top of the round of As added in step 7.

[10] Pick up a B, a 2 mm pearl, and a B, and sew through the next A in the previous round. Repeat this stitch to complete the round, and end the working thread and tail.

[11] Repeat steps 1–10 to make a total of eight color C bezeled chatons and eight color D bezeled chatons.

Assembly

[1] Center 2 yd. (1.8 m) of thread through the center A in the last row of the "Edge embellishment" along the edge without the pearls. Wrap half of the thread around a bobbin or small piece of cardboard if desired.

[2] With the working thread, pick up two Bs, and sew through the next A of the edge embellishment. Pick up 20 11ºs, and sew through a B, a 2 mm pearl, a B, an A, a B, a 2 mm pearl, and a B in a color C bezeled chaton. Pick up 20 11ºs, skip the next seven As along the edge of the band, and sew through the following A. Pick up two Bs, and sew through the next A in the band (photo b, center dangle). (Note: Photo b shows the back of the choker for placement). Repeat this step three more times.

[3] Using the other thread, repeat step 2 to make a mirror image on the other half of the band. End the threads.

[4] Add 1 yd. (.9 m) of thread to one end of the band, and sew through the beadwork to exit the fifth A from the A the last color C bezeled chaton is stitched to.

[5] Pick up 12 11ºs, and sew through a B, a 2 mm pearl, a B, an A, a B, a 2 mm pearl, and a B in a color D bezeled chaton. Pick up 12 11ºs, skip the next seven As in the band, and sew through the following A along the edge of the band (photo b, left dangle). Make sure you are working on top of the color C bezeled chatons; remember that photo b shows the back of the choker.

[6] Pick up two Bs, and sew through the next A. Repeat this stitch once.

[7] Repeat steps 5 and 6 to attach a total of seven color D bezeled chatons.

[8] Work row 5 of "Edge embellishment" to add the pearls to this edge of the band, and end the thread.

Adjustable clasp chain

[1] Add 15 in. (38 cm) of thread to the end of the necklace opposite the "Closure tab," and exit the end A. Pick up a repeating pattern of eight Bs and a 6 mm round crystal four times. Pick up eight Bs, and sew through a B, a 2 mm pearl, and a B in the remaining color D bezel.

[2] Pick up seven Bs, skip the last seven Bs picked up in the previous step, and sew back through the next B and the remaining 6 mms and Bs in the chain, stopping just before the first B in the chain. Pick up a B, and sew through the end A in the choker (photo c). Retrace the thread path, and end the thread.

DESIGN NOTE:
To make earrings, attach earring findings to a pair of bezeled chaton crystals. In the earrings above, I used 2 mm round crystals in place of the 2 mm pearls.

Midnight sun

Capture a crystal in a bezel nestled in a band of netted stars

designed by **Giorgia Scardini**

A lobster claw clasp at one end of the bracelet latches onto the loop at the other end.

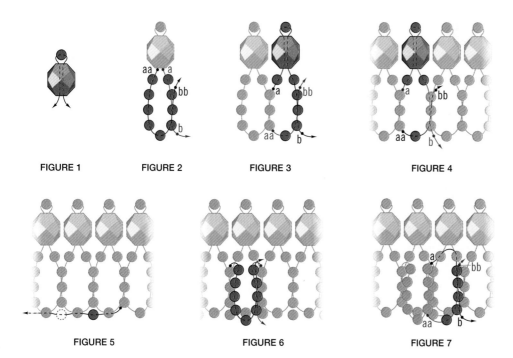

FIGURE 1   FIGURE 2   FIGURE 3   FIGURE 4

FIGURE 5   FIGURE 6   FIGURE 7

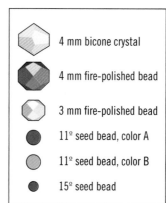
stepbystep

Rivoli bezel
Front

[1] Thread a needle on each end of 2 yd. (1.8 m) of Fireline, and center a 15º seed bead. Over both needles, pick up a 4 mm fire-polished bead (figure 1).

[2] With one needle, pick up four 15ºs (figure 2, a–b). With the other needle, pick up five 15ºs, and cross through the last three 15ºs picked up with the first needle (aa–bb).

[3] With the top needle, pick up a 15º, a 4 mm bead, and a 15º. Skip the last 15º, sew back through the 4 mm bead, and pick up four 15ºs (figure 3, a–b). With the bottom needle, pick up a 15º, and cross through the last three 15ºs picked up with the top needle (aa–bb).

[4] Repeat step 3 until you have a total of 21 4 mm beads.

[5] For the last stitch: With the top needle, pick up a 15º, a 4 mm bead, and a 15º. Skip the last 15º, sew back through the 4 mm bead, pick up a 15º, and sew through the corresponding three 15ºs of the first stitch (figure 4, a–b). With the bottom needle, pick up a 15º, and cross through the same three 15ºs (aa–bb).

[6] With the bottom needle, sew through the next 15º. Pick up a 15º, and sew through the next 15º (figure 5). Repeat to complete the round, and sew up through the next three 15ºs to exit the outer edge of the bezel.

Back

[1] With one needle, pick up four 15ºs. With the other needle, pick up five 15ºs, and cross through the four 15ºs picked up with the first needle (figure 6).

[2] With the outer needle, sew through the next two 15ºs in the outer rim before and after the next 4 mm bead, and pick up four 15ºs (figure 7, a–b). With the inner needle, pick up a 15º, and cross through the last four 15ºs picked up (aa–bb).

[3] Repeat step 2 around the bezel until you reach the first stitch.

[4] For the last stitch: With the outer needle, sew through the next two 15ºs in the outer rim before and after the next 4 mm bead, and sew

materials
pink-and-brown bracelet
6½ in. (16.5 cm)

- 18 mm crystal rivoli (Swarovski, vitrail light)
- **32** 4 mm bicone crystals (Swarovski, rose satin)
- **46** 4 mm Czech fire-polished beads (bronze)
- **16** 3 mm Czech fire-polished beads (bronze)
- 11º seed beads
  3–5 g color A (Ornela ALSB54, iris metallic dark gold)
  1 g color B (Miyuki 11-0031, 24-karat gold-plated Duracoat)
- 2–3 g 15º seed beads (Miyuki 15-457, metallic dark gold)
- lobster claw clasp
- Fireline 6 lb. test
- beading needles, #12 or #13

yellow-and-blue bracelet colors:
- 18 mm crystal rivoli (peacock eye)
- 4 mm bicone crystals (light topaz)
- 4 mm Czech fire-polished beads (smoky topaz AB)
- 3 mm Czech fire-polished beads (turquoise)
- 11º seed beads
  color A (Miyuki 11-458, metallic brown iris)
  color B (Toho 11R999, gold-lined rainbow black diamond)
- 15º seed beads (Miyuki 14-458, metallic brown iris)

Play up the pattern contrast with color.

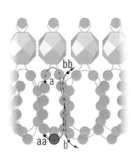

FIGURE 8

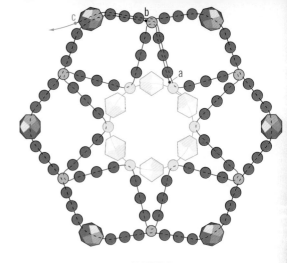

FIGURE 9

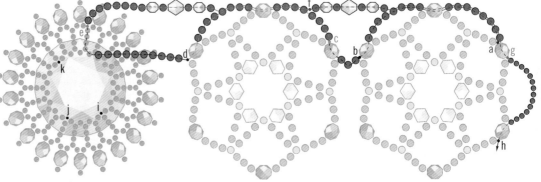

FIGURE 10

through the first four 15ºs in the next stitch **(figure 8, a–b)**. With the inner needle, pick up a 15º, and cross through the same four 15ºs **(aa–bb)**.

[5] Insert the rivoli into the bezel facing "Front."

[6] With the inner needle, sew through the next 15º in the inner rim of the bezel. Repeat around the inner rim. With the outer needle, sew through the next two 15ºs in the outer rim and the next five 15ºs to exit the inner rim. Sew through all the 15ºs in the inner rim in the opposite direction until you reach the other thread. Tie the threads with a square knot (Basics), and end the threads (Basics).

Star motifs

[1] On 24 in. (61 cm) of Fireline, pick up an alternating pattern of a color B 11º seed bead and a 4 mm bicone crystal six times, and tie the beads into a ring with a square knot, leaving a 1-in. (2.5 cm) tail. Sew through the next few beads, pulling the knot into a 4 mm to hide it, and exit a B. Trim the tail.

[2] Pick up three color A 11º seed beads, a B, and three As, skip the next 4 mm bicone in

the ring, and sew through the following B in the ring.

[3] Repeat step 2 around the ring, and step up through the first three As and B **(figure 9, a–b)**.

[4] Pick up three As, a 4 mm bead, and three As, and sew through the next B in the previous round. Repeat to complete the round, and step up through the next three As and 4 mm bead **(b–c)**. Don't end the working thread.

[5] Repeat steps 1–4 to make four "Star motifs."

Assembly

[1] Lay out the components with the "Rivoli bezel" in the center and two "Star motifs" on each side.

[2] With the working thread exiting a 4 mm bead on an end "Star motif," pick up eight As, and sew through the next 4 mm bead. Repeat once **(figure 10, a–b)**.

[3] Pick up three As, and

sew through a 4 mm bead in the next "Star motif" **(b–c)**.

[4] Repeat step 2 **(c–d)**.

[5] Pick up 10 As, and sew through a 15º in the inner ring on the back of the "Rivoli bezel" and the next four 15ºs to exit the outer rim **(d–e)**.

[6] Pick up eight As, a 3 mm fire-polished bead, an A, a 4 mm bicone, an A, a 3 mm, and an A. Skip the last four As added in step 4, and sew through the next four As, 4 mm bead, and four As **(e–f)**.

[7] Pick up an A, a 3 mm, an A, a 4 mm bicone, an A, a 3 mm, and an A. Skip the next 13 beads, and sew through the following four As, 4 mm bead, eight As, and 4 mm bead of the first "Star motif" **(f–g)**.

[8] Pick up 14 15ºs, and sew through the next 4 mm bead **(g–h)**.

[9] Repeat steps 2–7 to connect the remaining edge of this half of the bracelet, using the remaining working thread of the other motif if necessary. When connecting the "Star motif" to the "Rivoli bezel" in step 5, leave seven 15ºs on the inner rim of the bezel between the connectors **(point i)**.

[10] Repeat steps 2–9 for the remaining half of the bracelet, but in step 8, pick up six 15ºs, a lobster claw clasp, and six 15ºs. Leave four 15ºs on the inner rim of the "Rivoli bezel" between the connectors on one half of the bracelet and the connectors on the other half **(points j and k)**. End all remaining threads.

Belle
of the ball

A necklace, bracelet, or beaded bead: Go where your imagination takes you.

Stitch a versatile beaded motif that exudes romantic sophistication

designed by **Cathy Lampole**

materials

beaded motif 1 in. (2.5 cm) diameter
- crystal pearls
  4 8 mm
  12 3 mm
- **8** 4 mm bicone crystals
- **1 g** 15º seed beads
- nylon beading thread, size B
- beading needles, #12

beaded bead ⅞ x 1 in. (2.2 x 2.5 cm)
- crystal pearls (Swarovski, light gold or white)
  8 8 mm
  4 6 mm
  24 3 mm
- **12** 4 mm bicone crystals (Swarovski, light Colorado topaz AB 2X)
- **1 g** 15º seed beads (gold)
- nylon beading thread, size B
- beading needles, #12

necklace 17½ in. (44.5 cm)
- **7** beaded motifs (Swarovski, bright gold pearls and lime AB 2X bicone crystals)
- additional crystal pearls (Swarovski, bright gold)
  18 8 mm
  12 6 mm
  26 3 mm
- **12** 4 mm bicone crystals (Swarovski, lime AB 2X)
- clasp
- **4** crimp beads
- **4** crimp covers
- **2** wire guards
- flexible beading wire, .019
- chainnose pliers (optional)
- crimping pliers
- wire cutters

bracelet 7½ in. (19.1 cm)
- **5** beaded motifs (Swarovski, light gold pearls and light Colorado topaz AB 2X bicone crystals)
- **100–120** 3 mm crystal pearls (Swarovski, light gold)
- **10 g** 11º seed beads (Toho 1300, transparent alexandrite)
- **1 g** 15º seed beads (gold)
- 3-strand tube clasp
- nylon beading thread, size B
- beading needles, #12

Made with pearls, crystals, and metallic seed beads, this rich embellishment makes any piece an instant classic. Attach two motifs for a beaded bead, line them up for a necklace centerpiece, space them along a bracelet band, or invent your own ways to flaunt them in your jewelry.

step by step

Motif

[1] On 1 yd. (.9 m) of thread, pick up four 8 mm pearls, leaving a 1-in. (2.5 cm) tail. Tie the 8 mms into a ring with a square knot (Basics), pull the thread through an adjacent 8 mm, and trim the tail.

[2] Pick up four 15º seed beads, a 4 mm bicone crystal, and four 15ºs, and sew through the 8 mm your thread exited at the start of this step and the next 8 mm in the ring (**figure 1, a–b**).

[3] Pick up four 15ºs, a 4 mm, and a 15º, and sew through the first three 15ºs picked up in the previous step, the 8 mm your thread exited at the start of this step, and the next 8 mm in the ring (**b–c**). Repeat this step once (**c–d**).

[4] Sew through the adjacent three 15ºs in the first stitch. Pick up a 15º, a 4 mm, and a 15º, sew through the corresponding three 15ºs in the third stitch, and continue through the 8 mm your thread exited at the start of this step (**d–e**).

[5] Sew through the beadwork to exit a 4 mm. Pick up a 15º, and sew through the next 4 mm (**figure 2, a–b**). Repeat this step three times (**b–c**), and then sew through the beadwork to exit an 8 mm (**c–d**).

[6] Pick up a 3 mm pearl, and sew through the next 8 mm (**d–e**). Repeat this step three times, and continue through the first 3 mm picked up in this step (**e–f**).

[7] Pick up a 15º, a 3 mm, a 15º, a 4 mm, a 15º, a 3 mm, and a 15º, and sew through the next 3 mm in the previous round (**f–g**). Repeat this step three times (**g–h**). Tie a half-hitch knot (Basics) to secure the thread, but do not trim.

Beaded bead

[1] On 1½ yd. (1.4 m) of thread, work one motif. Sew through the beadwork to exit an outer-edge 4 mm.

[2] Pick up a 15º, a 6 mm pearl, and a 15º, and sew through the next outer-edge 4 mm (**figure 3, a–b**). Repeat this step three times (**b–c**), and tie a half-hitch knot, but do not trim the thread. Set this motif aside.

[3] On 1 yd. (.9 m) of thread, work steps 1–6 of "Motif."

[4] With the working thread exiting a 3 mm from step 6, pick up a 15º, a 3 mm,

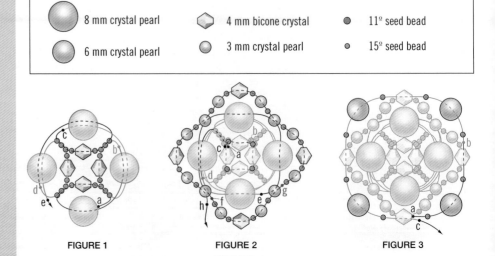

8 mm crystal pearl	4 mm bicone crystal	11º seed bead
6 mm crystal pearl	3 mm crystal pearl	15º seed bead

FIGURE 1

FIGURE 2

FIGURE 3

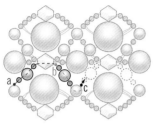

FIGURE 4

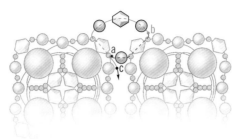

FIGURE 5

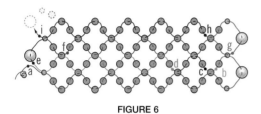

FIGURE 6

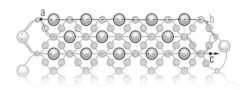

FIGURE 7

and a 15º, and sew through an outer-edge 4 mm of the first motif previously set aside (figure 4, a–b). Pick up a 15º, a 3 mm, and a 15º, and sew through the corresponding 3 mm of the second motif (b–c). Repeat this step three times to join the two motifs, and end the threads.

Necklace
[1] Make seven motifs, leaving the working thread on each motif.
[2] Sew through the beadwork of a motif to exit a 15º next to an outer-edge 4 mm (figure 5, point a).
[3] Pick up a 3 mm, and sew through a corresponding 15º, 4 mm, and 15º of another motif (a–b). Pick up a 3 mm, a 4 mm, and a 3 mm, and sew through the corresponding 15º, 4 mm, and 15º of the previous motif (b–c). Retrace the thread path to reinforce the join, and end the thread.
[4] Repeat step 3 to join all seven motifs, making all the connections along the same edge, and end all the threads.
[5] On 8 in. (20 cm) of beading wire, string a crimp bead and two 3 mms. Go through a corner 4 mm of an end motif, pick up two 3 mms, and go back through the crimp bead. Adjust the wire to leave a ¼-in. (6 mm) tail, and crimp the crimp bead (Basics).

[6] Over the wire and tail, string a 6 mm pearl, three 8 mms, a 6 mm, and a 4 mm. Repeat twice. String a crimp bead, half of a wire guard, and half of the clasp. Feed the wire through the other half of the wire guard, the crimp bead, and the next few beads strung. Adjust the wire for tension, crimp the crimp bead, and trim the tail.
[7] Repeat steps 5 and 6 on the other end of the motifs.
[8] Using chainnose or crimping pliers, close a crimp cover over each crimp.

Bracelet
[1] Make five motifs.
[2] On a comfortable length of thread, attach a stop bead (Basics), leaving a 12-in. (30 cm) tail. Pick up a 15º, 21 11º seed beads, a 15º, a 3 mm pearl, a 15º, and an 11º (figure 6, a–b).
[3] Working in netting, skip the last five beads picked up, and sew back through the next 11º (b–c).
[4] Pick up three 11ºs, skip the next three 11ºs in the previous row, and sew back through the following 11º (c–d). Repeat this step four times to the end of the row, but in the last repeat, sew through the end 15º (d–e).
[5] Pick up a 3 mm, a 15º, and an 11º, and sew through the middle 11º in the previous stitch (e–f). Work as in step 4 to the end of the row (f–g).

[6] Pick up a 3 mm, a 15º, and an 11º, and sew through the middle 11º in the previous stitch (g–h). Work as in step 4 to the end of the row (h–i).
[7] Repeat step 6 for the desired length of the bracelet.
[8] Sew half of the clasp to the backside of one end of the bracelet, and then sew pearls to fill in the gaps between the netted stitches at the end of the bracelet (figure 7, a–b).
[9] Sew two rows of pearls between the netted stitches on the front of the bracelet at this end (b–c).
[10] Using the tail, repeat steps 8 and 9 on the remaining end.
[11] Space the motifs evenly on the front of the bracelet. Using the tail of a motif, sew through the motif to exit an outer-edge 4 mm. Sew the motif to the netted band by stitching through 11ºs in the band that align with the holes of the 4 mm. Repeat to attach all four 4 mms of the motif, and end the thread. Repeat this step to attach all five motifs.

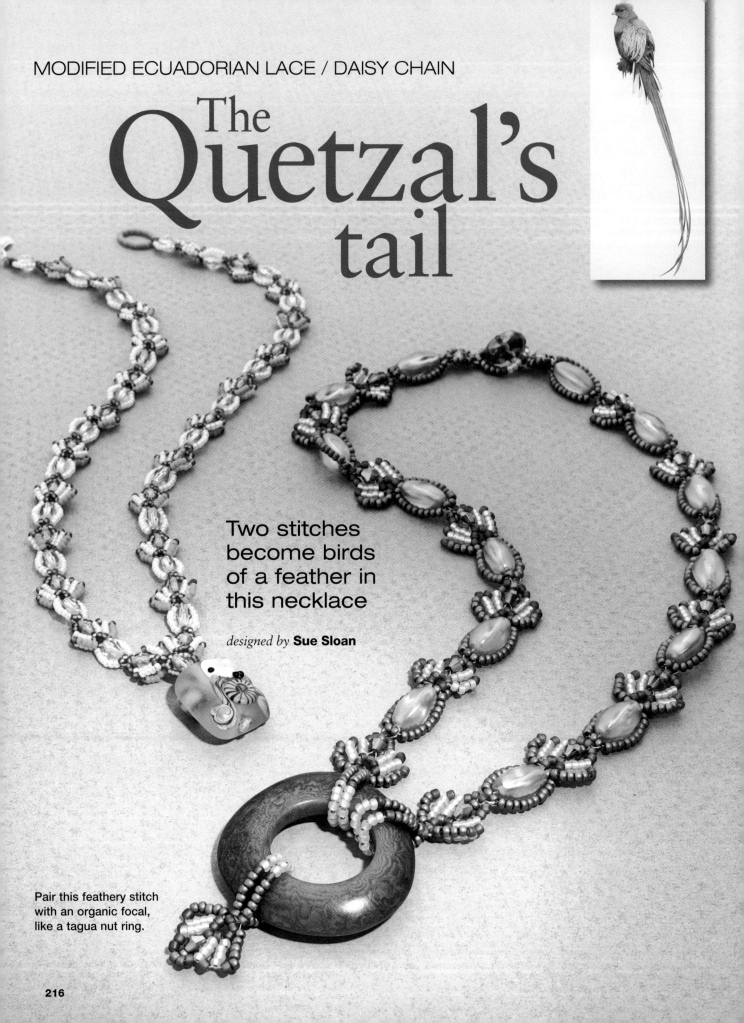

The Quetzal's tail

Two stitches become birds of a feather in this necklace

designed by **Sue Sloan**

Pair this feathery stitch with an organic focal, like a tagua nut ring.

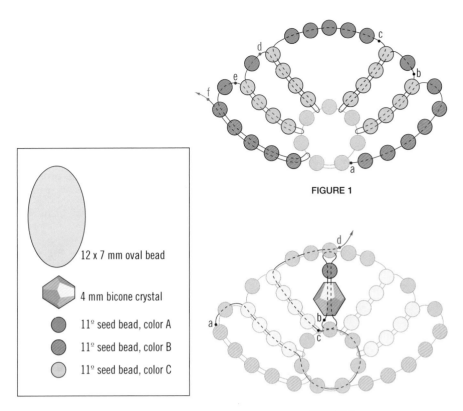

FIGURE 1

12 x 7 mm oval bead

4 mm bicone crystal

11º seed bead, color A

11º seed bead, color B

11º seed bead, color C

FIGURE 2

materials

necklace with tagua ring 20 in. (51 cm)
- 35–40 mm tagua nut ring (ecobeadstagua.etsy.com)
- 11 x 7 mm fire-polished glass rondelle (Preciosa, honey; item H20-4872GL, firemountaingems.com)
- **14** 12 x 7 mm pressed-glass oval beads (Preciosa, ocean blue with pearlized coating; item H20-4689GL, firemountaingems.com)
- **17** 4 mm bicone crystals (Swarovski, topaz)
- 11º seed beads
  4 g color A (Toho 710, matte raku vine/green iris)
  6 g color B (Toho 513F, matte nickel-plated bronze/plum iris)
  5 g color C (Toho 2217, gilt-lined aqua opal)
- Fireline 6 lb. test
- beading needles, #12

necklace with bird focal 18 in. (46 cm)
- 12 x 19 mm glass bead by Kathy Lowe (etsy.com/shop/allfiredupglassbeads)
- 11 x 7 mm fire-polished glass rondelle (Preciosa, clear; item H20-3272GL, firemountaingems.com)
- **25** 6 mm faceted fire-polished round beads (Preciosa, lemon; item H20-1208GL, firemountaingems.com)
- **26** 3 mm faceted fire-polished round beads (Preciosa, teal; H20-1133GL, firemountaingems.com)
- 15º seed beads
  2 g color A (Miyuki 158, transparent olive)
  1 g color B (Miyuki 412, opaque turquoise green)
  3 g color C (Miyuki 527, butter cream Ceylon)
- Fireline 6 lb. test
- beading needles, #13

Found in the tropical forests of Central America, the Resplendent Quetzal is a brightly colored bird with a knack for accessorizing: During mating season, males grow a pair of trailing tail feathers. This stitch, aptly based on the Ecuadorian lace technique and crossed with daisy chain, creates bright plumage perfect for capturing a tagua nut ring.

stepbystep

Neck straps

[1] On a comfortable length of Fireline, pick up seven color A 11º seed beads, and tie them into a ring with a square knot (Basics), leaving a 12-in. (30 cm) tail. Sew through the first two As in the ring.

[2] Pick up five color B 11º seed beads, an A, and four color C 11º seed beads. Sew under the thread between the next two As in the ring, and sew back through the four Cs **(figure 1, a–b)**.

[3] Pick up an A and four Cs, sew under the thread between the next two As in the ring, and sew back through the four Cs **(b–c)**.

[4] Pick up five As and four Cs, sew under the thread between the next two As in the ring, and sew back through the four Cs **(c–d)**.

[5] Repeat step 3 **(d–e)**.

[6] Pick up an A and five Bs, sew under the thread between the next two As in the ring, and sew back through the five Bs just added **(e–f)**. Continue through the A just picked up, the four Cs picked up in the previous step, and the next six As in the ring **(figure 2, a–b)**.

[7] Pick up a 4 mm bicone crystal and a B, sew through the center A in the loop above the A your thread is exiting, sew back through the B and 4 mm, and sew through the same A in the ring **(b–c)**. Retrace the thread path through the crystal embellishment, and sew through the next four Cs and three As to exit the center A in the loop above the 4 mm **(c–d)**.

[8] Pick up two Bs, sew through the A your thread exited at the start of this step, and continue through the two new Bs.

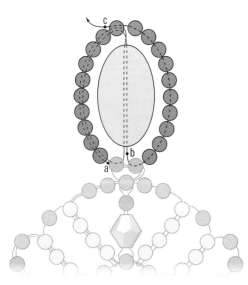

FIGURE 3

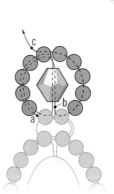

FIGURE 4

[9] Pick up nine or 10 Bs, an A, and a 12 x 7 mm oval bead. Sew through a B added in step 8, and sew through the Bs, A, and oval just picked up, positioning the loop of beads around one side of the oval (figure 3, a–b). Sew through the other B added in step 8, pick up nine or 10 Bs and an A, and sew through the A at the top of the first loop of beads, positioning the new loop around the other side of the oval (b–c). Sew through all the beads around the oval, exiting the two As at the top.

[10] Pick up five As, and sew through the two As at the top of the oval to form a new ring of As.

[11] Repeat steps 2–10 six more times or to the desired length neck strap, but in the last repeat of step 9, pick up 10 or 11 Bs to encircle each side of the oval instead of nine or 10 Bs and an A. End and add thread (Basics) as needed while you stitch, but do not end the working thread or tail when you complete the strap. Make sure you end with at least 12 in. (30 cm) of working thread, otherwise end the thread and add a new length.

[12] Make a second neck strap.

Toggle bead

[1] With the working thread from one of the neck straps, pick up two Bs, sew through the two Bs above the last oval in the strap, and continue through the two new Bs.

[2] Pick up five Bs and a 4 mm. Sew through one of the Bs added in step 1, and sew through the five Bs and 4 mm

again, positioning the loop of beads around one side of the 4 mm (figure 4, a–b). Sew through the other B picked up in step 1, pick up five Bs, and sew through the B at the top of the first loop, positioning the new loop around the other side of the 4 mm (b–c). Sew through all the beads around the 4 mm, exiting the two Bs at the top.

[3] Pick up two Bs, sew through the two Bs at the top of the 4 mm, and sew through the two new Bs again. Retrace the thread path of the connection, exiting the two new Bs.

[4] Pick up a B, an 11 x 7 mm rondelle, and an A. Skip the A, and sew back through the rondelle, the B, and the two new Bs your thread exited at the start of this step, sewing in the same direction as before. Retrace the thread path of the toggle bead, and end the working thread.

Toggle ring

[1] With the working thread from the remaining neck strap, work steps 1–3 of "Toggle bead."

[2] Pick up four Bs, an A, three Cs, an A, three Cs, an A, three Cs, an A, three Cs, an A, and four Bs. Sew through the two new Bs above the 4 mm, sewing in the same direction as before. Retrace the thread path of the toggle ring, and end the working thread.

Pendant

[1] Using the tail from a neck strap, pick up two As, sew through the two As at the bottom of the ring of As in the first stitch, and continue through the first A just added. Work a ladder stitch thread path (Basics) through the two new As to position them side by side.

[2] With your thread exiting one of the

DESIGN NOTE:

In step 9 of "Neck straps," check to make sure that each loop of beads just encircles each side of the oval. If there is thread showing between the beads in the loops, add Bs as necessary. If the loops do not hug the oval, omit Bs as needed.

DESIGN NOTES:

- To make a dainty necklace with 15° seed beads (above), use smaller fire-polished beads, and pick up fewer Bs at the start of step 9 of "Neck straps."

- To make an earring (left): Start with a ring of six color B 11° seed beads. Pick up two Bs, sew through two Bs in the ring, and continue through the two new Bs. Work as in steps 9, 10, and 2–7 (in that order) of "Neck straps," end the threads, and attach an earring finding.

new As with the needle pointing away from the beadwork, pick up five Bs, an A, nine Cs, an A, five Bs, and the tagua donut, and sew through the A your thread exited at the start of this step. Sew through the beadwork to retrace the thread path of this connection.

[3] Sew through the beadwork to exit the other A added in step 1, and repeat step 2. End the tail.

[4] Repeat steps 1–3 with the other neck strap.

Dangle

[1] On 20 in. (51 cm) of Fireline, work steps 1–7 of "Neck straps," but leave only a 6-in. (15 cm) tail in step 1. When you complete step 7, sew through the beadwork to exit the two As at the bottom of the ring of As.

[2] Work steps 1–3 of "Pendant," and end the working thread and tail.

Echoes of Nefertiti

Regal components evoke
visions of the past

designed by **Helena Tang-Lim**

Use a variety of stitches to create this regal yet wearable
design. Perfect spacing allows square beads to make
rounded components that drape beautifully.

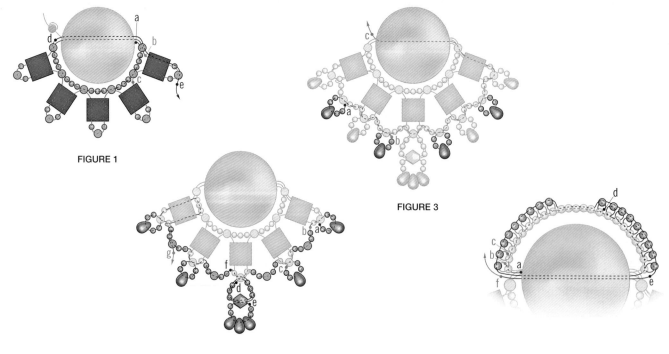

FIGURE 1

FIGURE 3

FIGURE 2

FIGURE 4

Create a museum-worthy necklace by weaving gentle curves into fan-shaped components and a coordinating toggle ring. A right-angle weave toggle bar adds an interesting element, and a twisted herringbone rope completes this lovely design.

⬤	14 mm disk bead
◼	5 mm Tila bead
⬠	3 mm bicone crystal
⬭	3 mm fringe/drop bead
●	11º seed bead
○	15º seed bead, color A
●	15º seed bead, color B

stepbystep

Small pendants

[1] On 1 yd. (.9 m) of Fireline, attach a stop bead (Basics), leaving a 6-in. (15 cm) tail. Pick up a 14 mm disk bead.
[2] Pick up an 11º seed bead and three color A 15º seed beads. Repeat this pattern four more times, and then pick up an 11º. Sew through the disk bead and the first 11º picked up in this step **(figure 1, a–b)** to create a half-ring around one edge of the disk bead.
[3] Pick up a 5 mm Tila bead, an A, an 11º, and an A, and sew through the remaining hole of the Tila bead. Sew through the next 11º in the half-ring of beads picked up in step 2 **(b–c)**. Repeat this step four times **(c–d)**.
[4] Sew through the disk bead and the next four beads, exiting the center 11º at the end of the Tila bead **(d–e)**.
[5] Pick up two As, a 3 mm drop bead, and two As. Sew through the 11º your thread exited at the start of this step to form a loop around it, and then sew through the next A at the end of the Tila bead **(figure 2, a–b)**.
[6] Pick up two As, an 11º, and two As,

and sew through the next A and 11º at the end of the next Tila bead **(b–c)**.
[7] Repeat steps 5 and 6 once **(c–d)**.
[8] Pick up three As, a 3 mm bicone crystal, and three As. Sew through the 11º your thread exited at the start of this step, and then sew through the first three As and the 3 mm crystal picked up in this step **(d–e)**. Pick up two As, three drop beads, and two As. Sew through the 3 mm crystal, the next three As, the 11º your thread exited at the start of this step, and the next A at the end of the Tila bead **(e–f)**.
[9] Repeat steps 6 and 5 twice, and then sew through the beadwork to exit the center 11º picked up in the previous stitch **(f–g)**.
[10] Pick up two As, a drop bead, and two As, and sew through the 11º your thread exited at the start of this step. Sew through the next three As, an 11º, three As, and an 11º **(figure 3, a–b)**. Repeat this step three times, but in the last repeat, sew through the beadwork to exit the disk bead **(b–c)**. End the working thread and tail (Basics).
[11] Make a total of three small pendants, but for the third small

pendant, start with 1½ yd. (1.4 m) of Fireline instead of 1 yd. (.9 m), and don't end the working thread.
[12] Pick up 23 As, and sew through the disk bead to form a half-ring around the remaining edge of the disk bead. Sew through the first A picked up in this step **(figure 4, a–b)**.
[13] Pick up an A, and sew through the A your thread exited at the start of this stitch and the next A in the half-ring **(b–c)**. Repeat this stitch eight times, sew through the next five As in the half-ring **(c–d)**, and then stitch nine As to the last nine As in the half-ring. Sew through the disk bead, the first nine As added in this step, the next five As, and the last nine As added in this step **(d–e)**. Sew through the disk bead **(e–f)**, and end the working thread.

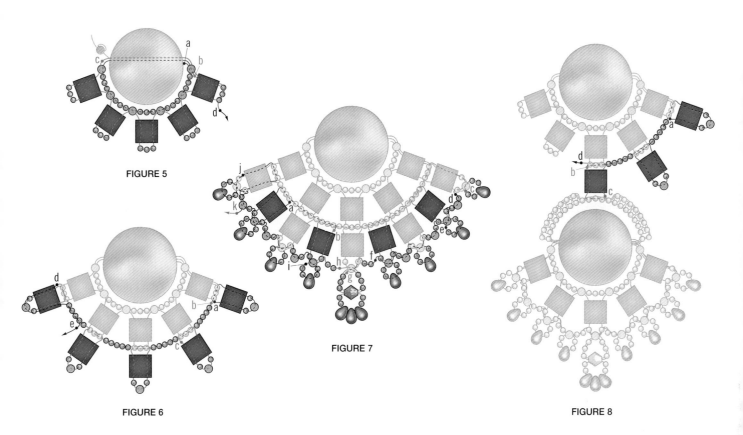

FIGURE 5

FIGURE 6

FIGURE 7

FIGURE 8

Large pendants

[1] On 2 yd. (1.8 m) of Fireline, work as in steps 1 and 2 of "Small pendants" (figure 5, a–b).

[2] Work as in step 3 of "Small pendants," but pick up three As at the end of each Tila instead of an A, an 11º, and an A (b–c).

[3] Sew through the disk bead and the next five beads, exiting the three As at the end of the Tila bead (c–d).

[4] Pick up a Tila bead, an A, an 11º, and an A. Sew through the remaining hole of the Tila bead just picked up and the three As at the end of the Tila bead in the previous row (figure 6, a–b).

[5] Pick up five As, and sew through the three As at the end of the next Tila bead in the previous row (b–c).

[6] Repeat steps 4 and 5 three times, work step 4 once more (c–d), and then sew through the beadwork to exit the last four As picked up in the previous stitch (d–e).

[7] Pick up a Tila bead, an A, an 11º, and an A, and sew through the remaining hole of the Tila bead just picked up and the three center As your thread exited at the start of this step. Sew through the next eight As (figure 7, a–b).

[8] Repeat step 7 three times, but in the last repeat, sew through only four As instead of eight.

[9] Sew through the next three beads, exiting the center 11º at the end of the Tila bead in the second row (b–c).

[10] Pick up two As, a drop bead, and two As. Sew through the 11º your thread exited at the start of this stitch and the next A (c–d).

[11] Pick up an A, an 11º, and an A, and sew through the A and 11º at the end of the next Tila bead in the second row (d–e).

[12] Repeat steps 10 and 11 twice, and then repeat step 10 (e–f).

[13] Pick up two As, and sew through the A and 11º at the end of the next Tila bead in the second row (f–g). Work as in step 8 of "Small pendant" (g–h). Pick up two As, and sew through the A and 11º at the end of the next Tila bead in the second row (h–i).

[14] Repeat steps 10 and 11 three times, and then repeat step 10 (i–j). Sew through the beadwork to exit the last 11º picked up in the previous stitch (j–k).

[15] Work as in step 10 to add a loop of two As, a drop bead, and two As to the remaining center 11ºs on both sides

of the center drop. End the working thread and tail.

[16] Repeat steps 1–15 to make a second large pendant.

[17] To begin the center large pendant, repeat steps 1–3.

[18] Repeat steps 4 and 5 twice (figure 8, a–b). Pick up a Tila bead, and sew through the three center As from the half-ring at the top of the small center pendant (b–c). Sew through the remaining hole of the Tila bead just picked up and the three As at the end of the Tila bead between the first and second rows (c–d). Retrace the thread path, exiting the three As between the Tila bead just picked up and the corresponding Tila bead in the first row of Tila beads.

[19] Repeat step 5 and 4 twice. Sew through the beadwork to exit the last four As picked up in the previous stitch.

[20] Repeat steps 7–15, but in step 13, sew through the three As between the Tila beads, omitting the crystal-and-drop embellishment.

Toggle ring

[1] On 2 yd. (1.8 m) of Fireline, pick up an 11º and three As. Repeat this pattern

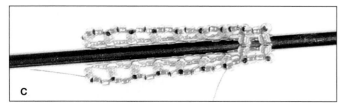

nine more times. Sew through all the beads again to form a ring, leaving a 6-in. (15 cm) tail. Exit an 11º.

[2] Pick up a Tila bead, an A, an 11º, and an A, and sew through the remaining hole of the Tila bead. Sew through the next 11º in the ring. Repeat this step nine times to complete the round.

[3] Pick up three As, and sew through the next 11º in the initial ring. Repeat to create a second layer of As in the initial ring, and exit an 11º.

[4] Pick up a Tila bead and an A. Sew through the center 11º at the top of the corresponding Tila bead in the first round of Tila beads. Pick up an A, sew through the remaining hole of the Tila bead just added, and continue through the next 11º in the initial ring **(photo a)**. Repeat this step to complete the round, and then step up through the beads to exit a center 11º at the top of a pair of Tila beads. Sew through the adjacent A above a Tila bead added in the round.

[5] Pick up two As, an 11º, and two As, and sew through the A, 11º, and A at the end of the next Tila bead in the initial ring **(photo b)**. Repeat this step nine times, exiting an 11º at the top of one of the Tila bead spokes. Sew through the adjacent 15º that you didn't sew through in the previous round.

[6] Pick up two As, and sew through the center 11º in the stitch before the next Tila bead spoke. Pick up two As, and sew through the A, 11º, and A at the end of the next Tila bead spoke. Repeat this step nine times, exiting an 11º at the top of one of the Tila spokes.

[7] Pick up nine As, and sew through

the 11º your thread exited at the start of this step. Retrace the thread path to secure the loop of As.

[8] Sew through the beadwork to exit the next 11º along the outer edge of the ring. Pick up two As, a drop bead, and two As. Sew through the 11º your thread just exited. Repeat this step 18 times, and then end the working thread and tail.

Toggle bar

[1] On 2 yd. (1.8 m) of Fireline, pick up eight As, leaving a 12-in. (30 cm) tail. Sew through the first six As again to form a ring.

[2] Working in modified right-angle weave (Basics) with two beads per side, stitch a strip eight units long. You will pick up six As per stitch and sew through the first four As picked up in each stitch to get in position to start the next stitch.

[3] Work a second row (Basics) off of the first using six As for the first stitch and four As for the subsequent stitches. Repeat this step to stitch a third row.

[4] If desired, wrap the rows of right-angle weave around a form, or fold the beadwork lengthwise to form a tube. Pick up two As per stitch **(photo c)** to work a connecting row off of the pairs of edge As in the first and third rows.

[5] Sew through a pair of As along the long edge of the tube. Pick up a color B 15º seed bead, and sew through the next pair of As along the same edge. Repeat this stitch twice, and then work one stitch with an 11º. Work three more stitches using Bs **(photo d)**.

[6] Sew through a pair of end As to

embellish the next edge as in step 5, and then use only Bs along the next edge. Repeat to embellish all the edges, and then sew through the beadwork to exit the 11º added to the center of the first edge.

[7] Pick up 10 As, and sew through the 11º your thread exited at the start of this step to form a loop. Retrace the thread path, and then sew through the beadwork to exit a pair of As along the end of the tube opposite the tail.

[8] Pick up a B, and sew through the next pair of As along the end of the tube. Repeat to add a B to each corner of the end round. Exit a corner B. Pick up an A, a 4 mm bicone crystal, and an 11º. Skip the 11º, sew back through the 4 mm and A, and sew through the corner B your thread exited at the start of this step. Sew through the next pair of As and corner B.

[9] Pick up an A, and sew through the 4 mm and 11º above it. Sew back through the 4 mm and the A just picked up, and continue through the B your thread exited at the start of this step. Sew through the next pair of As and corner B. Repeat this step twice, and then end the working thread.

[10] Repeat steps 8 and 9 using the tail.

Twisted ropes

On a comfortable length of Fireline, use alternating As and Bs to make a four-bead ladder (Basics), leaving a 20-in. (51 cm) tail. Using the ladder as a base, make a twisted tubular herringbone rope (Basics) 4¼ in. (10.8 cm) long. End and add thread (Basics) as needed, making sure to end with at least 8 in. (20 cm) of working thread when you complete the rope. Repeat to make a second rope.

Assembly

[1] Using the 20-in. (51 cm) tail from one of the ropes, pick up an 11º, a 4 mm, and an 11º, and sew through the disk bead from one of the small pendants. Pick up a repeating pattern of an 11º and a 4 mm four times, and then pick up an 11º. Sew through the disk bead from a large pendant. Pick up a repeating pattern of an 11º and a 4 mm five times, and then pick up an 11º. Sew through the disk bead from the large center pendant. String the second half of the necklace as a mirror image of the first, ending with an 11º, a 4 mm, and an 11º.

[2] Sew through an end stitch of the other rope, sewing through the end the 20-in. (51 cm) tail is exiting. Sew through the beadwork to retrace the thread path, and then end the first 20-in. (51 cm) tail. Using the 20-in. (51 cm) tail from the other rope, retrace the thread path of the strung pendants, sew through the beadwork of the first rope, and then retrace the thread path a second

time. End the second 20-in. (51 cm) tail.

[3] Using the remaining thread on one of the ropes, pick up a 4 mm, an 11º, three As, an 11º, a 4 mm, an 11º, and 10 As. Sew through the loop of As from the toggle bar, and sew back through the last 11º, 4 mm, and 11º just picked up. Pick up three As, and sew through the first 11º picked up and the following 4 mm. Sew through the beads in the last few rounds of the rope to exit a bead in the stitch opposite the one your thread exited at the start of this step. Retrace the thread path of the toggle connection, and end the thread.

[4] With the remaining thread on the other rope, pick up a 4 mm, an 11º, and 10 As. Sew through the loop of As from the toggle ring, and sew back through the last 11º and 4 mm picked up. Sew through the beads in the last few rounds of the rope to exit a bead in the stitch opposite the one your thread exited at the start of this step. Retrace the thread path, and end the thread.

materials

necklace 18 in. (46 cm)

- **6** 14 mm disk beads (Czech, matte bronze peacock)
- **77** 5 mm Tila beads (Miyuki 2006, matte metallic dark bronze)
- **25** 4 mm bicone crystals (Swarovski, crystal Dorado)
- **5** 3 mm bicone crystals (Swarovski, crystal Dorado)
- **5 g** 3 mm fringe/drop beads (Magatama, metallic bronze)
- **2 g** 11º seed beads (gold)
- **15º** seed beads
  8 g color A (Toho 557, metallic gold)
  4 g color B (Miyuki 462, metallic rainbow bronze)
- Fireline 6 lb. test
- beading needles, #12

Fool for flowers

This handsome bracelet is a great project if you want to use up those odds and ends in your bead stash.

At first glance, this fetching floral cuff appears to be bead embroidery, but don't be fooled

designed by **Tamara Scott**

The dramatic elements in this bracelet are stitched separately and then sewn to a suede or leather cuff and embellished with a few simple back-stitched swirls.

step by step

Vine

[1] On 1 yd. (.9 m) of Fireline, pick up a color B 15º seed bead and a color A 11º seed bead, and sew through the B again (figure 1, a–b), leaving a 6-in. (15 cm) tail.

[2] Pick up a B and an A, sew down through the A added in the previous stitch (b–c), and sew up through the B added in the previous stitch and the B just picked up (c–d). Repeat this stitch for a total of 10 rows. The vine will begin to curve.

[3] Continue to work the vine:

Rows 11–27: Work as in step 2 using all As. This will create a straight section in the vine.

Rows 28–34: Work as in step 2, but flip-flop the As and Bs to form a curve going in the opposite direction of the first curve.

Rows 35–48: Use all As.

Rows 49–55: Work as in step 2.

Rows 56–71: Use all As.

Rows 72–78: Work as in step 2, but flip-flop the As and Bs.

Rows 79–95: Use all As.

Rows 96–102: Work as in step 2, and end the threads (Basics).

Leaves

[1] On 12 in. (30 cm) of nylon thread, pick up two Bs, and sew through the first B again (figure 2, a–b), leaving a 6-in. (15 cm) tail.

[2] Pick up two As, and sew through the Bs in the previous row and the first A just added (b–c).

[3] Pick up two As, and sew through the As in the previous row and the first A just added (c–d).

[4] Pick up two Bs, and sew through the As in the previous row and the first B just added (d–e).

[5] Pick up a B, and sew through the next B in the previous row (e–f) and the rest of the beads in the column (f–g).

[6] Pick up an A, and sew through the adjacent B (g–h). End the threads.

[7] Make a total of six leaves.

materials

bracelet 7¼ in. (18.4 cm)

- **2** 10 x 2½-in. (25 x 6.4 cm) strips of suede, leather, or Ultrasuede
- **2** 4 mm pearls (Swarovski, antique gold)
- **3** mm pearl (Swarovski, antique gold)
- **6** 3 mm bicone crystals (Swarovski, turquoise AB2X)
- **8º** seed beads
  2 g color C (Miyuki 1052, galvanized gold)
  1 g color H (Miyuki 457L, metallic light bronze)
  4 g color I (Toho 1700, gilded marble white)
  1 g color K (Miyuki 2426, silver-lined Montana blue)
- **11º** seed beads
  8 g color A (Toho 512F, metallic nickel-plated sage)
  2 g color D (Toho 1201, marbled opaque beige)
  9 g color E (Toho 46L, opaque terra cotta)
  6 g color F (Toho 152F, matte transparent grey AB)
  6 g color H (Miyuki 457L, metallic light bronze)
  2 g color L (Miyuki 592, antique ivory pearl Ceylon)
- **15º** seed beads
  3 g color B (Miyuki 2008, matte metallic patina)
  3 g color G (Miyuki 429, opaque salmon)
  5 g color H (Miyuki 457L, metallic light bronze)
  1 g color J (Miyuki 2002, matte metallic silver grey)
  3 g color M (Miyuki 551, Ceylon silver)
  2 g color N (Miyuki 003, silver-lined gold)
- 10 mm snap
- Fireline 6 lb. test
- nylon beading thread
- beading needles, #12
- glovers needles, #12

● 4 mm pearl	
● 8º seed bead, color C	
● 8º seed bead, color I	
● 8º seed bead, color K	
● 11º seed bead, color A	
● 11º seed bead, color D	
● 11º seed bead, color E	
● 11º seed bead, color F	
● 11º seed bead, color H	
● 15º seed bead, color B	
● 15º seed bead, color J	
● 15º seed bead, color G	
● 15º seed bead, color N	
● 15º seed bead, color H	

FIGURE 1

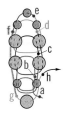

FIGURE 2

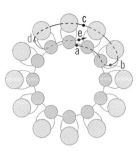

FIGURE 3

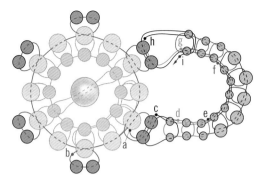

FIGURE 4

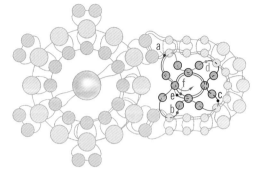

FIGURE 5

Large flower

[1] On 1 yd. (.9 m) of nylon thread, pick up a color E 11º seed bead and a color C 8º seed bead, and sew through the E again, leaving a 6-in. (15 cm) tail.

[2] Pick up an E and a C, and sew down through the C in the previous row, up through the E in the previous row, and up through the E just added. Repeat this step for a total of 12 rows.

[3] Join the ends to form a ring: Sew through the first two Es at the starting end of the strip **(figure 3, a–b)**, and sew through the first two Cs in the opposite direction **(b–c)**. Sew through the last two Cs on the other end of the strip **(c–d)**, being careful not to twist the strip. Sew back through the last two Es on this end of the strip **(d–e)**. Retrace the thread path to secure, and sew through the beadwork to exit an E on the inside of the ring. The Es will sit up on the Cs.

[4] Pick up a 4 mm pearl, and sew through an E on the opposite side of the ring. Sew back through the 4 mm and the E your thread exited at the start of this step. Retrace

the thread path, and sew through the beadwork to exit a C.

[5] Pick up two color F 11º seed beads, and sew through the C your thread exited at the start of this step and the next two Cs in the ring **(figure 4, a–b)**. Repeat this step to complete the round, and step up through the first two Fs added in this step **(b–c)**.

[6] Pick up two color G 15º seed beads, and sew through the previous two beads and the first G just added **(c–d)**. Repeat this step two more times **(d–e)**.

[7] Pick up a G and a color D 11º seed bead, and sew through the previous two beads and the G just added. Repeat this step four more times **(e–f)**.

[8] Pick up two Gs, and sew through the previous two beads and the first G just added. Repeat this step two more times **(f–g)**.

[9] To form a petal, sew through the next two Fs along the outer edge of the original ring **(g–h)** and the last two Gs added in step 8. Retrace the thread path, and exit the inside G in the last stitch added in step 8 **(h–i)**.

[10] Pick up three Gs, and sew through the corresponding G on the other side of the petal **(figure 5, a–b)**. Pick up three Gs, skip the next two Gs along the inside edge of the petal, and sew through the next G **(b–c)**. Repeat this last stitch twice, but in the first repeat skip three Gs **(c–d)**, and in the second repeat skip two Gs, and then step up through the first two Gs added in this step **(d–e)**.

[11] Sew through the center G in each set of three picked up in step 10 **(e–f)**. Retrace the thread path through all four center Gs. Sew through the beadwork to exit the next pair of Fs along the outer

edge of the original ring.

[12] Repeat steps 6–11 five times, and end the threads.

Medium flower

[1] On 18 in. (46 cm) of nylon thread, leaving a 6-in. (15 cm) tail, work as in steps 1–4 of "Large flower" using color H 11º seed beads and color K 8º seed beads.

[2] With the thread exiting a K, pick up two color J 15º seed beads, and sew through the K again and the first J just added **(figure 6, a–b)**.

[3] Pick up two color I 8º seed beads, and sew through the previous two Js and the first I just added **(b–c)**. Pick up an F, and sew through the two Is added in this step **(c–d)**.

[4] Pick up five Fs, and sew through the next I **(d–e)**, the following J, the K your thread exited in step 2, and the next two Ks in the original ring **(e–f)**.

[5] Repeat steps 2–4 for a total of six petals. End the threads.

[6] Repeat steps 1–5 to make another medium flower, but substitute Gs for Js, Hs for Ks, and a 3 mm pearl for the 4 mm pearl.

DESIGN NOTE:
The bead colors listed in the Materials list on p. 225 can be used simply as a guide to make this cuff using small amounts of beads you have left over from other projects.

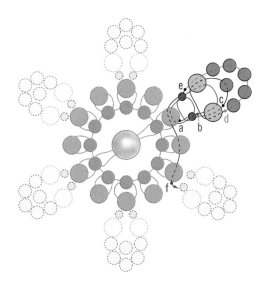

FIGURE 7

FIGURE 8

FIGURE 6

Small flower

[1] On 18 in. (46 cm) of nylon thread, pick up 10 color B 15º seed beads, leaving a 6-in. (15 cm) tail. Tie the beads into a ring with a square knot (Basics), and sew through the next three Bs in the ring, tugging gently on the working thread to hide the knot in a bead.
[2] Pick up two color H 11º seed beads, sew through the next B in the ring and the B your thread exited at the start of this step, and then sew through the first H just added (figure 7, a–b).
[3] Pick up a color N 15º seed bead, and sew through the previous two Hs (b–c).
[4] Pick up five Ns, sew through the adjacent H, the two Bs sewn through in step 2, and the next two Bs in the original ring (c–d).
[5] Repeat steps 2–4 for a total of five petals.
[6] With the thread exiting a B in the original ring, pick up a 3 mm bicone crystal, sew through a B on the opposite side of the ring, and sew back through the 3 mm and the B your thread exited at the start of this step. End the threads.

[7] Repeat steps 1–6 for a total of three small flowers.
[8] Repeat steps 1–6 to make three more flowers, but substitute color M 15º seed beads for the center N in step 3 and color L 11º seed beads for the Ns in step 4.

Band

[1] Measure your wrist. Cut a 2¼-in. (5.7 cm) wide band of suede, leather, or Ultrasuede that is equal to the length of your wrist plus 2 in. (5 cm). If desired, round one end by trimming the corners.
[2] Cut a second band exactly the same size for the backing.
[3] Determine which side of the top band is the front, and place the vine in the desired position. Tie a knot at one end of 12 in. (30 m) of nylon thread, and thread a #12 glovers needle on the other end. Tack the vine to the top band by sewing from back to front through the band near the center of the vine. Sew over the thread bridge between a 15º and an 11º, and then sew back down through the band. Repeat two or three times to secure the center of the vine, and

end the thread by tying a knot on the back side of the band.
[4] Repeat step 3 for each of the curves in the vine. End the thread after each curve; do not run it across the back of the band as this will cause it to pucker. Make sure the vine lies flat on the band.
[5] Working in beaded back-stitch (Basics), sew a swirl at each end of the vine using As and Bs, and end the thread after each one.
[6] Position the other components as desired, and tack them down to the top band, working from one end of the band to the other.
[7] Position the ball half of the snap at the center of the straight end on the top side of the band, approximately ½ in. (1.3 cm) from the edge, and sew it in place securely.
[8] Determine the outer surface of the backing band. Mark the desired position of the socket half of the snap on the outer surface of the backing in the center near the curved end. Align the backing and the embroidered top band back to back, checking that the ball half of

the snap lines up with the mark for the socket half.
[9] Sew the socket half of the snap in place securely.

Edging

[1] Position the top and bottom bands back to back, matching the edges. Add 2 yd. (1.8 m) of nylon thread by sewing through the top band from back to front and making several small stitches along the edge, leaving a 2-in. (5 cm) tail.
[2] Pick up a color E 11º seed bead, a color H 15º seed bead, and an E, and sew down through both layers of the band from front to back. Sew back through the last E added, and snug up the beads (figure 8, a–b).
[3] Pick up an H and an E, and sew through both layers of the band from front to back about 3 mm from where your thread exited. Sew back through the last E (b–c).
[4] Repeat step 3 for the entire edge of the bracelet. End the thread.

Natural surroundings

A multi-stitch beaded bezel and tubular bracelet straps provide the perfect environment for a stone cabochon

designed by **Deborah Hermanson-Pulos**

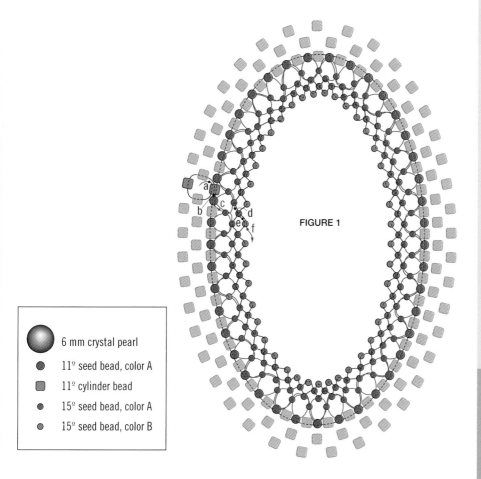

FIGURE 1

materials

copper bracelet 7½ in. (19.1 cm)

- 28 x 40 mm oval cabochon (brecciated jasper, firemountaingems.com)
- 12 6 mm crystal pearls (Swarovski, dark grey)
- 6–7 g 11º seed beads in each of **2** colors: A (metallic dark copper), B (gunmetal)
- 1–2 g 11º cylinder beads (gunmetal iris)
- 1 g 15º seed beads in each of 2 colors: A (metallic dark copper), B (gunmetal)
- 3-strand slide clasp
- nylon beading thread, size D
- beading needles, #12

Legend:

- 6 mm crystal pearl
- 11º seed bead, color A
- 11º cylinder bead
- 15º seed bead, color A
- 15º seed bead, color B

DESIGN NOTE:

A cabochon has a flat back and rounded front, but the height of the front varies from cab to cab. As you work, adjust the number of rounds to customize the beaded bezel to fit snugly against both the front and the back.

An organic focal deserves a custom setting, such as this fitted bezel made by combining right-angle weave and peyote stitch. Herringbone straps accented with crystal pearls show off the centerpiece to maximum effect.

stepbystep

Beaded bezel

[1] On 3 yd. (2.7 m) of thread, center four 11º cylinder beads. Working in right-angle weave (Basics), make a strip of beadwork 41 stitches long, or until the strip surrounds the outer edge of the 28 x 40 mm cabochon. Form the strip into a ring (Basics and **figure 1, a–b**), and exit an edge cylinder.

[2] Pick up a color A 11º seed bead, and sew through the next edge cylinder in the ring. Repeat this stitch to complete the round, and then step up through the first A 11º picked up in this step (**b–c**).

[3] Add a round of right-angle weave (Basics) using color A 15º seed beads, working off the A 11ºs in the previous round. Exit an edge A 15º (**c–d**).

[4] Pick up an A 15º, and sew through the next edge A 15º in the previous round. Repeat this stitch to complete the round, and then step up through the first A 15º picked up in this step (**d–e**).

[5] Pick up a color B 15º seed bead, and sew through the next A 15º in the previous round. Repeat this stitch to complete the round, and then step up through the first B 15º picked up in this step (**e–f**). Don't end this thread.

[6] Place the cabochon face up in the center of the bezel so that the back of the cabochon sits on the rounds just completed. If the cabochon has a tall profile, use the tail to add another round of right-angle weave using cylinders, working off the edge cylinders in the initial ring. Exit an edge cylinder in the new round.

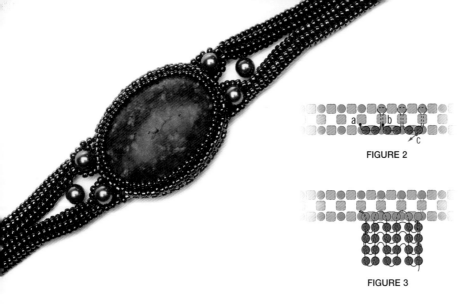

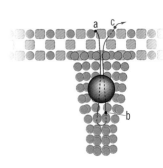

FIGURE 2

FIGURE 3

FIGURE 4

[7] Using the tail, repeat steps 2, 3, and 5 around the front surface of the cabochon. Retrace the thread path through the last round to snug up the beads against the front surface of the cabochon. End the tail (Basics).

[8] Using the remaining thread, retrace the thread path through the last round on the back of the bezel to snug up the beads against the back surface of the cabochon. End the thread.

Herringbone straps

[1] Add 1 yd. (.9 m) of thread (Basics) to one end of the bezel, leaving a 12-in. (30 cm) tail. Sew through the beadwork to exit a center cylinder in the initial ring where you would like to attach the first strap, with your thread pointing toward the bottom of the bezel (figure 2, point a). If you stitched another round of cylinders in step 6, exit the center cylinder in the round closest to the front surface.

[2] Pick up two A 11ºs, sew through the next cylinder in the opposite direction, sew through the adjacent A 11º in the bezel, and then sew back through the cylinder your thread just exited (a–b). Repeat this stitch two more times, exiting the last A 11º added (b–c).

[3] Working off the A 11ºs picked up in the previous step, work four rows of flat herringbone stitch (Basics) using A 11ºs for a total of five rows. Make an invisible turn at the end of each row by sewing under the thread bridge between the two previous edge beads and exiting the last two edge 11ºs (figure 3).

[4] Switch from flat herringbone to tubular herringbone stitch: Work a row of A 11ºs, but after the last stitch, fold the strip of beadwork in half so the edges face upward, toward the front surface of the cabochon, creating a space for a pearl embellishment. Sew up through the last two A 11ºs along the opposite edge.

[5] Continue in tubular herringbone (Basics) for a total of 14 rounds using A 11ºs. End the working thread.

[6] Using the tail, sew through the beads in the bezel to exit a cylinder or an A 11º along the top edge opposite the end pair of A 11ºs at the top of the herringbone tube. Pick up a 6 mm pearl, and sew through the end pair of A 11ºs in the tube (figure 4, a–b). Sew back through the pearl and the bead adjacent to the bead your thread exited at the start of this step (b–c). Retrace the thread path. End the tail.

[7] Repeat steps 1–6 next to the first row of As with the following changes:
• In step 1, add 3 yd. (2.7 m) of thread instead of 1 yd. (.9 m), and exit a center cylinder in the initial ring adjacent to the one you exited for the previous tube.
• Use color B 11º seed beads instead of A 11ºs.
• In step 5, don't end the working thread.
• In step 6, don't end the tail.

[8] To add a pearl embellishment between the two tubes, use the tail to sew through the beadwork, exiting a B 11º in the third round of tubular herringbone closest to the tube of A 11ºs. Pick up a pearl, and sew through a corresponding A 11º in the third round of the other tube. Sew back through the pearl and the B 11º your thread exited at the start of this step. Retrace the thread path a few times, and end the tail.

[9] Flatten the ends of the two tubes so there are three As and three Bs across the front and back of the tubes. Using the working thread, work a herringbone stitch thread path through the last round to connect the two tubes without picking up any new beads.

[10] Continue working in tubular herringbone to create one large tube by picking up A 11ºs and B 11ºs in the established pattern. Work a total of 22 rounds or until the tube is 1 in. (2.5 cm) short of the desired length.

[11] Retrace the thread path through the last round until you reach the back of the tube (opposite the front surface of the cabochon). Work five rows of flat herringbone using A 11ºs and B 11ºs in the established pattern, creating a short tab. Sew through the beadwork to exit an end bead in the last round on the front of the tube.

[12] Pick up a pearl, sew through the corresponding bead in the last row of the tab, continue through the adjacent bead, sew back through the pearl, and sew through the bead adjacent to the bead your thread exited at the start of this step. Sew through the next bead in the last round on the front of the tube.

[13] Repeat step 12 twice to add a total of three pearls, and then sew through the beadwork to exit the end bead in the last row of the tab.

[14] Sew through an end loop of half of the clasp and the next two beads in the end row. Repeat this connection twice, retrace the thread path to secure the connections, and end the thread.

[15] Repeat steps 1–14 on the other end of the bezel.

Supernova

Bezeled crystal stones and embellished ladders create an exciting explosion of beadwork

designed by **Kelli Burns**

Metal seed beads surround rivolis in a fine setting, while carefully placed glass seed beads incorporate just the right amount of color.

materials

silver necklace 18 in. (46 cm)

- 27 mm crystal stone (Swarovski, peacock)
- 4 18 mm rivolis (Swarovski, peacock)
- 8 4 mm rondelles (Chinese crystal, brown iris)
- 2 g 11º triangle beads (Toho 714, metallic silver)
- 5–6 g 11º metal seed beads, color A (silver)
- 2–3 g 11º seed beads, color B (Toho 714, metallic silver)
- 1–2 g 11º seed beads, color C (Toho 929, light yellow/capri-lined rainbow)
- 2 g 15º metal seed beads, color D (silver)
- clasp
- 12 in. (30 cm) chain
- 4 6 mm jump rings
- Fireline 6 lb. test
- beading needles, #12
- 2 pairs of pliers
- wire cutters

gold necklace colors:

- 27 mm crystal stone (Swarovski, crystal AB)
- 18 mm rivolis (Swarovski, crystal AB)
- 4 mm round beads, substituted for rondelles (Chinese crystal, blue iris)
- 11º triangle beads (Toho 712, metallic gold)
- 11º metal seed beads, color A (gold)
- 11º seed beads, color B (Toho 712, metallic gold)
- 11º seed beads, color C (Toho 2224, silver-lined purple)
- 15º metal seed beads, color D (gold)

Incorporate ladder stitch, modified herringbone stitch, picot techniques, and tubular peyote to turn bezeled rivolis into a solar system to orbit your neck.

step by step

Bezeled crystals
18 mm rivolis

[1] On 1 yd. (.9 m) of Fireline, pick up 36 color A 11º metal seed beads, leaving a 12-in. (30 cm) tail. Sew through all the beads again to form a ring, and sew through the first A again.

[2] Work four rounds of tubular peyote stitch (Basics) using As and two rounds using color D 15º metal seed beads, stepping up after each round. Retrace the thread path through the last two rounds, and end the working thread (Basics).

[3] Place the 18 mm rivoli into the bezel so the back of the crystal sits against the rounds of Ds.

[4] Using the tail, work two rounds using As and one round using Ds. Retrace the thread path through the last two rounds, and end the tail.

[5] Bezel a total of four 18 mm rivolis.

27 mm crystal stone

[1] On 1½ yd. (1.4 m) of Fireline, pick up 54 As, leaving a 12-in. (30 cm) tail. Sew through the first A picked up.

[2] Work a total of four rounds of tubular peyote stitch using As and two rounds using Ds, stepping up after each round. Retrace the thread path through the last two rounds, but don't end the working thread.

[3] Place the 27 mm crystal stone into the bezel so the back sits against the round of Ds.

[4] Using the tail, work one round using As and one round using Ds. Retrace the thread path through the last two rounds, and end the tail.

Embellished links
Sunburst links

[1] On 1½ yd. (1.4 m) of Fireline, work in ladder stitch (Basics) using triangle beads to make a ladder 18 beads long, leaving a 10-in. (25 cm) tail. The triangle beads will nestle together as shown in **figure 1**. Flip the ladder over so the working thread is exiting the top of the end triangle.

[2] Work in accelerated herringbone stitch: Pick up an A, two color B 11º seed beads, and an A. Sew down through the next triangle in the ladder and up through the following triangle **(figure 2, a–b)**. Repeat this step to complete the row, exiting the last triangle in the ladder **(b–c)**. The beadwork will begin to curve as you add subsequent rows.

[3] Flip the beadwork over, and add a picot edging on the opposite side of the ladder: Pick up a color C 11º seed bead, a B, and a C, and sew down through next triangle in the ladder, up through the following triangle, and then back through the last C added **(figure 3, a–b)**. Pick up a B and a C, and sew down through the next triangle in the ladder, up through the following triangle, and

---

4 mm rondelle

11º triangle bead

11º metal seed bead, color A

11º seed bead, color B

11º seed bead, color C

15º metal seed bead, color D

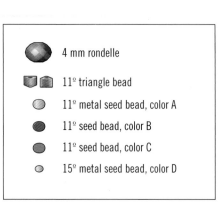

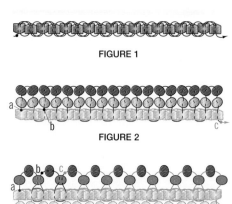

FIGURE 1

FIGURE 2

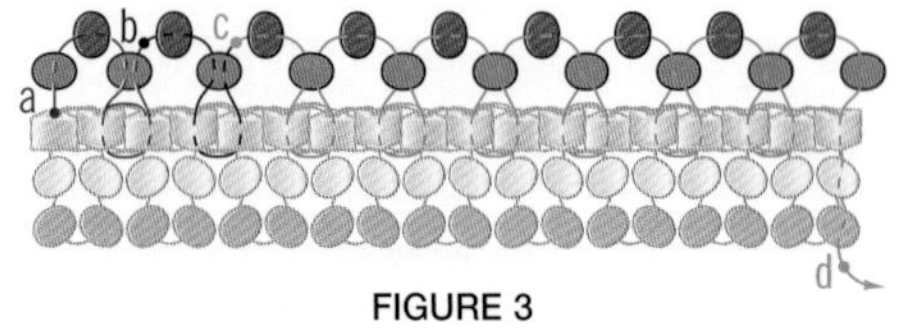

FIGURE 3

then back through the last C picked up
(b–c). Repeat this last stitch to complete
the row, but for the last repeat, sew
down through the last triangle, and
continue through the next A and B
on the other side of the ladder (c–d).
[4] Pick up an A, a B, a 4 mm rondelle,
and three Ds. Skip the three Ds, and sew
back through the rondelle. Pick up a B
and an A, and sew down through the
next B, A, and triangle (figure 4, a–b).
Sew up through the next triangle in the
ladder and the adjacent A and B (b–c).
[5] Pick up an A, a B, three Ds, a B, and
an A, and sew down through the next B,
A, and triangle. Sew up through the next
triangle in the ladder and the adjacent A
and B (c–d). Repeat this step twice (d–e).
[6] Repeat steps 4 and 5 once (e–f), and
then repeat step 4, exiting the last triangle
in the ladder (f–g). Sew through the
beadwork so the working thread and
tail are exiting opposite ends of the link.
Don't end the working thread or tail.
[7] Make a second sunburst link.

Curved links

[1] Work as in steps 1–3 of "Sunburst
link," but in step 1, make a ladder 14
beads long instead of 18.
[2] Work step 5, then step 4, and then
step 5 again. Sew through the beadwork
so the working thread and tail are exiting opposite ends of the link. Don't end
the working thread or tail.
[3] Make a second curved link.

Assembly

[1] Using the working thread from a
curved link, sew through three As along
the outer edge of an 18 mm bezeled

Gold lends a regal
feel and allows the
crystal tones to
really shine.

rivoli and through the end triangle
your thread exited at the start of this
step. Retrace the thread path, and sew
through the As along the outer edge of
the bezel to exit the A before the three
corresponding As opposite the join. To
make a loop that you'll use to attach a
chain, pick up six As, skip three As in
the bezel, and sew through the next A in
the bezel. Sew through the beadwork to
retrace the thread path through the loop
of As, and end the working thread.
[2] Using the tail from the same curved
link, sew through three As along the
outer edge of a new 18 mm bezeled
rivoli and back through the end triangle
of the curved link. Retrace the thread
path, and end the thread.
[3] Using the tail from a sunburst link,
sew through an A on the opposite edge
of the bezeled rivoli joined in step 2
so the sunburst link will sit centered
opposite the join of the curved link.

Sew back through the end triangle
of the sunburst link, retrace the thread
path, and end the tail. Using the working
thread from the same sunburst link,
repeat the join, and sew through the
beadwork to exit the center D of the
middle herringbone spoke.
[4] Repeat steps 1–3 with the remaining
links and 18 mm bezeled rivolis.
[5] Connect the bezeled 27 mm crystal
stone: Using the working thread from one
of the sunburst links, pick up a D, and
sew through an A along the outer edge
of the 27 mm crystal bezel. Continue
through the next 10 As in the bezel, and
pick up a D. Sew through the center D
of the middle herringbone spoke of the
other sunburst link. Pick up a D, and
sew through the next A along the outer
edge of the bezel. Continue sewing
through the outer edge of the bezel until
you reach the first sunburst link added.
Pick up a D, sew through the center D
of the middle herringbone spoke, sew
back through the beadwork of the
sunburst link, and end the thread. Use
the working thread from the other
sunburst link to retrace the thread path
of the join of the two sunburst links to
the 27 mm bezeled crystal stone.
[6] Cut two 6-in. (15 cm) pieces of
chain. Open a jump ring (Basics), and
attach one end of a chain to the loop
on an end 18 mm bezeled rivoli. Open
a jump ring, and attach half of the clasp
to the other end of the same chain.
Attach the remaining chain and clasp
half on the other end of the necklace.

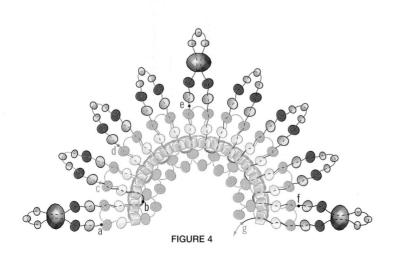

FIGURE 4

233

Other
Techniques

CROCHET
Floral abundance

Chain stitch seed beads and sequins into a bountiful necklace

designed by **Un-Roen Manarata**

An abundance of flower sequins float on airy strands of crocheted thread, creating a lovely, lightweight necklace with a bold but playful look.

step by step

[1] On a full spool of thread, string nine 11º seed beads and one sequin. Repeat this pattern, varying the number of 11ºs if desired (but always picking up a multiple of three), until you have strung all the beads and sequins.

[2] Leaving a 4-in. (10 cm) tail, make a slip knot (Basics), and insert the crochet hook into it. Crochet 20 chain stitches (Basics) without beads.

[3] Slide three beads up to the hook, and work a chain stitch (photo a), and then work six to eight chain stitches without beads. Repeat this step three times or until you reach a sequin.

[4] Slide a sequin up to the hook, and work a chain stitch (photo b), and then work six to eight chain stitches without beads.

[5] Repeat steps 3 and 4 (photo c), until the strand is about ¾ in. (1.9 cm) short

Enjoy the soothing rhythm of crochet with this multistrand necklace featuring seed beads and sequins.

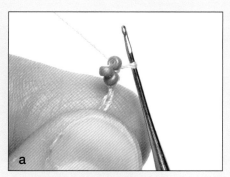

a

b

c

d

materials

necklace 17 in. (43 cm)

- 125–250 (2–4 g) 10 mm flower sequins (green/blue rainbow; Craftaroo, craftaroo.com)
- 10–14 g 11º seed beads (Toho 412, opaque turquoise)
- 2 8 mm fold-over cord crimp ends
- 2 5 mm jump rings
- lobster claw clasp with tag or soldered ring
- C-Lon beading thread, size D
- beading needle, #12
- crochet hook, 1.25–1.5 mm
- 2 pairs of pliers, including chainnose
- G-S Hypo Cement

DESIGN NOTES:

- If you don't want to string all the beads and sequins at once, string enough for a single strand (about 15 sequins), and then crochet it to the desired length. Repeat for the remaining strands.
- If desired, finish the necklace with cones instead of crimp ends: Cut 3 in. (7.6 cm) of 22-gauge wire, and make a wrapped loop (Basics). Slide one end of each cord into the loop, and tie them all with a square knot (Basics). Trim the cords close to the knot, and dot the knot with glue. Slide a cone and an accent bead onto the wire, and make the first half of a wrapped loop. Attach half of the clasp, and complete the wraps. Repeat on the other end.

of the desired length. Work 20 stitches without beads, and trim the thread, leaving a 4-in. (10 cm) tail. Pull the tail through the last loop, and set the strand aside.

[6] Repeat steps 2–5 to crochet a total of 10–15 separate strands with the remaining beads and sequins strung in step 1.

[7] Bundle the strands at one end, place them into a crimp end, dot them with

G-S Hypo Cement, and use chainnose pliers to fold the sides over the cords (**photo d**). Trim the cords close to the crimp end. Repeat on the other end of the strands.

[8] Open a jump ring (Basics), and attach one crimp end and half of the clasp. Repeat at the other end, attaching the other half of the clasp.

Byzantine balance

Alternating
Byzantine links
take a plain jump
ring bracelet to the
next level

designed by **Scott David Plumlee**

At first glance, Byzantine chain appears very complex, but it is actually considered to be a good beginning weave. Easily recognizable by its intriguing textural design, the Byzantine pattern has also been called "Bird cage," "Fool's dilemma," and "Bird's nest."

a

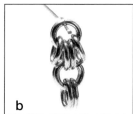

b

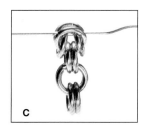

c

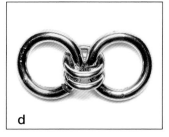

d

e

f

materials

bronze bracelet 7½ in. (19.1 cm)

- **290** 3.1 mm inner-diameter (ID) jump rings, 19-gauge (bronze)
- **21** 5 mm ID jump rings, 15-gauge (bronze)
- S-clasp
- 2 pairs of flatnose pliers

tri-colored bracelet colors:

- 3.1 mm inner-diameter (ID) jump rings, 19-gauge
  252 (silver)
  38 (copper)
- 5 mm ID jump rings, 15-gauge (bronze)

stepbystep

Byzantine links

[1] Open 180 and close 72 3.1 mm jump rings (Basics).

[2] Slide two closed rings onto an open ring, and close it. Slide another open ring through the same two closed rings, and close it. This is called doubling. Separate the ring pairs to make the start of a 2+2 chain.

[3] Slide an open ring through a pair of rings, slide on two more closed rings, and close the open ring. Double the new ring. Continue in this manner until the 2+2 chain is five pairs long (photo a).

[4] Flip back the last two rings added, letting them fall one to each side (photo b). Separate the uppermost rings. Using a piece of scrap wire, reach between the uppermost rings, and thread the wire through the two flipped rings (photo c). Slide an open ring into this spot, replacing the scrap wire, and close the ring. Double the new ring.

[5] Repeat step 4 on the other end of the chain, creating a Byzantine link.

[6] Repeat steps 2–5 to make 18 Byzantine links.

Assembly

[1] Open 38 3.1 mm jump rings, and close 20 5 mm jump rings. Slide two closed 5 mm rings onto an open 3.1 mm ring, and close it. Double the 3.1 mm ring. Spread out the rings to make a 1+2+1 chain (photo d). Continue in this manner until you have attached all the 3.1 mm rings.

[2] Open the 5 mm ring on one end of the chain, slide on the clasp and two end rings of a Byzantine link, and close it.

[3] Skip the next 5 mm ring in the chain, and open the third 5 mm ring. Slide on the end rings of the first Byzantine link and two end rings of a new Byzantine link, and close it (photo e).

[4] Open the second 5 mm ring, slide on the end two rings of a Byzantine link, and close it. Skip the next 5 mm ring in the chain, and open

the fourth 5 mm ring. Slide on the other two end rings of the first Byzantine link added on this side of the bracelet and two end rings of a new Byzantine link, and close it (photo f).

[5] Continue in this manner, adding a Byzantine link to one side of the bracelet and then the other.

[6] Open a 5 mm ring, and slide it through the final 5 mm ring in the bracelet, and close it.

DESIGN NOTES:

- **Byzantine chain is a 4-in-1 chain, which means each ring passes through four other rings.**
- **The designer made his bracelet using sterling silver, copper, and brass rings. Our bracelet is made of all brass rings to show a budget-friendly option.**

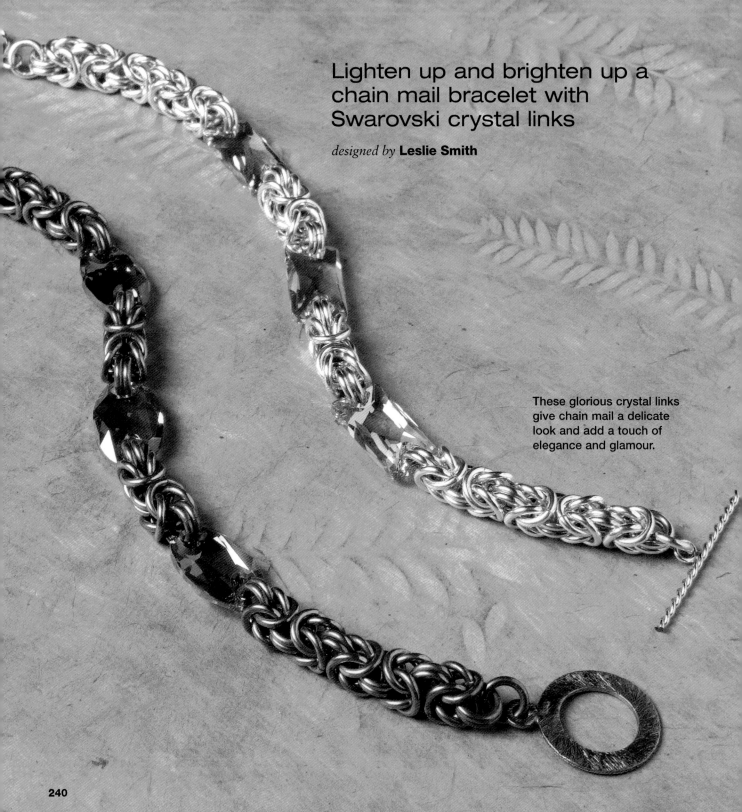

CHAIN MAIL

Crystal-linked chain mail

Lighten up and brighten up a chain mail bracelet with Swarovski crystal links

designed by **Leslie Smith**

These glorious crystal links give chain mail a delicate look and add a touch of elegance and glamour.

stepbystep

Copper bracelet

[1] Open 66 jump rings (Basics), and close the remaining rings.

[2] Slide two closed rings and one end of an 18 x 11 mm owlet crystal link onto an open ring, and close it. Slide another open ring through the same two closed rings and crystal link, and close it **(photo a)**. This is called doubling.

[3] Slide an open ring through the end pair of rings, and close the open ring. Double the new ring **(photo b)**. You now have three pairs of rings.

[4] Flip back the last two rings added, letting one fall to each side. Separate the uppermost rings. Using a piece of scrap wire, reach between the uppermost rings, and thread the wire through the two flipped rings **(photo c)**. Slide an open ring into this spot, replacing the scrap wire, and close the ring. Double the new ring **(photo d)**.

[5] Slide an open ring through the last pair of rings, slide on two more closed rings, and close the open ring. Double the new ring.

[6] Work as in step 4, but slide the end of another crystal link onto the open ring before closing it. Double the new ring. This completes one Byzantine segment connecting two crystal links.

[7] Working off the available end of the second crystal link, repeat steps 2–6 to attach another Byzantine segment and a third crystal link.

[8] Working off of the available end of either the first or third crystal link, make another Byzantine segment as in steps 2–5, and then work step 4. Repeat this sequence of steps to work another Byzantine segment off of the previous one, keeping in mind that you're working off the end two rings of the previous segment, not a crystal link. Then work half of a Byzantine segment as in steps 2–4.

[9] Slide an open ring through the last pair of rings and half of the clasp. Close the ring.

[10] Repeat steps 8–9 on the available end of the remaining crystal link.

Gold-and-silver bracelet

[1] Open all the gold-filled jump rings and 28 sterling silver rings (Basics), and close the remaining silver rings.

[2] Slide two closed silver rings and one end of an 18 x 9 mm space-cut crystal link onto an open gold ring, and close it. Slide another open gold ring through the same two closed silver rings and crystal link, and close it. This is called doubling.

[3] Slide an open silver ring through the pair of silver rings, and close the open ring. Double the new ring.

[4] Work as in steps 4–10 of "Copper bracelet," but follow the established silver-and-gold pattern.

a

b

c

d

materials

copper bracelet 7½ in. (19.1 cm)
- 3 18 x 11 mm owlet crystal links (Swarovski, crystal copper)
- 96 4.5 mm inner-diameter (ID) jump rings, 16-gauge (copper)
- clasp
- 2 pairs of pliers

gold-and-silver bracelet 7½ in. (19.1 cm)
- 3 18 x 9 mm space-cut crystal links (Swarovski, golden shadow)
- 4.5 mm inner-diameter (ID) jump rings, 16-gauge
  38 gold-filled
  58 sterling silver
- clasp
- 2 pairs of pliers

DESIGN NOTE:

When making the gold-and-silver bracelet, keep this in mind: Any time you add two closed rings, they will be silver.

Sequins aren't strong enough to hold up in a chain mail design on their own, but you can still use them as a design element. Enlarge the holes in the sequins, and pair each one with a closed ring in this weave.

materials

bracelet 7½ in. (19.1 cm)

- **96** 12 mm sequins in assorted colors
- ⅜-in. inner diameter (ID) jump ring, 14-gauge
- **173** ¼-in. ID jump rings, 18-gauge
- **9** ³⁄₁₆-in. ID jump rings, 18-gauge
- 36 x 22 mm (large) anodized aluminum scale
- **2** 22 x 14 mm (small) anodized aluminum scales
- lobster claw clasp
- 2 pairs of pliers
- ¼-in. (6 mm) circle paper punch

DESIGN NOTES:

- **Tape the paper punch closed or empty it often to prevent unruly punched-out centers from flying all over as you work.**
- **Save the punched-out centers for other projects using sequins.**

features

Using a mix of sequin colors allows the light to dance across this lively bracelet

designed by **Amanda Shero Granstrom**

a

b

c

d

e

f

g

step by step

Base

The base of the bracelet uses only ¼-in. ID jump rings, so steps 3–7 refer to jump rings without giving a size.

[1] Hold a 12 mm sequin cup side up, and punch a hole in the center with a ¼-in. (6 mm) circle paper punch **(photo a)**. Repeat for the remaining sequins.

[2] Open 69 and close 96 ¼-in. jump rings (Basics).

[3] Determine your color pattern, and lay out a row of four sequins on your work surface, cup side up. Place a closed jump ring on each sequin **(photo b)**. Each sequin and jump ring pair will be called a "sequin unit" in subsequent steps. The side of the unit with the jump ring is the back of the unit. The base will be worked with the back of the units facing up. Flip the finished bracelet over to hide the supporting jump rings.

[4] Working from one end of the row, slide an open jump ring through the first sequin unit from back to front, and the second sequin unit from front to back **(photo c)**, and close the jump ring.

[5] Slide an open jump ring through the second sequin unit from back to front, and the third sequin unit from front to back, and close the jump ring. Repeat this step with the remaining sequin unit **(photo d)**.

[6] For each subsequent row: Lay out four sequin units in your desired color pattern as in step 3. Attach the sequin units as follows:

• Slide an open jump ring through the second new sequin unit from back to front, the first new sequin unit from front to back, the first sequin unit in the previous row from front to back, and the second sequin unit in the previous row from back to front. Close the jump ring **(photo e)**.

• Slide an open jump ring through the third new sequin unit from back to front, the second new sequin unit from front to back, the second sequin unit in the previous row from front to back, and the third sequin unit in the previous row from back to front. Close the jump ring **(photo f)**.

• Slide an open jump ring through the fourth new sequin unit from back to front, the third new sequin unit from front to back, the third sequin unit in the previous row from front to back, and the fourth sequin unit in the previous row from back to front. Close the jump ring **(photo g)**.

[7] Repeat step 6 until you have a total of 24 rows of sequin units.

h

i

j

k

l

m

n

o

The jump rings picked up in step 6 are both attached through jump rings on the back surface of the base, but are shown from the top surface in photo n.

p

Clasp ends

[1] Open nine ³⁄₁₆-in. ID jump rings and eight ¹⁄₄-in. jump rings, and close one ³⁄₈-in. ID jump ring.

[2] Slide a ³⁄₁₆-in. jump ring through a small scale, and close the jump ring. Repeat to attach a ³⁄₁₆-in. jump ring to the remaining small scale (photo h).

[3] Slide a ³⁄₁₆-in. jump ring through the ³⁄₈-in. jump ring and the large scale. Close the jump ring (photo i).

[4] Slide a ³⁄₁₆-in. jump ring through the ³⁄₈-in. jump ring and large scale and through a small scale. Make sure the jump ring previously attached to the small scale falls to the outside edge and that all the scales are facing the same way. Close the jump ring. Repeat to attach the remaining small scale (photo j).

[5] On the end of the base where the last row of sequins lays under the second-to-last row (on the working side of the base), slide a ¹⁄₄-in. jump ring through the end sequin unit from front to back and the second sequin unit from back to front, and close the jump ring (photo k). Repeat to slide a ¹⁄₄-in. jump ring through the second and third sequin units in the last row, but attach the five ³⁄₁₆-in. jump rings from the top of the scales, making sure the rounded side of the scales are on the same side as the front surface of the sequins before closing the jump ring (photo l). Slide a ¹⁄₄-in. jump ring through the third and fourth sequin units in the last row as for the first jump ring in this step, and close the jump ring (photo m).

[6] Slide a ¹⁄₄-in. jump ring through the first two ¹⁄₄-in. jump rings added in step 5, and close the jump ring. Repeat to attach a ¹⁄₄-in. jump ring to the second and third ¹⁄₄-in. jump rings attached in step 5 (photo n). Slide a ³⁄₁₆-in. jump ring through the two ¹⁄₄-in. jump rings added in this step, and close the jump ring (photo o).

[7] Repeat steps 5 and 6 on the other end of the bracelet, with the following changes:
• In step 5, omit the scales, attaching the ¹⁄₄-in. jump ring to the second and third sequin units.
• In step 6, use all ³⁄₁₆-in. jump rings, and attach a lobster claw clasp to the last ³⁄₁₆-in. jump ring before closing it (photo p).

Wonder Woman cuff

Fight off evildoers with a bold cuff made of metal and wire

designed by **Ana V. Pizarro**

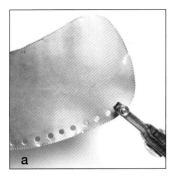

a

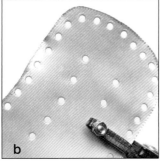

b

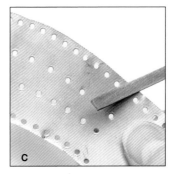

c

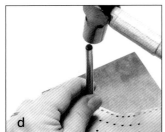

d

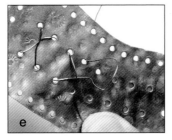

e

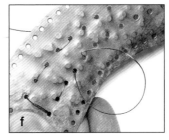

f

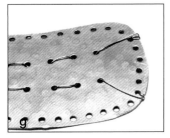

g

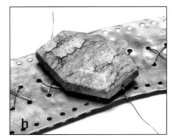

h

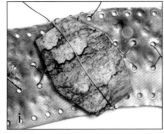

i

stepbystep

[1] Copy the template, p. 248, or make your own template: On a piece of thick paper, draw a wavy line that is about ½ in. (1.3 cm) shorter than the circumference of your wrist. Draw another wavy line parallel to the first, about 1½ in. (3.8 cm) away. Connect the ends, rounding the corners if desired.

[2] Cut out the template, and trace it onto the metal sheet with a marker. Use metal shears to cut the shape.

[3] Using the 1.8 mm hole punch, punch holes around the perimeter of the metal shape, placing them about ⅛ in. (3 mm) from the edge of the metal and 4 mm apart (photo a). The number of holes isn't important.

[4] Beginning about ½ in. (1.3 cm) from one end, punch two parallel rows of holes about ½ in. (1.3 cm) from each edge (photo b).

[5] File the entire edge of the metal shape with a metal file (photo c), and smooth with sandpaper.

[6] Hammer the metal shape to give it texture, and stamp it with patterns, if desired (photo d).

[7] If desired, patinate the metal shape with liver of sulfur, following the manufacturer's instructions. Rinse the metal shape, and polish it with a polishing cloth.

[8] Cut about 3 ft. (.9 m) of 24-gauge wire, and center it in an end pair of parallel holes, going from the back of the cuff to the front. Cross each wire over the front, and guide it down through the next hole in the adjacent parallel row (photo e) and up through the following hole

in the same row (photo f). Repeat along the length of the metal shape. At the end, guide each wire through a nearby edge hole, wrap it two or three times, and trim (photo g). Press the wire ends close to the metal shape.

[9] Cut 1 ft. (30 cm) of wire, and center the 25–30 mm bead. Position it in the middle of the metal shape, and attach it by wrapping each wire end through an edge hole a few times (photo h). Cross one wire end diagonally over the bead, and wrap it through a hole on the other edge (photo i). Repeat with the other wire end, wrapping it around the first wire on the front of the bead before attaching it to the other edge of the metal shape (photo j). Trim the ends, and press them in.

p. 248,

materials

cuff 3-in. (7.6 cm) diameter

- 3 x 7½ in. (7.6 x 19.1 cm) 26-gauge metal sheet
- 25–30 mm bead with flat back
- **15–25** 3–4 mm glass or crystal accent beads
- **30–60** 3 mm metal spacers or 8º seed beads
- 7 ft. (2.1 m) 24-gauge wire
- anvil or bench block
- bracelet mandrel or bracelet-forming pliers (optional)
- hammer
- liver of sulfur patina with glass or plastic container, hot water, and polishing cloth (optional)
- marker
- metal files
- metal hole punch, 1.8 mm
- metal shears
- metal stamps (optional)
- sandpaper, 600 grit
- thick paper
- wire cutters

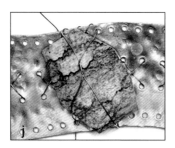 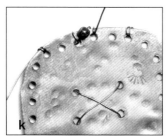 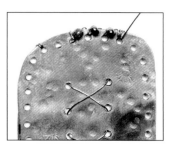

[10] Cut 3 ft. (.9 m) of wire, and center it in an edge hole at one end of the metal shape. Wrap it once or twice, and string a 3–4 mm accent bead. Guide the wire through the next edge hole, and wrap it around the edge **(photo k)**. String a 3 mm metal spacer or 8º seed bead, go through the next edge hole, and wrap the wire around the edge. Repeat **(photo l)**. Continue adding a pattern of an accent bead and two spacers or seed beads around the perimeter. When you run out of wire on this end, secure it to the metal shape with a few wraps, trim, and press the end in. Continue in this manner with the other wire end until the entire perimeter is embellished.

[11] Using your fingers, a bracelet mandrel, or bracelet-forming pliers, bend the metal into a cuff shape.

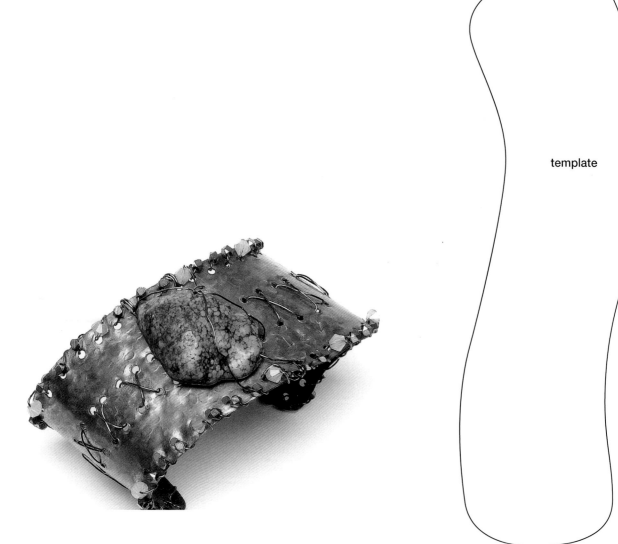

template

WRAPPED LOOPS

Chained reaction

Combine large-
and small-link chain
in mixed metals with
wire-wrapped
briolettes

designed by **Angela Casaccio**

Needle-like
threads of
golden rutile
glitter in
these quartz
briolettes,
bringing an
opulent
quality to this
necklace.

materials

necklace 18 in. (46 cm) with
3-in. (7.6 cm) dangle

- **12** 10–16 mm faceted
  gemstone briolettes or
  crystal drop beads
- **2** 4 mm beads
- 18 in. (46 cm) large-link circle
  chain (artbeads.com)
- **5–7** 24-in. (61 cm) lengths of
  small-link chain, various styles
  and finishes
- 34 in. (86 cm) 24- or
  26-gauge wire (choose the
  thickest gauge that will go
  through the holes of the
  briolettes or drops)
- clasp
- chainnose pliers
- roundnose pliers
- wire cutters
- Chain Sta (optional)

DESIGN NOTE:
Drape your necklace
on a neckform or attach
it to a Chain-Stā before
attaching the briolettes
or drop beads. It will
be easier to see how
the beads will fall if the
necklace is hanging as
it would be worn.

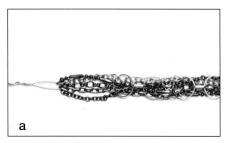

a

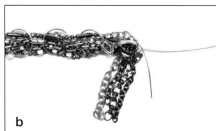

b

c

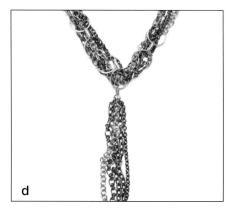

d

e

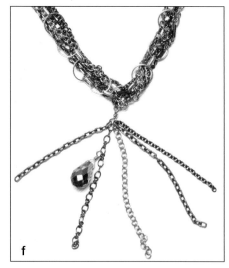

f

step by step

[1] Cut 2 in. (5 cm) of wire, fold it in half, and string an end link of each small-link chain. Twist the wire ends together to secure.

[2] Weave the wire through the links of the large-link chain, going up through the first link, down through the second link, up through the third link, and so on, pulling the bundle of small-link chains all the way through the large-link chain. Stop when the bundle of chains extends about ½–1 in. (1.3–2.5 cm) beyond the large-link chain (photo a). Remove the wire.

[3] Trim the other end of the small-link chains so they also extend about ½–1 in. (1.3–2.5 cm) beyond the large-link chain.

[4] Cut 3 in. (7.6 cm) of wire, and make the first half of a wrapped loop (Basics). On one end of the necklace, slide the end link of the large-link chain into the loop. Slide a link of each small-link chain into the loop, allowing the ½–1-in. (1.3–2.5 cm) ends to dangle **(photo b)**. Complete the wraps. String a 4 mm bead on the wire, and make

the first half of a wrapped loop. Attach half of the clasp, and complete the wraps **(photo c)**.

[5] Repeat step 4 on the other end of the necklace, attaching the other half of the clasp.

[6] Select five chain segments left over from step 3, and cut them so they vary from 2–3 in. (5–7.6 cm) in length. Cut 2 in. (5 cm) of wire, make the first half of a wrapped loop, slide an end link of each chain segment into the loop, and complete the wraps. Make the first half of a wrapped loop at the other end of the wire, attach it to a couple of chains at the middle of the necklace, and complete the wraps **(photo d)**.

[7] Cut 2 in. (5 cm) of wire, and string a 10–16 mm briolette or drop bead. Make a set of wraps as for a top-drilled bead (Basics). Make the first half of a wrapped loop with the remaining wire **(photo e)**, attach it to any link on a chain in the dangle, and complete the wraps **(photo f)**.

[8] Repeat step 7 with the remaining briolettes or drop beads, attaching them to the dangle and the center portion of the necklace as desired.

A little bit of sparkle

Add a splash of color with crystals and beading wire

designed by **Tea Benduhn**

materials

15 in. (38 cm) necklace
- **3** 8 mm pearls (white or cream)
- **10** 6 mm bicone crystals (crystal)
- **17** assorted crystals (Crystazzi) for dangles: 11 x 8 mm twisted ovals (crystal), 10 mm twisted rounds (crystal), 9 x 6 mm ovals (crystal), 8 mm twisted rounds (crystal), 6 x 6 mm fancy cubes (crystal), 4 x 6 mm rondelles (crystal), 6 mm bicones (crystal and Siam)
- clasp
- 2-in. (5 cm) eye pin
- **19** 2-in. (5 cm) head pins
- 2 crimp beads
- flexible beading wire, .018 (red)
- chainnose pliers
- crimping pliers
- roundnose pliers
- wire cutters

DESIGN NOTES:
- Use the crystals you have left over from other projects to make this necklace.
- Try this design using all the same color or shape crystals.

stepbystep

[1] On a head pin, string one of the assorted crystals, and make a wrapped loop (Basics). Repeat to make a total of 17 assorted crystal dangles and two pearl dangles.
[2] Make the center dangle: Open the loop of the eye pin (Basics), and attach a crystal-colored dangle, a red dangle, and a crystal-colored dangle. Close the loop. On the eye pin, string an 8 mm pearl, and make a wrapped loop.

[3] Cut 18 in. (46 cm) of beading wire, and center the dangle made in step 2.
[4] On each end, string a crystal-colored 6 mm bicone and two dangles from step 1. Repeat three times with the desired dangles, and then string a 6 mm bicone.
[5] On one end of the beading wire, string a crimp bead and half of the clasp. Go back through the crimp bead, and crimp it (Basics). Trim the excess wire. Repeat this step on the remaining end.

Contributors

Marcia Balonis is a jewelry artist residing in central Florida. Contact her via email at marcia@baublesbybalonis.net or visit www.baublesbybalonis.net.

Tea Benduhn is a former associate editor at *Bead&Button* magazine. Contact her in care of Kalmbach Books.

Jimmie Boatright is a retired school teacher and lifelong crafter who designs and teaches jewelry-making at local bead stores in the Atlanta, Ga. area. Contact Jimmie at (770) 967-6974 or via email at dboatri931@aol.com.

Suzanne Branca owns the online bead source A Grain of Sand. Contact her via email at suzanne@agrainofsand.com, or visit agrainofsand.com.

May Brisebois is the owner of BEADiful LLC in Cumming, Ga. She loves using simple techniques to display various elements to great results. Contact her at BEADiful, (678) 455-7858, or visit her website, www.beadifulgifts.com.

Cary Bruner remembers crafting at her grandma's house as a child and credits that experience as the reason she first entered a bead store. Now she works and teaches at Bead Haven Las Vegas. Email Cary at creationsbycary@aol.com.

Kathleen Burke took up beading after admiring a handmade crystal bracelet at a party. She lives in Portage, Mich., with her husband, a dog, and a cat who enjoys knocking bead containers on the floor. Email her at kat.burke2u@yahoo.com.

Kelli "Rae" Burns owns The Hole Bead Shoppe in Bartlesville, Okla., and has been beading and teaching since 2004. Kelli's creations range from Lucite bracelets to woven faux bangles to bead embroidery. Visit her website, theholebeadshop.com, or contact her at (918) 338-2444 or theholebeadshop@aol.com.

Angela Casaccio has been designing jewelry since 2002. She loves working with all mediums for her designs. She owns and operates Cela Creations Boutique in La Grange, Ill. Follow her work on Pinterest, or read her blog at celacreations.blogspot.com.

Carolyn Cave is a self-taught bead artist from Alberta, Canada, who loves to fulfill her creative passions by making jewelry and other articles with beads. Contact her via e-mail at carton@nucleus.com, or see her work on Facebook at Lady Beadle Designs.

Contact **Janice Chatham** at bighjh2@aol.com.

Lorraine Coetzee has been a full-time jewelry artist since 2006. She designs and fabricates jewelry items, as well as bead patterns and tutorials for all skill levels. Contact her at trinitydjsales@gmail.com or visit www.trinity-dj.blogspot.com.

Jane Danely Cruz is an associate editor at *Bead&Button*. Contact her via email at jcruz@beadandbutton.com.

Anna Elizabeth Draeger is a jewelry designer, former associate editor for *Bead&Button* magazine, and the author of *Crystal Brilliance, Great Designs for Shaped Beads,* and *Crystal Play.* Since 2009, Anna has been an ambassador for the Create Your Style with Swarovski Elements program. Her website is originaldesignsbyanna.squarespace.com.

Kris Empting-Obenland is a proud mom of four and a trained fashion designer. She enjoys sewing, knitting, and painting, and was infected with beadomania three years ago. Contact Kris at krisdesign.fsp@googlemail.com, or visit her websites, kris-design.de and krisdesignfsp.etsy.com.

Cheryl Erickson teaches beading classes and is the owner of Artistic Bead in West Des Moines, Iowa. Contact her at cheryl@artisticbead.com, or visit artisticbead.com.

Julia Gerlach is editor of *Bead&Button* magazine. Contact her via e-mail at jgerlach@kalmbach.com.

Amanda Shero Granstrom lives in Portland, Ore. She has been designing and crafting since 2001, and loves working with beads, fibers, polymer clay, glass, and chain mail. Contact her via e mail at amanda@redeftshibori.com, or visit craftycatjumprings.com.

Smadar Grossman lives in Israel, where she is designing jewelry using beads, her favorite material. Visit Smadar's website, smadarstreasure.blogspot.com, to see more of her work.

Aasia Hamid is a bead weaver and jewelry designer who loves to create unique jewelry in her home studio in Gilbert, Ariz. She enjoys teaching bead weaving, and sharing her knowledge of color and beading techniques. Contact her at (480) 586-1843 or aasia@aasiajewelry.com, or visit her website at aasiajewelry.com.

Deborah Hermanson-Pulos started beading when she decided to make a rosary for her daughter's First Communion. From that moment, she became an unrepentant beading junkie. She has taught beading classes in Illinois, and now enjoys teaching from her new home base on the shores of Lake Michigan. Contact Deborah at dpulosdesigns@att.net, or visit her website, deborahpulosdesigns.com.

Email **Carole Horn** at carolehorn@nyc.rr.com.

Darci Aryd'ell Hotelling lives on the edge of the Great Smoky Mountain National Park in North Carolina. Every day provides inspiration for her beadwork. Email Aryd'ell at gypsylight17@yahoo.com, or visit her blog, http://gypsysramblings.blogspot.com.

Amy Johnson draws inspiration from her background in tapestry weaving and graphic design to create her beaded jewelry. Three of her pieces have been finalists in *Bead&Button's* annual Bead Dreams competition. E-mail her at amy@amyjohnsondesigns.com, or visit her website, amyjohnsondesigns.com.

Barbara Klann has been beading for more than 20 years, and is constantly amazed at what can be accomplished with a small pile of beads and a needle and thread. Her main materials of choice are seed beads with a few crystals or pearls sprinkled in here and there. Contact Barbara in care of Kalmbach Books.

Amy Kohn worked in graphics and desktop publishing for 15 years before transferring her skills to wire and beadwork. She has been designing and teaching her creations in Israel since 2002. Visit Amy's website at amykohndesigns.etsy.com, or email her at amykohndesigns@bezeqint.net.

Isabella Lam began beading in 2004 and now owns two bead stores in Israel with her husband. She loves mixing traditional techniques with modern influence, aiming to design pieces that delight the wearer and grab the attention of everyone around her. Email Isabella at scarlet@actcom.co.il, or visit her website, isabella-lam.com or etsy.com/shop/bead4me.

Cathy Lampole of Newmarket, Ontario, Canada, enjoys the fine detail that can be achieved with beadweaving, especially with crystals. Besides designing jewelry, Cathy owns a bead shop, That Bead Lady. Visit her website, thatbeadlady.com, or email her at cathy@thatbeadlady.com.

Laura Landrum has been beading for 20 years. She loves experimenting with different styles of beaded beads. Contact her by email at landrumjewelry@gmail.com, or visit her website, lauralandrum.biz.

Teri Dannenberg Lawson began beading with semiprecious stones, and later discovered even more ways to play with color and texture using seed beads and crystals. She loves unexpected combinations and using simple patterns with great materials for eye-catching effects. Contact her at teridann@gmail.com.

Wendy Lueder lives in South Florida. She holds degrees in philosophy and graphic design technology, and for 15 years she has created custom jewelry under the initial inspiration of Carol Wilcox Wells' book, *Creative Bead Weaving*. Contact Wendy at wendy@capturedglimpse.com, or visit capturedglimpse.com.

Un-Roen Manarata of Belgium is a Create Your Style with Swarovski Elements ambassador and makes jewelry in several mediums, including crochet, bead stitching, and metal clay. Contact her at un-roen@elfen.be.

Alla Maslennikova likes to incorporate unusual elements in her beadwork. Contact her at beadlady.ru@gmail.com, or visit beadlady.ru to view her designs.

Contact **Lauren M. Miller** at lalabirddesigns@gmail.com, or visit her website, lalabirddesigns.com.

Samantha Mitchell designs jewelry as a way to express her creativity when she's not busy caring for her son. Contact her at samantha@crystyles.com, or visit her website, crystyles.com.

Grace Nehls is a jewelry designer who teaches her creations at Bead Haven in Las Vegas. She finds inspiration for designs in her everyday surroundings. Contact her via email at gnehls@beadmegracefully.com.

Sara Oehler is a well-known jewelry designer residing in sunny Phoenix, Ariz. With Jamie Hogsett, she is the author of *Show Your Colors!* She has designed jewelry and written for numerous publications, and appears as "Ask Sara" of Soft Flex® Company. To ask a beading question, visit wwwSoftFlexCompany.com and click on "Ask Sara," or visit softflexgirlblogspot.com.

Nealay Patel has been beading for eight years and enjoys the challenge of rendering his architectural designs in beads. He is the author of *Jewelry for the New Romantic*. View more of his designs at behance.net/nealayjewelry or facebook.com/nealay.

LindaMay Patterson gets her inspiration from *Bead&Button* magazine. Contact LindaMay in care of Kalmbach Books.

Huib Petersen got bit by the beading bug more than 14 years ago when he bead-embroidered a wedding dress for his friend. He works in a variety of mediums, and he is well known for his beaded sculptures. See more of his work at petersenarts.com, or contact him via email at huib@petersenarts.com.

Ana V. Pizarro has been beading since 2004 and is a teacher at Caravan Beads in Chicago. To see more of her work, visit avpjewelry.com. Contact Ana at anavpizarro@hotmail.com.

"Equation in a tangible form," is how **Scott David Plumlee** describes chain mail design. This mathematician create countries in preparation for his books, *Handcrafting Chain and Bead Jewelry*, and *Chain and Bead Jewelry: Creative Connections*. Contact Scott via email at info@davidchain.com, or visit his website, davidchain.com.

Melanie Potter is the director of School of Beadwork and a national artist and instructor teaching unique off-loom jewelry designs. Her background in couture sewing provided a natural foundation for her jewelry making, and her recent venture into watercolor painting has further inspired her art. Her designs are published in a number of magazines and books. Learn more about Melanie at melaniepotter.com.

Ludmila Raitzin is a renowned sweater designer with work featured at Saks Fifth Avenue, Neiman Marcus, Bloomingdales, and more. Her background in fashion led her to become a successful jewelry designer known for her color sense and strong design abilities. Her work has been exhibited in the Museum of Art and Design and has been published in several books and magazines. Contact Ludmila via email at raitzinl@yahoo.com.

Anu Rao is a dentist and mother of three girls. She began beading just a few years ago. Contact Anu via email at anu7rao@yahoo.com.

Maggie Roschyk teaches at many venues, including the Bead&Button Show in the U.S. and the Bead Art and Jewelry Accessory Fair in Germany. Maggie is a contributing editor to *Bead&Button* magazine, the author of an online column called "Maggie's Musings," and the author of the book *Artistic Seed Bead Jewelry*. Contact her via email at blueroses@wi.rr.com.

Cynthia Rutledge has been sharing the art of beading for 19 years. Her focus is using off-loom beadweaving stitches to create jewelry designs that have a contemporary yet timeless elegance. She teaches around the U.S. and internationally. Contact Cynthia at (909) 338-0296, email her at info@cynthiarutledge.net, or visit her website, cynthiarutledge.net.

Giorgia Scardini was born in Rome, Italy. She is a multimedia artist who now lives in Pleasant Hill, Calif.,with her husband, son, and dog.Visit her website, giorgiajewelry.com, or contact her via email at giorgiascardini@ sbcglobal.net.

Jackie Schwietz has been beading for more than eight years. She lives in Florida, where she is surrounded by inspiration. Contact Jackie by email at rjschwietz@comcast.net.

Tamara Scott has been a professional artist and teacher for more than 20 years. When she's not teaching, Tamara is busy designing in her studio in Atlanta, Ga. To see more of her designs and to purchase kits, visit tamarascottdesigns.net.

Sherry Serafini is a full-time artist and international instructor in the art of beading. Sherry has written *Sensational Bead Embroidery*, and co-authored *The Art of Bead Embroidery*. She has embellished the stage wear of several well-known musicians. Visit her website, www.serafinibeadedjewelry.com.

Laura Shea has been beading for 18 years and teaching beaded beads since 2001. She is an active member of several bead societies and a math-in-art group. She sells kits on her website, adancingrainbow.com, and teaches internationally.

Sue Sloan is a beader based in Portland, Ore. Contact her in care of Kalmbach Books.

Leslie Smith has been beading for more than eight years and creating chain mail jewelry for five years, beginning with a design from *Bead&Button* magazine. She lives in Encinitas, Calif. Email her at leslie@925maille.com, or visit her website, 925maille.com.

Donna Sutton is excited by color, texture, and design. She started beading in 2008 after relocating from Michigan to Englewood, Fla., where she began to work at My Bead Gallery. The atmosphere of the shop as well as the talented instructors constantly inspire and challenge her. Contact Donna at dragonflydreamdesign@hotmail.com.

From her studio in southern N.H., **Amee K. Sweet-McNamara** creates one-of-a-kind pieces of textile art-jewelry, writes, and teaches. Her soutache bead embroidery book is forthcoming from Kalmbach Books. To reach Amee, see more of her work or peruse the current class schedule, visit ameerunswithscissors.com.

Hiroe Takagi taught herself beadwork while working as a freelance nail artist. She is now a certified instructor of beadwork at the Gakusyu Forum of the Japanese Association of Leisure and Cultural Development. Contact her via e-mail at beads-fan@be-pal.com.

Helena Tang-Lim lives in sunny Singapore and got the beading bug after making her first pair of beaded shoes in 1996. She now designs and sells her beadwork jewelry, kits, and patterns online at Manek-Manek Beads. Contact her at helena@manek-manek.com, or visit her website, manek-manek.com.

A part-time beader with a full-time love of jewelry design and creation, **Ellen Tihane** also teaches through the Toronto Bead Society. Contact her via email at fortytwo.pieces@yahoo.com.

Michele Trondsen lives in Washington with her husband, Robert, and their dog, Cherry. She has done crafts all her life, but beading is her favorite. Designing patterns and watching them transform into jewelry excites her, and she especially loves netted patterns because they go so quickly. Contact Michele via email at r_trondsen2010@ comcast.net.

Jenny Van is a microbiologist and jewelry designer based in Huntington Beach, Calif. Contact her via e-mail at jenny@beadsjcom, or visit her website, beadsjcom.

As a Create Your Style with Swarovski Elements Ambassador, **Diane Whiting** is also moderator of the Create Your Style Sparkling Community, which reaches DIY jewelry enthusiasts around the world, and she writes a blog, "Sparkles and Smiles." Diane attends numerous bead shows annually.

Connie Whittaker is associate editor for *Bead&Button* magazine. Contact her via email at cwhittaker@kalmbach.com.

Emi Yamada has loved making jewelry and beaded insects since her childhood. She is a bead instructor in Hiroshima City, Japan, and she is also a member of the Bead Society of Japan. Email her at pipi-07@nifty.ne.jp, or visit homepage3.nifty.com/chocoo/.

Sheryl Yanagi channels her detail-oriented skills as a computer programmer into the detailed beadwork she designs. Her beads of choice are 15º seed beads. Contact Sheryl at syanagi@comcast.net.

Index